HOUSING

Design, Research, Education

Edited by
MARJORIE BULOS
AND
NECDET TEYMUR

Routledge
Taylor & Francis Group
LONDON AND NEW YORK

First published in 1993 by Avebury (Ashgate Publishing Limited)

This edition first published in 2025
by Routledge
4 Park Square, Milton Park, Abingdon, Oxon OX14 4RN

and by Routledge
605 Third Avenue, New York, NY 10158

Routledge is an imprint of the Taylor & Francis Group, an informa business

British Library Cataloguing in Publication Data
A catalogue record for this book is available from the British Library

ISBN: 978-1-032-86590-4 (Set)
ISBN: 978-1-032-86388-7 (Volume 9) (hbk)
ISBN: 978-1-032-86399-3 (Volume 9) (pbk)
ISBN: 978-1-003-52733-6 (Volume 9) (ebk)

DOI: 10.4324/9781003527336

New Series Introduction to *RLE: Ethnoscapes*

The neologism *Ethnoscapes*[1] was created by David Canter and David Stea in 1987 when they happened both to be in Yogjakarta at the same time. They wanted a term to cover the rapidly emerging multidisciplinary field of research into many aspects of how individuals, groups and cultures interact and transact with their surroundings. It was derived as follows:

Ethno (combining form) indicating race, people or culture.

Scape (suffix-forming nouns) indicating a scene or view of something.

Ethnoscapes (plural noun) Scholarly and/or scientific explorations of the relationships people and their activities, have with the places they create and/or inhabit; historical, psychological, anthropological, sociological, and related disciplines that study the experiences of places, attitudes towards them, or the processes of shaping, managing, or designing them. The term was subsequently used to provide an umbrella for a series of books. These cover topics that are so multidisciplinary that they do not sit comfortably in any of the constrained silos of academic and scholarly research. As indicated on the opening page of the first book in the series, many disciplines "have developed marauding sub-groups who move freely across each others' borders, carrying ideas almost like contraband, without declaring that they have crossed any disciplinary boundaries."

They include domains labelled as Behavioural or Perceptual Geography, Environmental/Architectural Psychology, Urban History, Social Ecology, Behavioural Archaeology, Urban Planning, Behavioural Architecture, and Landscape Architecture. There are also many other areas of research and practice that, whilst not being overtly psychological, social, or cultural, do explore and act on the built and natural environment in a way that recognises the importance of the human transactions with those settings. These professions include interior and product design, comparative linguistics, and even aspects of criminology and mental health providers.

Like all such implicit and explicit transactions between different domains, a community of interest and support has emerged in which those who cross the boundaries often find they have more in common with other transgressors than with their mother disciplines. This has given rise to common means and forms of communication, with a shared understanding of the issues and approaches that are of value. Although, of course, these are not always understood in the same way by all those involved,

The *Ethnoscapes* series of books provides a forum for these multifarious, cross-disciplinary, determinedly international, studies and practices. Each of the books takes on board one or more of the environmental challenges that that individuals, societies and cultures are facing. Emphasising a social perspective, rather than the dominant 'hard' science viewpoints embedded in physical, geological and climate changes.

It may now be regarded as rather prescient that it was over three decades ago that the need and importance was recognised of bringing together the many strands of environmental social research and practice. But there is no doubt that there were academics and professionals exploring Ethnoscape topics, going back to the 1960s, often in isolation and with little recognition, that are today front-page, and podcast, news. The challenges in the environmental social sciences that Ethnoscapes explores are just as pertinent now as they were when initially identified.

The series, in essence, deals with four challenges the environmental social sciences embrace.

1. Addressing "the awareness of governments and public alike of the problems of environmental degradation and pollution."

This includes the challenge of providing acceptable housing and related environmental conditions that also encompassed the support for environmental and related cultural heritage. It also requires detailed consideration of the assessment and evaluation of designs and design proposals as well as background research on policy related issues.

2. Developing ways of conceptualising human interactions with the physical surroundings.

This may seem somewhat abstract but has practical implications. The dominant view that people are passively controlled by their surroundings supports a paternalistic, management of what it is assumed people need. That ignores the active way in which people make sense of their environment, drawing on cultural and historical influences. This recognises the importance of user participation in decisions about built and natural settings. That, in turn, requires a much richer understanding of how people interact with where they are or want to be.

3. A much wider range of ways of exploring people's transactions with the environment is needed to contribute to policy and practice as well as developing richer insights into human experiences.

The stock in trade of surveys, or the inevitably artificial laboratory-based experiments, whilst of value for some explorations, need to be augmented by methodologies that enrich an understanding of what the experiences are of being in, acting on, and developing places. They need to connect not just with the endeavours of individuals but also with how cultures and societies express these transactions.

4. Finding ways to enable practitioners and researchers to express their own encounters with the contexts they are influencing or studying.

Much of the research that is carried out in what are curiously called 'Ivory Towers', even when it is studying the big wide world, allows the pretence of distancing from the direct experiences of the issues being studied. Yet the challenges of moving across disciplinary boundaries are as much personal challenges of finding new ways of thinking, communicating, and acting, as an academic demand to develop more effective intellectual systems. The Ethnoscapes series recognises the value of exploring these challenges by hosting a variety of formats. Many of these go beyond the staid and limited formulations that academic discourse assumes to be the norms.

The Ethnoscapes series brings together a vibrant mix of cutting-edge explorations, from all over the world, of human transactions with the built and natural environments. This includes, for example, consideration of vernacular architecture that contrasts with the architecture and urbanism of the colonial enterprise, the meaning of home, aesthetics, well-being and health, and consideration of how environmental psychology has become 'green'. All of these topics, and more, provide an exciting basis for dealing with current challenges in the environmental social sciences.

Note

[1] Not to be confused by the term *Ethnoscape* later concocted by Arun Appadurai in 1990, to refer to **human migration**, the flow of people across boundaries. This includes migrants, refugees, exiles, and tourists, among other moving individuals and groups, all of whom appear to affect the politics of (and between) nations to a considerable degree. Ignorant of the lexicographical origins of the term 'scape' he rather confusingly added it to many ideas of flow, such as the flow of technology – technoscapes and the flow of ideas ideoscapes. Appadurai, A. (1990). "Disjuncture and difference in the global cultural economy." *Theory, Culture and Society* 7(2–3): 295–310.

Routledge Library Editions: Ethnoscapes

1. *Environmental Perspectives* David Canter, Martin Krampen & David Stea (Eds) (1988) ISBN 978-1-032-81616-6

2. *Environmental Policy, Assessment, and Communication* David Canter, Martin Krampen & David Stea (Eds) (1988) ISBN 978-1-032-81635-7

3. *New Directions in Environmental Participation* David Canter, Martin Krampen & David Stea (Eds) (1988) ISBN 978-1-032-81646-3

4. *Vernacular Architecture: Paradigms of Environmental Response* Mete Turan (Ed.) (1990) ISBN 978-1-032-82023-1

5. *Forms of Dominance: On the Architecture and Urbanism of the Colonial Enterprise* Nezar AlSayyad (Ed.) (1992) ISBN 978-1-032-84164-9

6. *The Meaning and Use of Housing: International Perspectives, Approaches and Their Applications* Ernesto G. Arias (Ed.) (1993) ISBN 978-1-032-84781-8

7. *Placemaking: Production of Built Environment in Two Cultures* David Stea & Mete Turan (1993) ISBN 978-1-032-86434-1

8. *Environmental Psychology in Europe: From Architectural Psychology to Green Psychology* Enric Pol (1993) ISBN 978-1-032-83324-8

9. *Housing: Design, Research, Education* Marjorie Bulos & Necdet Teymur (Eds) (1993) ISBN 978-1-032-86388-7

10. *Architecture, Ritual Practice and Co-determination in the Swedish Office* Dennis Doxtater (1994) ISBN 978-1-032-81774-3

11. *On the Aesthetics of Architecture: A Psychological Approach to the Structure and the Order of Perceived Architectural Space* Ralf Weber (1995) ISBN 978-1-032-82034-7

12. *The Home: Words, Interpretations, Meanings and Environments* by David N. Benjamin (Ed.) (1995) ISBN 978-1-032-86411-2

13. *Tradition, Location and Community: Place-making and Development* Adenrele Awotona & Necdet Teymur (Eds) (1997) ISBN 978-1-032-84608-8

14. *Aesthetics, Well-being and Health: Essays within Architecture and Environmental Aesthetics* Birgit Cold (Ed.) (2001) ISBN 978-1-032-86577-5

Other Ethnoscapes series titles also available:

Integrating Programming, Evaluation and Participation in Design: A Theory Z Approach Henry Sanoff (1992) HBK 978-1-138-20338-9; EBK 978-1-315-47173-0; PBK 978-1-138-20339-6

Directions in Person-Environment Research and Practice Jack Nasar & Wolfgang F. E. Preiser (Eds) (1999) HBK 978-1-138-68674-8; EBK 978-1-315-54255-3; PBK 978-1-138-68677-9

Psychological Theories for Environmental Issues Mirilia Bonnes, Terence Lee & Marino Bonaiuto (Eds) (2003) HBK 978-0-75461-888-1; EBK 978-1-315-24572-0; PBK 978-1-138-27742-7

Housing Space and Quality of Life David L. Uzzell, Ricardo Garcia Mira, J. Eulogio Real & Joe Romay (Eds) (2005) HBK 978-0-81538-952-1; EBK 978-1-351-15636-3; PBK 978-1-138-35596-5

Doing Things with Things: The Design and Use of Everyday Objects Alan Costall & Ole Dreier (Eds) (2006) HBK 978-0-75464-656-3; EBK 978-1-315-57792-0; PBK 978-1-138-25314-8

Rethinking the Meaning of Place: Conceiving Place in Architecture-Urbanism Lineu Castello (2010) HBK 978-0-75467-814-4; EBK 978-1-315-60616-3; PBK 978-1-138-25745-0

ETHNOSCAPES
Current Challenges in the Environmental Social Sciences

Series Editors: *David Canter and David Stea*

1 Environmental Perspectives
2 Environmental Policy, Assessment and Communication
3 New Directions in Environmental Participation
4 Vernacular Architecture
5 Forms of Dominance
6 Integrating Programming, Evaluation and Participation in Design
7 The Meaning and Use of Housing
8 Placemaking
9 Environmental Psychology in Europe
10 Environmental Evaluation and Planning in the Third World

Housing: Design, Research, Education

Edited by

MARJORIE BULOS
School of Land Management and Urban Policy
South Bank University

NECDET TEYMUR
Centre for International Architectural Studies
School of Architecture, University of Manchester

Avebury

Aldershot · Brookfield USA · Hong Kong · Singapore · Sydney

Published by
Avebury
Ashgate Publishing Limited
Gower House
Croft Road
Aldershot
Hants GU11 3HR
England

Ashgate Publishing Company
Old Post Road
Brookfield
Vermont 05036
USA

British Library Cataloguing in Publication Data

Housing: Design, Research, Education. —
(Ethnoscapes: Current Challenges in the Environmental Social Sciences)
I. Bulos, Marjorie II. Teymur, Necdet III. Series
307.3

ISBN 1 85628 515 4

Typeset by
School of Land Management and Urban Policy
South Bank University
Wandsworth Road
London SW8 2JZ

Printed and Bound in Great Britain by
Athenaeum Press Ltd, Newcastle upon Tyne.

Contents

Introduction

It is not long since housing has been recognised as a researchable and teachable subject. Now, however, housing appears as an increasingly important subject in University courses, attracts a significant amount of research funding and, in most societies, remains as a key political issue. In the future, how people should be housed, whether houses are 'homes' or merely 'shelter' and the role design and education contribute to the knowledge we have on these matters will become increasingly key issues. As the pace and direction of economic and social restructuring becomes faster and sharper the need for new thinking about the relations between housing, design and education will become more urgent.

This collection of papers demonstrates some of the diversity and richness of the research being undertaken which takes as its starting point peoples' notion of home and the way in which a sense of home is captured, distilled and expressed through various facets of design, and conversely the urgent need for architects and planners to take seriously the everyday scale and scope of peoples' home experience.

The breadth of subject background and cultural location from which these papers are drawn provides stimulating reading at the same time as presenting a challenging choice of perspectives. This challenge of how to handle and use knowledge from different disciplines is the focus of those papers which grapple with the epistemological and practical matters of developing appropriate theoretical and pedagogic frameworks within which these various strands can be fruitfully brought together.

The opportunity to produce and bring together such a range of materials initially occured through a symposium at which earlier versions of these papers were presented and discussed. Two agencies were instrumental in bringing together such interdisciplinary and culturally diverse materials: The International Association for People-Environment Studies (IAPS) who initiated and carried forward the onus of the symposium and South Bank University which hosted the symposium in the summer of 1991 and subsequently provided the necessary resources to put these papers into a publishable form.

Thanks are due to: all the authors of the papers who have revised them for this volume, Gilles Barbey and Roderick Lawrence and the executive committee of IAPS for their involvement and support, Nicola Hallas for her organisation and production of the papers, Josephine Gooderham of Ashgate Publishers for support and guidance in their preparation and, finally, Professor M. Gibson of The School of Land Management and Urban Policy at South Bank University for committing resources of a variety of kinds to this enterprise.

1 Learning housing designing: The *home-less* design education

N. Teymur

Background

This paper is neither primarily about housing or 'housing research' nor simply about 'design education', but about a juxtaposition, or an intersection, of them.

The background to this has been an observation that although an overwhelming majority of the members of international, interdisciplinary associations such as IAPS or EDRA as well as the participants of conferences are involved in education, as a research topic education is not more than a minority interest and only a small number of papers that are presented at these conferences tend to deal with their *educational* experiences. This therefore leaves us with an unanswered question as to how, exactly, their research work finds (or does *not* find) its way *into* (or originates *from*) studios or classrooms.

To give some substance to my provocation I would like to start with some pretty obvious facts and make the following arguments:

- Housing is the one building type which literally every human being (even the so-called 'homeless' ones!) use most of their lives and most hours of their days.
- Houses (or housing) are the most common, the smallest, and the most 'ordinary' of the buildings, yet, they make up the bulk of the physical fabric of cities, towns and villages, and have the richest social and cultural meanings embedded in them.
- Often, the largest part of most families' budgets go to paying for their homes - whether as mortgage payments or as rent.

- They therefore contain the most reliable bodies of evidence about everyday lives of people.
- Furthermore, and contrary to the accusations of determinism attached to such views, housing quality (in whatever way it is defined) can be variously associated, even correlated, with quality of life, mental and physical health and social well-being in general.

Housing lack poses health risk

THE Royal College of Physicians is calling on the Government to build more affordable homes, in a report by the college's public health faculty.

The report claims that living in poor quality and overcrowded housing increases the spread of infectious and respiratory diseases and the problem of homelessness increases stress.

It predicts that the housing shortage will get worse and calls for an increase in both private and public house building programmes.

Figure 1.1 *Source: Building Design*, 24 May, 1991

One might think that even just one of these facts would be more than enough to make housing a most prominent research area and a popular design topic in schools of architecture and planning, but, alas, that is not the case. Neither its social and urban significance not its sheer quantity is deemed sufficient to make housing more than a minor building type, and one that is *not* considered by educators and the educated alike to be the stuff of which 'great architecture' is made. It is therefore seen neither worthy of substantial study programmes nor of creative, innovative and challenging design exercises. (As I will discuss later, the mere existence of housing research and design education under the same roof is neither a substitute nor a guarantee for an integration of the two areas).

In this paper I will try to substantiate some of these observations and offer some explanations on the basis of brief sociological, epistemological and pedagogical analyses putting the current attitudes in their historical, ideological and political contexts. I must make it clear that my point of view here is primarily *educational* and my observations largely derive from my experience of the British architectural education.[1]

In the end I will attempt to briefly suggest how we can bring these two areas of work closer with a view to integrating them.

Organization of the paper

Because of the scope that I am trying to cover, I will have to be brief and precise at the same time, but it is not easy to achieve both in dealing with a subject matter that provokes a lot of emotions as well as touching a variety of academic and professional expertise.

For example, my first generalized observation would be that housing is an area where a detachment, even a separation, between *knowledge* and *design*, the *world* and the *School* and *research* and *education* seems to have been highly entrenched. This observation can be taken as a serious theoretical challenge just as much as a polemical statement. It may provoke gut reactions as well as positivistic scrutiny. The questions that may arise could include: 'why does it matter?' or, 'what is wrong with getting on with our housing research or design teaching; surely nobody is stopping those who want to do both, or to use research findings in the studio?, or, more pedantically, 'what do you really mean with 'the world' and 'knowledge'?

In response to such questions, I will be both polemical, hence, occasionally overstating a case to provoke reactions, and analytical, hence, attempting to be accountable. I will therefore be analytical in my polemics, and somewhat polemical in my analysis.

Inspired by such questions, the order of the paper will be as follows;

1. Observations and contexts;
2. Analysis;
3. Criticism;
4. Expansion;
5. Integration.

A contextual introduction

We, the academics and researchers tend to behave as if we operate in a context which is our own making. We weave our networks, build up our associations, establish our institutes, and develop our discourses and disciplines almost solely around bibliographical (or architectural) references.

The internal workings of this self-referential and almost incestuous 'academy' of ours inevitably generate two epistemological problems that are relevant to our topic:

i. the *wider world*, which includes and effects the very objects of our work, is either reduced to an optional interest that we indulge in outside working hours (we may read about it, paint it, participate in it, ...) in a way that does not much influence our research or teaching; or it is reduced to manageable research topics or architectural commissions.
ii. our self-referential, funding-stimulated, client-orientated, market-led or institutionally sanctioned work naturally tends to concentrate on what *is* already published, designed, built or taught, and seldom on what is *not*.

When our work on housing and education is seen under these two perspectives, two attitudes emerge: We become more aware of the context ranging from G7 summit to the most recent pronouncements from the Royal Architectural Critic, from the house prices to the recent developments in CAD, from the RIBA's recent deal with the Government on architectural education to the 'post-deconstructivist' fashions in Schools of Architecture, or from EC Directive on architectural education to the homelessness in London, and try to establish the links between our work and this wider world. Secondly, by identifying gaps, absences and silences in our work, we become more acute in our perception, more self-critical in our assessment and somewhat negative in our analysis.

Figure 1.2 Exhibition poster, 1969

Analysis of education and housing

I propose that rather than asking how housing research (hereafter HR) and design education (hereafter DE) are *related* - as, obviously, they must be, we should be asking how and why, in practice, they seem to be treated as *un-related*?

But, why this negativity? Would it not be more useful if I did gratefully acknowledge those rare cases of teaching housing design that are indeed informed by research. Or, couldn't I have cited individual research projects that concern themselves with the transmission of research knowledge into design process? The answer is that, what analytical work should primarily do is to expose what *is*, rather than imagine what one thinks the things *ought to be*. I therefore feel obliged to highlight the overwhelming cases of *ignoring* knowledge rather than to celebrate the few that do not.

But, where do these methodological judgements and strategic decisions come from and which theoretical premises they are based on?

Firstly, they come from an understanding that architectural and planning educations are practices with their own specificities, in other words, they are distinct both from architectural or planning practices and from the education of other disciplines.

Secondly, my observations and the analysis on the relationship between architectural education (hereafter AE) and HR are based on a two-fold theoretical framework on which I have been working for some time:

1. *A disciplinary framework (SIEP):* according to which architectural practice (AP, architectural education (AE), housing practice (HP) and HR can be identified as the objects of SOCIOLOGY, IDEOLOGY, EPISTEMOLOGY, and PEDAGOGY; and

2. *An analytical model (OoMm):* according to which AP, AE, HP and HR can be seen in terms of their OBJECTIVES, OBJECTS, METHODOLOGIES, and MANAGEMENT.

Let me go through these briefly:

SIEP Framework

- **SOCIOLOGY** of AP, AE, HP and HR refers to the social organization and the constitution of these practices;

- **IDEOLOGY** of AP, AE, HP and HR refers to the ways these practices see and represent themselves to themselves;

- **EPISTEMOLOGY** of AP, AE, HP and HR refers to the process and the produces of knowledge production in and about these practices;

- **PEDAGOGY** of AP, AE, HP and HR refers to the processes by which they are taught and learned.

OOMM Model

- **OBJECTIVES** of AP, AE, HP and HR refers to the questions of why and with what purpose and aims do these practices operate?

- **OBJECTS** of AP, AE, HP and HR refers to the questions of what is designed, built, studied and taught (eg. physical objects, pedagogical packages and bodies of knowledge, ...)

- **METHODOLOGY** (and the medium) of AP, AE, HP and HR refers to the questions of how the objects are studied, taught, researched in what mediums they express themselves?

- **MANAGEMENT** of AP, AE, HP and HR refers to the questions of who administers the designing, building, researching or teaching activities, hence, who controls the resources, frameworks, decisions, and knowledge?

A juxtaposition, possibly on a matrix, of these two sets of dimensions prompts some interesting, albeit complicated further questions that would not readily arise when H, HR, A and AE are considered from mono-disciplinary points of view. Additionally, such a juxtaposition generates some insights concerning the operations and organization of AE and HR with respect to each other. For example:

- How is H *defined* by different disciplines, practices, social groups and cultures?
- What effect does this differential definition have on the way in which H is valued, studies, funded, designed, produced, distributed, ...?
- What constitutes H knowledge?
- Where does H knowledge enter (or fail to penetrate) the design process?

To be able to identify individual issues to see the range of problems associated with HR and DE we may attempt an analytical matrix of observations under the two frameworks mentioned.

AE & HR	SOCIOLOGY	IDEOLOGY	EPISTE-MOLOGY	PEDAGOGY
OBJECTIVES	j🔫☺🕯🗣🚃 🚃 jhhgkk	🐁✍📖_♡ jh	🚂🚃🕯⌀⇨ ⌀	Plngc••77
OBJECTS	🔫🚌🌴👁〰✍ ⌀▥jko🏠	bu🐿ψ🌲🏠	¶8∞ ??	JHj⇨⌀🕯⌀ 🏠🏠
METHO-DOLOGY	@£gb≤˚¬🚃 🚂	jhf🦇✾	xcrvtrhf⇨🕯 🔫	,jh8i
MANAGE-MENT	K';.hυfo	kª1🌳🍂🌲🐈	.,m◇🦉🐿 🚃🐿te	=8VɃĦVHu

Figure 1.3

It must be declared that the contents of the matrix that follows represents what I think the dominant situation at present *is*, rather that what it *should be*.

AE & HR	SOCIOLOGY	IDEOLOGY	EPISTEM-OLOGY	PEDA-GOGY
O B J E C T I V E S	**AE>** A legal hurdle to get into and socialize within an established profession ... **H & HR>** Producing knowledge and information on housing production and distribution or on housing conditions, ... mainly for policy-making, but also for guiding housing design, ...	**AE>** 'Architecture' as distinct from 'building' design as unique and 'core' component, Architectural design as primarily an activity of formal composition, ... **H & HR>** House/housing as a socially defined, politically dominated resource; culture, space and form are dealt with apolitically and often separate from economics, ...	**AE>** Using existing knowledge in design; not aimed to produce new knowledge, ... **H & HR>** Producing new knowledge on H, identifying patterns of change in legal and cultural definitions, ...	**AE>** Training professional architects (mainly for private practice); 'good designer' being the expected end product, ... **H & HR & AE>** Housing studied by academics; few courses on housing, selective mention in history; design projects seldom based on HR, and criticism seldom informed by research knowledge, ...

AE & HR	SOCIO-LOGY	IDEO-LOGY	EPISTEM-OLOGY	PEDA-GOGY
O B J E C T S	**AE>** 'Society' does not exist except as undifferentiated and largely conflict-free abstractions, e.g., 'community', 'users', 'clients', etc; 'Architect' as leader of construction team (fast eroding and replaced by other professionals) ; ... **H & HR>** Housing either as a sociological problem or an economic resource - without urban, spatial and architectural specificity, or in terms of minute use and life patterns of inhabitants, ...	**AE>** 'Architect' as the visionary, know-all, multi-disciplinarianartist/ scientist; being challenged and forced to become business*men* (which they already are!); fear and rejection of the ordinary, ... **H & HR>** HR to highlight the inequalities; or to romanticize meaning of home; yet, housing not as *produced*, but as already-existing backdrop; ...	**AE>** Buildings as the source *and* the object of knowledge; EPISTEMOLOGICAL OBJECTS, concepts and 'theories' are derived from client-orientated private practice, beliefs, manifestos, personal views or professional guidelines, (eg *RIBA Plan of Works*); history, practice and technology as separate corpus of knowledge; knowledge and information from other disciplines are used and referred to, but seldom criticized, added to or reciprocated; ... **H & HR>** Housing knowledge produced and fragmented among various disciplines and professions; seldom integrative, often blind to others; ...	**AE>** Educational material: traditionally codified/ received wisdom of architecture (expressed in Architectural discourse), privileged 'works of A' (hence, little or no housing), 'aesthetic/ formal theories of A'; environmental design and construction techniques but no social and little urban knowledge; ... **H & HR>** Fragmentation of housing knowledge reproduced in H education; divided between Departments;

AE & HR	SOCIOLOGY	IDEOLOGY	EPISTEM-OLOGY	PEDA-GOGY
METHODOLOGY (& MEDIUM)	**AE>** A sociology of AE is non-existent, knowledge of its relationship with architectural profession undeveloped; ... **H & HR>** Fairly analytical, quantitative; institutions or policy-oriented, domestic scope, macro and demographic, or micro-cultural, ethnographic, historical, but seldom theory-led;	**AE>** Combined ideologies of Architectural profession, 'A', design; and periodic changes of fashion militating against sustained and informed awareness; ... **H & HR>** Quantitative certainty vs. doctrinaire prescriptions; or purely formal approaches; impossibility of experimentatio ndetachment from design practice; ...	**AE>** Reproduction of received perceptions, canonic precedents or repetition of one-liners, '6 points', '10 Commandment s', etc, as substitute for analytical knowledge of buildings and cities; impatience with and rejection of knowledge that does not immediately prove itself *in practice*; ... **H & HR>** Fragmented housing knowledge produced and expressed in different mediums (eg. numerical, graphical, verbal, emotional; ...	**AE>** Curriculum divided between design and lectures, hence studio and lecture rooms, hence drawing board and slide screen, hence verbal and graphical; ... criticism confined to design as drawing; ... **H & HR>** Housing design not researched for teaching;

AE & HR	SOCIOLOGY	IDEOLOGY	EPISTEMOLOGY	PEDAGOGY
MANAGEMENT	**AE>** AE as 'serving' the profession; market as the determinant of the number and type of graduates; architectural practice background often seen as sufficient to teach most subjects or run Schools; studio teachers seen as key (or core) staff, others 'supporting' the studio; increasingly hierarchical with part-timers doing most teaching with little say, input or commitment; research staff isolated and temporary; ... **H & HR>** Research grants available for narrowly defined goals; research only on topics that are funded; ...	**AE>** Office practice (mainly private practice) as the source of inspiration, target of aspirations, pool of part-time tutors supposedly bringing in 'real-world' experiences or more well-known ones giving 'master classes'; ... **H & HR>** Research done to supply 'data' for policy makers, hence hands-off from politics as well as design and urban planning; tendency not to be critical of government policies, professional practices or business priorities; ...	**AE>** Curriculum organized to *support* and *feed* studio design work; knowledge and information from architectural and building subjects and from other disciplines called in, used and referred to, but non-architects or architects with multi-disciplinary training not allowed to influence what is taught and how; ... **H & HR>** Housing knowledge as official data open to manipulation research separate from teaching; ...	**AE>** Architectural practice background seen as almost sufficient to set curriculum and teach most subjects, even to run Schools; curriculum organized around the 'studio' research is rudimentary, criticism is visually oriented; ... **H & HR>** Research generally done separate from teaching and mostly by those not teaching design; design teachers seldom doing research; studios not organised in a way that would allow research continuity; ...

For all their brevity, axiomatic style and lack of empirical support, these working matrices are expected to help bring together the fields of housing and AE, reveal the gaps in our understanding of our own work, can lead to further research into specific areas identified and can stimulate informed criticism. They can also enable us to move from negative observations to positive propositions and integrative actions.

First some critical results of the analysis.

Criticism

While trying to understand whether and what AE was missing out in its exclusion of housing ad HR from its scope I have not examined whether and what *housing* was missing out but not being seriously studied by architects. Pointing out the results of much of the architectural intervention into mass housing during recent decades, cynics might even say that it is not so bad if architects kept their skills to what they consider to be 'Architecture' and keep their hands off housing. For us, however, cynicism should only be the last resort when research and education both fail to analyse the role of architectural and planning professions along with other institutions and groups of people in generating less then satisfactory housing.

Absence of housing in design curriculum is not just a defect in meeting the pragmatic objectives of AE but has much wider consequences. Training good architects with the assumption either that they will seldom design housing or that housing is fairly easy to design, or worse, that housing is not 'Architecture' in the first place, is theoretically and pedagogically untenable as it is morally indefensible.

(Talking of the theoretical and the moral, I am aware of the danger of falling into an old trap: it is not tenable to suggest that socially-conscious individuals or Schools would research and design housing and the others would deal with other building types, or that housing is a more 'social' object than, say, office buildings or leisure centres. 'Social' is not an adjective denoting higher morality or responsibility, but an objective description of a concrete phenomenon).

But, we should not lose a sense of a *global* perspective either. It is not right to put the cart in front of the horse. If, even some of the most developed industrial societies still seem to have serious housing problems, it is not simply because *architects* have not been designing good housing, researchers have not been doing enough research or the schools have not been teaching mor housing projects. The housing problem is a problem that is part and parcel of the very social set-ups that fail to (or chose not to) tackle many other human problems - some more urgent even than housing.

Therefore, while housing is special in its *educational* content, an incomplete consideration of building types in general would mean an incomplete understanding of the built reality in general. A highly selective view of built reality leads to a defective grasp of what is necessary and what is possible, or what is important and what is not so important in architecture.

There can be no satisfactory explanation of the failures of public housing involving the lives of millions of people without a comprehensive understanding of the close links between cultural, political, technological, professional, pedagogical, cognitive and other processes around housing. But there is more to understanding what is really meant by this string of words than just listing them. After all, all course documents state that the courses are aiming to do precisely that.

The problem is therefore manifold and many sided: in addition to the declarations that architects normally deal with 'Architecture' (hence, not with ordinary buildings), there is the problem that even when they decided to promote housing to the rank of Architecture (as they occasionally did in recent decades), they may not be equipped to do justice to it.

BD Special report

GOOD DESIGN IN HOUSING?

The DoE's Good Design in Housing Awards were announced yesterday. Medals went to 15 schemes, and another 35 were commended. Is the award really achieving the increase in standards that was hoped for by its sponsors? With Parker Morris standards increasingly under attack, and growing dissatisfaction with most types of housing, *Building Design* reports on the awards and the issues that lie behind them. Pages 17-27.

Figure 1.4 *Source: Building Design,* 27 October, 1978

News

Jim's Runcorn housing in shock demolition vote

By John Wood

Corporation decision 'ruthless and dictatorial' says Stirling

Figure 1.5 *Source: Building Design,* 3 March, 1989

Figure 1.6
(Collage by N. Teymur)

Similarly, even if the researchers research housing to the best of their abilities, the knowledge produced is not always in a form or medium that designers and planners can use, or students can digest. The respective shortcomings of the researchers and designers are characterized by a *symmetry or ignorance* and a *symmetry of incomprehension*. There are gaps of paradigm, gaps of medium, gaps of language, differences of point of view as well as differences of objectives and objects. There is even a mutual distrust that shows itself in dismissive (and largely anti-intellectual) remarks round such simplistic oppositions as theory vs. practice, writing vs. drawing, talking vs. designing or real world vs. academia.

From criticism to positive action

The analysis of the link (*and* neglect of the links) between housing and education, and research into the methodological issues in everyday teaching activities have revealed some unexpected possibilities for both research and teaching, but particularly for AE.

For example, I have observed that in addition to exposing the current state of the relationship between AE and HR, alternative matrices in terms of **OoMm** and **SIEP** models could b constructed to develop new relationships and present fresh starting points for establishing alternative educational policies. The resulting explanation would at first seem to be arbitrary, but by introducing an explicitly theoretical and comparative correlation (as opposed to a selectively empirical one) this approach can yield greater integration and rigour in both research and education.

Expansion: from a criticism of education to its practice

In order to project onto pedagogic practice the critical observations made, that practice itself has to be approached in a way quite different from the traditional ones such as pragmatism, professionalism, anecdotal experiences, Architectural partizanship, etc. In addition to introducing OoMm and SIEP models of examining education, I am proposing two parallel strategies to guide our architectural pedagogy and research into an *integrative* direction:

1. A re-definition of the *purpose* of AE, and
2. A re-charting of the scope of *knowledge* in architecture and education.

1. *A re-definition of the purpose of AE*

Over-professionalization of AE has long been suppressing and holding down an aspect of education that in fact distinguishes education from other human endeavours. To spell out this aspect and to explore the possibilities I want to introduce a dual concept of 'purpose' (as distinct from mere education objectives), comprising of a 'first' and a 'second', purpose.

i. 'The first purpose' of professional education:
(or, the bottom line of so-called 'learning by designing')

The design projects done in schools of architecture have the universally recognized purpose of teaching design by doing. Even with its inevitable status as *hypothetical,* rather than practical or real, problem solving, design project is considered to be the most useful vehicle for attaining the real-life design skills and developing the designerly working habits. For this purpose, it is obvious that the larger the variety of building types experienced the better it would be. Also for this purpose, every building can be experimented on (or, to use a common student expression, 'played with'). The question of what type of knowledge do the studio projects use, and whether and to what extent they use *research-based knowledge* is not difficult to investigate. What is likely to emerge is that, this view of design projects is largely based on pure pragmatism. After all, professional education is in the business not of producing wisdom, but institutionally sanctioned types and numbers of professionals!

ii. 'The second purpose' of education: housing as an educational object

'Second purpose' of education does not imply that it is secondary with respect to the pragmatic purposes. 'Second' here refers to the present status of the purpose of education repressed and suppressed under the ideology of 'professional training'.

Now, I would like to argue that besides the straight forward use of design projects in training architects, every project done in the schools context can also be useful in educating the minds, the eyes and the hands of our students in a variety of directions. These directions may be different from, but not necessarily incompatible with, other, more pragmatic, purposes. However, they are not limited by comparatively narrow professional objectives. Buildings seen as complex socio-technical objects and their designing as equally complex socio-cognitive processes can be the vehicles for educating enlightened, perceptive and creative individuals. In this respect housing has a special potential not matched by any number of building types.

Take any building type through which future designers learn the skills of designing; schools, hospitals, museums, offices, sports centres or, say, newspaper offices. These buildings all have cultural, social, technological, historical, human, ... contents. They can make up urban landmarks or constitute city blocks. They are highly visible, even assertive, with their large sizes and formal features, they may represent specific divisions of labour, or stand for and assist the dominance of a culture of a mode of production. They all have a variety of symbolic purposes, spatial and functional complexities, institutional intricacy, and behavioral multi-variancy - often all atone and the same time. In an ideal (that is, hypothetical) social world that values enlightenment, one could examine any or all of these aspects in the studio. One could unravel the layers of meaning and control embodied in the multi-levels of spatial and functional organization. One could explore the complex technology of knitting the bricks-and-mortar of the building fabric, and find out how it is interlaced with a multitude of financial, cultural and geographical determinants. Or, one can get pleasure out of analysing beauty (or ugliness) while trying to create new forms ...

In other words, there is no reason why buildings of all sorts could not be excellent *educational* material for what I call 'the second purpose' of education. Yet, none has the unique combination that houses have, of simple, quoditienne transparency on the one hand and subtle complexity, deep memory and multi-layered presence, on the other. The fact that people grow up *with* as well as *in* houses, and they change as well as are changed by the domestic extensions of their bodies is more than enough to make the houses and housing the repository of social knowledge learning of which would be highly rewarding.

2. *A re-charting of the scope of knowledge in architecture and education*

Now, in an effort to satisfy the two purposes of education I am advocating an open and critical state of mind or, what I propose to call, an *'epistemological maximalism'* which, briefly, implies the ideal of a more and wider body of knowledge than the traditional research, education and practice in architecture, planning and urban design would aim for. These two opposing attitudes to knowledge define two main strategies:

i. The minimum strategy

is to do with increasing the knowledge of the built form (which may or may not include a consideration of housing) through research and teaching, but primarily for *pragmatic* (ie utilitarian, technical, contractual, narrowly academic) purposes. What it aims to achieve is only the 'right' (that is, minimum necessary) degree and amount of accurate, reliable, classifiable, immediately usable ... knowledge - not too little, but not more than immediately called for either. Its implicit role model would be scientific, industrial or commercial knowledge geared to specific *extra-pedagogic* aims. In the case of architecture (with 'A'), this minimum also includes selective historical information, ideological notions and professional self-images that architects entertain in their minds and institutions, if not always in their deeds.

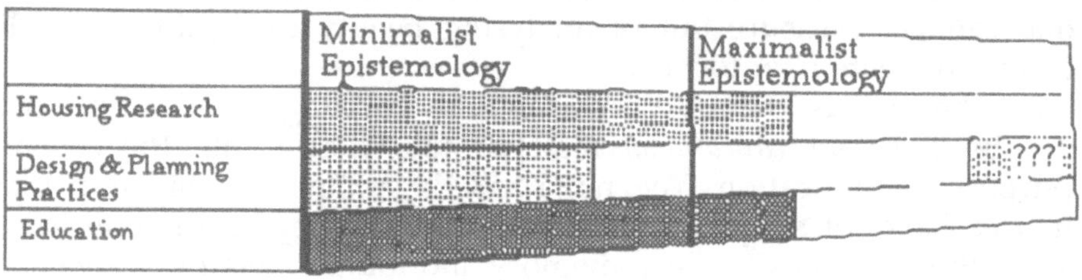

Figure 1.7 **Minimum strategy's treatment of two epistemologies in terms of their emphases, priorities and relative perspectives in research, design and planning practices and education**

ii. The maximum strategy

involves producing and using knowledge in ever increasing quality and quantity. This knowledge must of course be reliable, but not necessarily as accurate, as classifiable or as readily usable as in the case of minimum strategy.

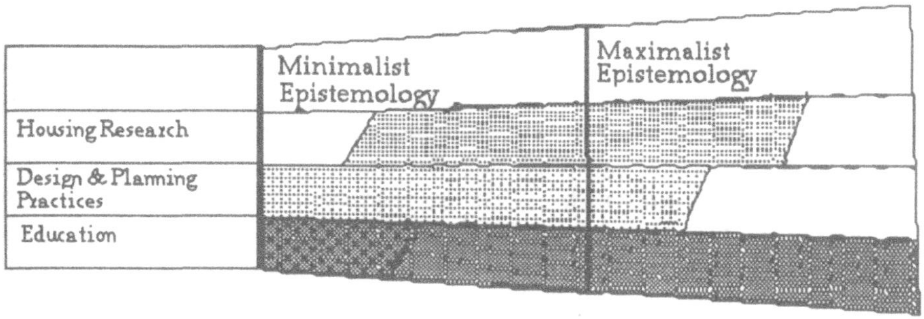

Figure 1.8 **Maximum strategy's treatment of two epistemologies in terms of their emphases, priorities and relative perspectives in research, design and planning practices and education**

Rather, it is a kind of knowledge that aspires to *advance learning* and *wisdom*. It questions and makes critical *its own* function outside the sphere of knowledge production. For example, 'impracticality' would not necessarily be synonymous with uselessness, long-term wisdom would not be subject to accusation of irrelevance, and the critical could not be equated with the disruptive. Its role model is traditional, liberal, academic activity with sources of inspiration ranging from arts to social idealism.

The first strategy is geared to satisfying the minimum necessary requirements of practices, but it is occasionally allowed to produce a bit of the second type too. Professional/vocational education (e.g. architectural education) is assumed (in effect, if not in intension) to need only a rudimentary knowledge of the built world for its primary purpose of training professional designers. If it also harbours some elements of the second type of knowledge, or research activity, its motive in doing so is seldom the advancement of knowledge.

The second strategy, on the other hand, aspires to higher wisdom, broader perspective and wider creativity.

Integration

Because of the institutional, ideological and pedagogical attitudes entrenched in both camps, alternative and more integrative modes of analysis, research, teaching and designing have not been given much of a chance in educational set-ups. For example, it is possible to study housing in the studio and go beyond mere 6B-sketch approach. It is possible to read and talk about, or survey, criticize quantify, even politicize architecture, .. while experimenting with forms, colours, proportions. For the same token, it is not unimaginable to promote design with a substantial knowledge-base as it is to study space and form 'scientifically'.

For example, analysis of buildings or urban spaces as independent of their formal or stylistic characteristics:

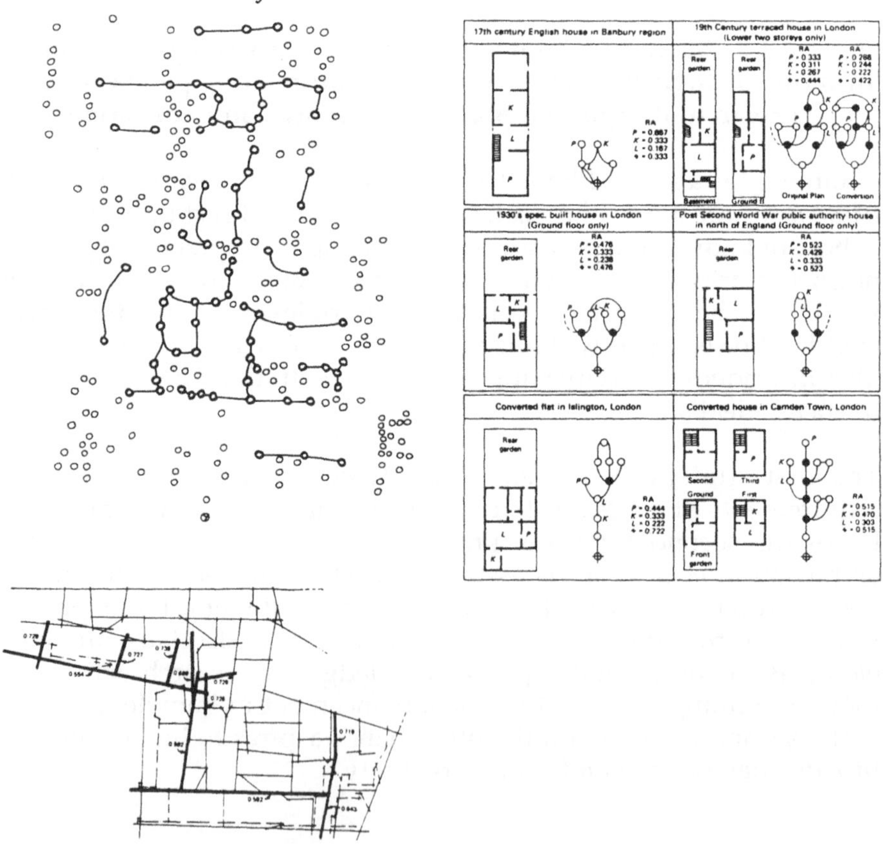

Figure 1.9 *Source*: Hillier, B. & Hanson, J. (1984), *Social Logic of Space*, CUP, pp. 131, 157).

or, studying a wide range of aspects in a comparative manner - and do so in the studio, as part of the 'design' programme:

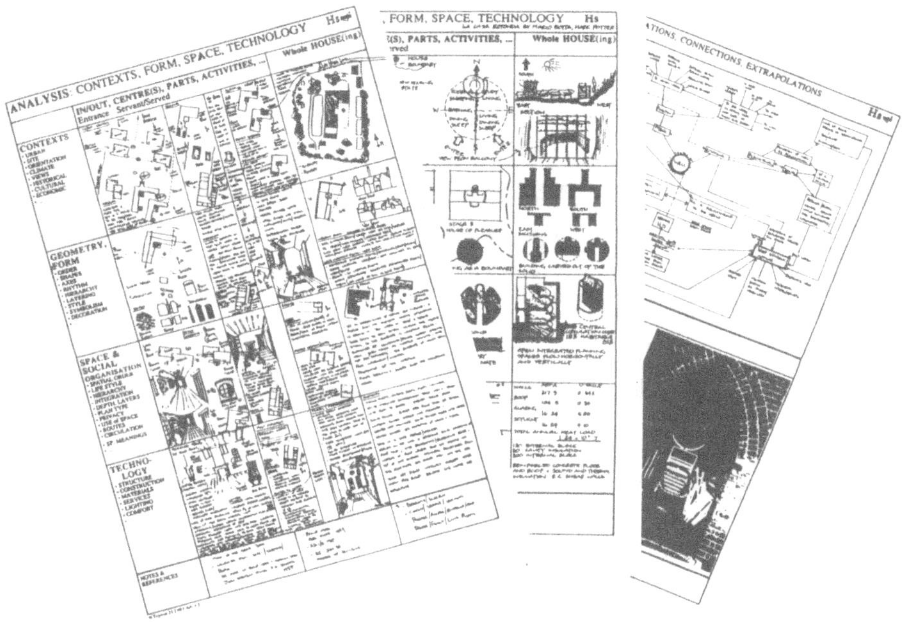

Figure 1.10 **Analytical design**

Yet, attempting to integrate knowledge and design has to go beyond traditional research and traditional design attitudes. Knowledge and design will not simply come together any more than elements of either can automatically come together to form greater wholes.

Figure 1.11 *Source: Behiç Ak, 'Cumhuriyet'*, 12 December, 1982

The 'Project' is a mode that must not be underestimated. 'Design' is an activity with great educational as well as creative potential. And research must stop being a highly specialized and highly developed tool with no built-in medium to communicate with its subject-matter.

Whilst one cannot change in the absence of changes in the other, neither case of change would be sufficient without integrating 'third parties'. These, however, require new occasions, new platforms and new vehicles to expose our ignorances and insularities while developing new modes of analysis, design and criticism.

Aiming to incorporate into design education *as full* a knowledge of *as much* of the built world as possible is not incompatible with deeper and specialist knowledge. Pragmatic purpose should not stop us enjoying a broader view. Recognition of the limits set by the commercial market is not an excuse for refusing enlightenment.

Learning about important issues such as housing even when there are no immediate 'customers' is probably more commendable than condemning our practice to irrelevance or our vision to a poverty of imagination.

Note

1. Many of the ideas and observations presented here have been explored in earlier work. For a recent attempt to integrate curricular issues with educational policy, see: Teymur, N. (1992) *Architectural Education: Issues in Educational Practice and Policy*, London, Question Press.

2 Housing and homes: Agenda for future research

R. Lawrence

Introduction

Housing and home are complex subjects of enquiry. Despite the rapid growth of studies in this field, academics and professional practitioners have rarely developed and applied innovative concepts and methods. Rather, they have usually reapplied traditional approaches which have seldom identified and studied the interrelations between all the different classes of dimensions that define and are mutually defined by the design, meaning and use of housing and homes. Moreover, a temporal perspective has been rarely applied. This paper requests and suggests a re-orientation of contemporary research founded on integrative principles that assist scholars to identify and study the multiple dimensions of housing and home. Furthermore, the reciprocal relations between all these dimensions can be taken into account to generate a contextual understanding, either at a specific point in time, or over an extended period.

Housing evokes a range of divergent images and concepts which reflect its multi-dimensional nature. Recent research collectively shows that the meaning of housing, like the meaning of home,is not only complex and elusive, but that is also varies from person to person, between social groups in the same society and across cultures (cf. Altman and Werner, 1985, Duncan, 1981, Kent, 1990, Kron, 1983, Lawrence, 1987, Low & Chambers, 1989)[1]. Some studies show that houses are commonly attributed economic values, exchange values, aesthetic values and use values whereas, in addition to these, homes are usually attributed symbolic and sentimental values. In this respect, home is not merely 'a territorial core' (Porteous, 1976) nor 'an ordering principle in space' (Dovey, 1978) defined by material characteristics, but a complex entity that defines and is defined by cultural, demographic, economic, material, political and psychological dimensions. Consequently, it is not surprising that research on housing and home has grown in scope and volume.

In recent decades many theoretical perspectives, concepts and research methods have been used by authors from a wide range of academic disciplines and professions. Although this paper is not meant to provide an exhaustive account of all these theoretical and methodological contributions, it is suggested that an overview of recent publications enables the formulation of two broad classes of studies:

i) research concerned with urban and housing history and sociology; and
ii) a range of studies of people and their surroundings at the scales of dwelling units and residential quarters.

This paper briefly outlines and comments on the underlying theoretical and methodological frameworks that have guided research in both these classes of studies. It identifies selective and interpretative biases which have meant that it has been extremely difficult to develop and apply a comparative perspective, or examine the interrelations between the complex array of dimensions that define and are mutually defined by the design, meaning and use of housing and homes. Although this paper does not provide prescriptions for future research, it tables theoretical and methodological principles, which are currently being applied to study housing and home in the Canton of Geneva, Switzerland.

Characterisations of contemporary research

Housing and home were not major subjects of enquiry for many researchers in the social sciences, nor professional planners and designers, until recently. Nonetheless, during the last two decades, both housing studies and research on home have grown rapidly in scope and volume. It is suggested that two broad classes of interpretations can be observed: research concerned with urban and housing history and sociology; and architectural, ergonomic, psychological and sociological studies of people and their dwelling units, and/or their residential neighbourhood. The characteristics of each of these two classes of studies are illustrated in figure 1 and they will now be briefly described.

Urban and housing history and sociology

During recent decades, a large volume of housing studies has examined the interrelations between broad societal dimensions and the layout and use of residential neighbourhoods and dwelling units. Themes including housing economics, national and local housing policies and legislation, housing construction methods and domestic technology have been examined. In general, this class of studies has examined broad societal dimensions related to mechanisms of 'supply and demand' and/or the housing conditions of specific categories of people in precise cities and towns (eg. the size of households and dwelling units, landlord-tenant relations, and official housing and land-use policies and practices). There are very few studies that explicitly include a study of morphological or spatial dimensions, but Daunton (1983) and Lawrence (1986) are two exceptions. Both these studies aim to identify changes in the design and use of dwelling units over time, and relate these changes to broad societal dimensions. In some cases, including Lawrence (1986), this approach leads to the formulation of housing typologies in precise cities or towns over an extensive period of time.

There has been a limited amount of demographic research concerning the structure and composition of households and families, (which have undergone significant changes in many industrialized and developing countries during this century, particularly with respect to the increase in the portion of one-person households, the decline in household size and the increase in one-parent families (cf. Haumont & Segaud, 1989). In general, many studies in this category of research give scant attention to the changing nature of the design and composition of the housing stock, or the values of residents concerning the meaning and use of domestic space and facilities. This oversight illustrates a more general shortcoming of this category of research: in general, the interrelations between cultural and societal dimensions and processes have rarely been associated or examined in conjunction with personal ideas and values, as well as household customs, either at one point in time, or over an extended period.

TIONS	(Synchronic usually)	
	MORPHOLOGICAL STUDIES (Synchronic and Diachronic)	Morphology of residiential quarters Layout and size of dwelling units (so with households) Architecture of housing types (somti larger context)
AND THEIR JNDINGS	PSYCHOLOGICAL & SOCIO-PSYCHOLGOICAL STUDIES (Synchronic approach)	Cultural, societal and individual hum How residents perceive, value and as residential environments
S	STUDIES OF DOMESTIC LIFE (Synchronic approach)	Architectural studies Ergonomic studies Socio-economic class, age, professiona Household demographics: structure a composition of households

e and interpretative biases in both categories of research)

.1 The design, meaning and use of housing and home

Studies of people and their surroundings

This category of housing research includes contributions from ergonomics, environmental psychology, architecture and behavior studies, and housing sociology, which have commonly examined the point-of-view of the resident using either:

i) psychological and socio-psychological concepts such as identity, place-identity, self, social-self and cosmic-self in order to interpret how people perceive, use and value residential environments, from the geographical scale of specific rooms to neighbourhoods; or
ii) architectural and sociological interpretations stemming from surveys, including interpretations of housing aspirations and 'needs', and lifestyles, in terms of the age, gender, education, household composition, socio-economic class and residential mobility of the studied population. These studies have enabled differences between residents in the same and different localities to be identified and interpreted in terms of cultural, demographic and socio-economic variables. Yet, the majority of these studies in this category have examined biological and psychological dimensions without explicitly accounting for the broader societal context in which the studied population resided. This means that ideologies concerning housing and home, in general, and housing policies, economics, and domestic life, in particular, are not integrated into these studies. Moreover, research of this kind has frequently adopted a selective bias by focusing on the so-called 'typical' or 'norm', while rarely examining representative samples of resident populations (eg. single-parent households, the unemployed) or representative samples of the housing stock (eg. studying single-family houses or recurrent apartment buildings at the expense of other types of residential accommodation). Last, but not least, and in contrast to the first category of studies, this kind of research has rarely adopted a temporal perspective (Lawrence, 1985) and, consequently, it has not provided a theoretical or methodological framework for an integrative approach or the study of housing and home.

Principles for a re-orientation of future studies

The two preceding sections of this paper have classified and given a broad assessment of studies of housing and home. Some limitations of the two categories of studies have been briefly presented. Given these limitations, the task of some researchers, during the last decade, has been the redefinition and the reinterpretation of housing and home. Some of these researchers (cf. Deprés, 1989, Lawrence, 1987) argue that an integrative perspective is necessary. This kind of perspective ought to overcome the either/or dualist approach shared by the two categories of studies presented above. It is suggested that this goal can be achieved if (and only if) the dimensions of study in any particular research project are explicitly related to and comprehended with respect to the contextual conditions in which they occur. These contextual conditions define and are mutually defined by a range of cultural, societal and individual human dimensions that are interrelated, that occur at diverse scales, and that are susceptible to change during the course of time. In order to study these dimensions, and the interrelations between them, a redefinition and reorientation of much current research is required.

First, it is necessary to reject any **hierarchical model** used often in housing studies which is claimed to order 'variables' in terms of their weight or force. In this respect, and to cite but one example, it is noteworthy that Rapoport's (1969) claim that cultural variables have primacy over all others in the determination of house form is still frequently accepted *a priori* by scholars.

This hierarchical interpretation is not only partial (as Lawrence (1987) has shown) but it has also been illustrated that extremely broad conceptual tools, such as 'culture' need to be replaced by intensive analyses that define not only the dimensions operative in specific contexts but also the reciprocal relations between them.

Second, it is also necessary to reject any **atomistic-mechanistic model**, used in some housing studies to identify and study cause-effect interactions between two 'variables' isolated from the context in which they occur. One example of this kind of interpretation is the study of residential mobility and housing choice in terms of 'pushes and pulls'. This kind of study has been challenged by Michelson (1977, 1980).

In contrast to the two models just mentioned it is necessary to develop and apply a holistic, integrative, conceptual framework which not only reconciles the divergences between the two categories of housing studies presented earlier, but also accounts for the multiple dimensions of housing as well as the reciprocal relations between them, and the contextual conditions in which they occur.

These sets of principles have and still are being applied in an ongoing research project concerning the qualitative characteristics of rental housing in the Canton of Geneva[2]. This project includes two complementary studies;

1. First, an historical study of the evolving design and use of public, collective and private spaces and facilities in residential quarters built between 1860 and 1960; and a longitudinal study of household size and composition, the local housing stock, and housing tenure during this period. As this study has been published in french and english (Lawrence, 1986, 1990) only references or remarks will be made to it in the remainder of this paper. It is noteworthy that this study has identified many contextual conditions pertinent to housing in Geneva.
2. Second, an ongoing study of how inhabitants in the Canton of Geneva qualify the constituents of their residential environments and aspects of their daily lives. This study comprises a survey of 525 households from a representative sample supplied by the government statistical office. The survey includes plan analysis of residential buildings and their immediate surroundings; documentation of changes to the layout and furnishing of dwelling units; and a questionnaire with directed, semi-directed and open-ended questions about the daily activities of the household, and each respondent both inside and outside the dwelling unit; his or her residential biography; and questions about the dwelling unit, the residential building, and the neighbourhood.

From principles to applications

Bearing in mind earlier discussion in this paper about the pertinence of contextual understanding and the need for an integrative perspective, the content and structure of this ongoing study warrant further consideration, both in relation to those principles stated above and with respect to the initial results being obtained. The main issues include:

1. *What are the units of analysis?* Our reading of the literature on the meaning and use of home and neighbourhood underlines that there

are not prescribed boundaries that enable one to predefine that 'house is synonymous with home'. Rather than assuming, for example, that home can be equated with a dwelling unit, it is necessary to formulate a method of enquiry that can account for the multivariate meanings and uses of residential environments. This has been done in the ongoing survey, as well as the historical study.

Initial results suggest that this approach challenges recurrent interpretations of main and secondary residences by contemporary urban sociologists. They have commonly maintained that the dwelling unit in an urban setting is the main residence, whereas a property in the countryside that is used on weekends and during holidays is necessarily a secondary residence.

In the current study, 35% of households have access to two residences; in all cases the residence in the Canton of Geneva is rented, whereas in all but a few cases, the residence in the countryside is owned by the respondent or a close relative. There are clear indications from the initial results that although the majority of respondents spend much more of their time in their urban residence, this dwelling unit is not usually attributed the same emotional meaning as the residence in the countryside. In a few cases, respondents noted that they spend more time in their countryside residence - they cultivate it - and this was a consciously made pattern of living. Concurrently, they never used their urban residence on weekends nor during holidays, but only as a dormitory three or four evenings each week. In these cases the dwelling unit has a strong administrative and utilitarian value[3].

Last, but not least, the initial results suggest that those respondents who have access to two residences are generally less critical of both the design and management of their urban dwelling unit, as well as the qualitative aspects of the immediate surroundings, and the neighbourhood its services and facilities. Further multivariate analyses are being currently undertaken to examine other mediating variables that are interrelated to these relatively high levels of appreciation.

2. *How does one delimit the subject of study?* In relation to the preceding discussion, it is pertinent to examine how the qualitative characteristics of residential environments can be examined in terms of geographical areas that are frequently predefined in an arbitrary way by researchers. It has been commonplace for housing surveys to examine dwelling interiors without considering the external surroundings (beyond the plot) and especially the neighbourhood, its

services and facilities. Nonetheless, as there are not prescribed boundaries that define home, housing areas, or residential neighbourhood, alternative approaches ought to be formulated and applied. This is currently being done in the ongoing study in order to address some difficult issues, such as differences in the way respondents in the same and different neighbourhoods perceived and evaluate environmental problems (including air pollution and the propagation of noise), as well as access to public parks and natural reserves. Multivariate analyses are being undertaken and the in-depth study of open-ended questions may provide clues for further research.

3. *What characteristics are common to housing and daily life in a specific block, street, neighbourhood, city or region?* Previous studies suggest that there may be a shift in the relative weight or pertinence of those characteristics that residents use to qualify their surroundings as the geographical scale of the residential environment increases. This shift may occur irrespective of the age, gender, nationality or occupation of the residents.

The initial results of this study indicate that the way respondents qualify the environmental constituents of their dwelling, its site, and its immediate surroundings is different to the way they qualify the residential building in which that dwelling unit is located, as well as the neighbourhood and its services. Moreover, their is no linear relationship between the pertinence and appraisal of environmental constituents at these three different geographical scales. Reasons for this finding are still being examined.

4. *How does one account for consensual meanings and uses as well as individual differences?* The interrelations between people and their residential environment can be examined on four interrelated levels which have been presented in more detail elsewhere (Lawrence, 1986, 1987, 1990).

First, there are material and non-physical characteristics of the built environment and human life which are universal in a society. These include building regulations and some protocols for human behavior in specific situations.

Second, there are material and non-physical characteristics which are consistently shared by members of a community or a group during a specific period of time, such as prescribed ways of preparing and eating food.

Third, there are other characteristics shared by a few individuals, such as a household, an extended family, or a club, that can only be known and acted upon by those few individuals who are insiders.

Finally, any individual has certain ways of behaving and of evaluating which are idiosyncratic, and it is necessary to account for individual differences that mediate the ways people perceive and construe domesticity.

In order to accommodate these interrelated levels, the ongoing study is currently examining the responses to all sets of questions in relation to:

- age;
- gender;
- nationality;
- profession or occupation;
- housing management issues;
- length of tenancy;
- access to a secondary residence;
- appreciation of environmental problems;
- presence of kith and kin in the same neighbourhood.

The preceding discussion illustrates that the kind of approach advocated in this paper and currently being applied in ongoing research challenges some assumptions and raises several questions that have not been addressed by the majority of published studies of the qualitative aspects of housing. It is anticipated that most of these assumptions will be challenged and many questions will be answered by the application of qualitative and quantitative approaches that explicitly incorporate a temporal perspective.

5. How can a temporal perspective be applied? A small yet growing number of architectural and urban designers, housing administrators, and social scientists have refuted static interpretations of the relationships between people and their residential environments. Some share a viewpoint expressed by Michelson (1977) that challenges these static, positivistic, empirically based studies of a wide range of subjects, such as residential satisfaction, the personalisation of home interiors, privacy, security, well-being, 'user needs', and residential mobility. Apart from presenting a substantial amount of theoretical and empirical evidence that challenges many appraisal studies of residential environments, Michelson describes and illustrates the pertinence of a comprehensive approach which aims to:

1. establish what criterion people use for their choice and appraisal of housing;
2. relate these criteria to a temporal perspective, notably the residential biography of people and their long-term plans;
3. clarify whether the criteria support alternative housing conditions which may not be attained simultaneously at a specific point in time; and
4. establish those conditions which enable a synchronic appraisal of housing to be fruitful.

Therefore, although a temporal perspective is rarely incorporated in contemporary housing studies, it cannot be ignored. To correct this common shortcoming, the study reported here aims to identify and define one or more of the following processes:

1. those design related decisions prior to and during the planning of housing units and residential quarters;
2. the history of the built environment from occupation including all those modifications to its structure by the owner and/or tenant; and
3. an understanding of the residential biography of the inhabitants in terms of their aspirations and goals as well as their stage in the life-cycle.

Conclusion

The initial sections of this paper have characterised research on housing and homes in two main classes or categories which have different perspectives and research methods. Then some theoretical and methodological principles were presented with the aim of overcoming the limitations of many studies that are not founded on an integrative perspective. This perspective is founded on a holistic interpretation of those dimensions, and the reciprocal relations between them, which need to be examined in a precise situation. Given the complex nature of these dimensions it is too early to abandon this subject of enquiry. Hopefully, the integrative perspective outlined in this paper will be a focus of enquiry and discussion in the near future.

Notes

1. This paper is not intended to present a comprehensive overview or a complete reference bibliography of studies in this field. Rather, broad classes of studies are identified and one or two examples of these kinds of studies are cited merely as illustrative examples.
2. This study has deliberately examined rental housing because this sector is the dominant form of tenure in Switzerland, generally, and in Geneva, in particular. According to official census returns in 1980, 11% of the housing stock in Geneva was owner-occupied, 3.5% was co-operative tenure and 83% was rental tenure, and these proportions have changed insignificantly since 1960. The reasons for this structure of the housing stock are examined in Lawrence (1986).
3. It is noteworthy that public servants employed in the Canton of Geneva are expected to reside in the Canton (largely due to taxation collected by the Cantonal authority). Given the cost of housing in Geneva, as well as the relative lack of choice due to a low vacancy rate, there are many public servants who seek a formal dispensation or alternative arrangement.

References

Altman, I. & Werner, C. (eds.), (1985), 'Human Behavior and Environment', Home Environment, vol. 8, New York, Plenum Press.

Daunton, M. (1983), *House and Home in the Victorian City: Working-class Housing, 1850-1914*, London, Edward Arnold.

Deprés, C. (1989), 'Beyond theoretical purism: the search for an integrated paradigm in environmental meaning research', in Hardie, G., Moore, R. & Sanoff, H. (eds.), *Changing Paradigms*, Proceedings of the 20th Annual Conference of the Environmental Design Research Association, Washington DC, EDRA, pp. 82-87.

Dovey, K. (1978), 'Home: an ordering principle in space', *Landscape*, vol. 22, no. 2, pp. 24-30.

Duncan, J. (ed.), (1981), *Housing and Identity: Cross-cultural Perspectives*, London, Croom Helm.

Haumont, N. & Segaud, M. (eds.), (1989), *Families, modes de vie et habitat*, (Families, lifestyles and housing), Paris, Editions l'Harmattan.

Kent, S. (ed.), (1990), *Domestic Architecture and the Use of Space*, Cambridge, Cambridge University Press.
Kron, J. (1983), *Home-Psych: the social Psychology of Home Decoration*, New York, Clarkson N. Potter.
Lawrence, R. (1985), 'A more humane history of homes: research method and application', in Altman, I. & Werner, C. (eds.), *Home Environments*, 'Human Behavior and Environment', Vol.8, New York, Plenum Press, pp. 113-132.
Lawrence, R. (1986), *Le Seuil franchi: logement populaire et vie quotidienne en Suisse romande*, 1860-1960, (Stepping across the threshold: popular housing and daily life in the french-speaking region of Switzerland, 1860-1960), Georg Editeur, Geneva.
Lawrence, R. (1987), *Housing, Dwellings and Homes: Design Theory, Research and Practice*, John Wiley, Chichester.
Lawrence, R. (1990), 'Public, collective and private space: a study of urban housing in Switzerland', in Kent, S. (ed.), *Domestic Architecture and the Use of Space*, Cambridge University Press, Cambridge, pp. 73-91.
Low, S. & Chambers, E. (eds.), (1989), *Housing, Culture and Design*, University of Pennsylvania Press, Philadelphia.
Michelson, W. (1977), *Environmental Choice, Human Behavior and Residential Satisfaction*, Oxford University Press, New York.
Michelson, W. (1980), 'Long and short range criteria for housing choice and environmental behavior', *Journal of Social Issues*, vol. 36, no. 3, pp. 135-149.
Porteous, D. (1976), 'Home: the territorial core', *Geographical Review*, vol. 66, no. 4, pp. 383-390.
Rapoport, A. (1969), *House Form and Culture*, Prentice Hall, Englewood Cliffs, N.J.

3 Design Theory in the context of the recent history of housing research

E.S. Brierley

Introduction

The way in which design theorists perceive the value of research studies of the concepts involved in housing has changed over the past two decades. This is, in part, the result of a shift in emphasis from studies based upon empirical research of the meanings of concepts to people and of the utilisation of space to one in which recognition is given to the idea of precedent. To an extent the change in emphasis is due to a reaction to the notion of determinist controls over design in favour of the theory of an integrated approach to design. In the past research work that involved the study of phenomenon and of conceptual investigations was of interest to designers, however in recent theoretical studies of design experiential values have been an influence when formulating an integrated approach to design. The change in emphasis reflects a reaction to analytical studies in which the wider cultural context is given recognition.

Concepts of design theory

A conceptual approach to design theory derived from housing research has been that of setting out the possibilities available to design theorists in contrast to indicating determinist controls over design decisions. This approach has implied that rational thought, a logical philosophy, may be an aid to speculative invention. The conceptual approach has in the past resulted from studies of phenomenon and of both surveys of the meaning of concepts to people and from study of the utilisation of space.

The identification of the needs of people has been suggested by assessments of the probability of a response being made. That form of assessment has usually been elicited by means of questionnaire techniques and may involve scaler analysis. One benefit of this approach has been that, rather than simplistic analysis of satisfaction being obtained, a range of possibilities is presented which can be related to levels of tolerance, of adequacy and of satisfaction.

The implication of recent work for design theory is to place an emphasis upon the idea of design precedent. To an extent there has been a shift in studies from empirical research to experiential values to provide the basis for an integrated theory of design, yet such an approach should be modified by analysis of concepts and values. In order to indicate the significance of this change for both research workers and designers, the paper refers to inter-disciplinary studies made by social scientists and designers in the setting of observations of various social groups occupying varying dwelling types over the past two decades.

Arguably there has been a shift in emphasis by designers over the last twenty years from the influence of studies which relied upon deductive values to those based upon inductive experience. This change can be observed in the way designers have used both referential formal sources and studies of precedent. The basis of this can be found in the reaction to the analytical and economic values of design associated with C.I.A.M., the International Congress of Modern Architecture. That reaction resulted in a concern with cultural ideas and synthetic processes of design. One criticism of the movement away from analytical values is that there is an implication that formal elements have become to be considered as abstract devices. On the other hand, the formal dimension may result in delightful incidents in design.

Norberg-Schulz (1968) attempted to derive an integrated theory of design which was a development from analytical values. His conceptual approach was both empirical and relied upon the concepts being logically unified into a system. Yet the theory was not intended to provide particular solutions, rather it was intended to provide a search of possible factors and combinations. To an extent a parallel with this approach can be observed in social science investigations which indicate the probability of relationships occurring rather than in evaluations of satisfaction expressed in quantitative terms.

Studies of the relationship between the built environment and people's awareness have given some emphasis to the meaning of concepts to people. To an extent that is in contrast to the way in which guides to design describe standards. One difficulty has been that of assessing the imprecise needs of people to compare with that of physical standards. Studies of the needs of people indicate that standards of design are often based upon the minimum which people will accept or tolerate. A further problem in environmental studies is that due to the way standards are presented, they imply that one criteria will have precedence over related criteria. In addition to which the changes that occur in society and personality factors provide further variables when formulating and implemented guides to design decisions.

Invariably, standards of space both within the dwelling and in the environment are defined in terms of adequacy rather than of satisfaction. Yet to return to the theory of Norberg-Schulz (1968) such emphasis upon particular conditions belie the need to examine a range of possibilities in the context of an integrated concept of design. An example of the way in which factors can interact in unexpected ways is that satisfaction with the environment is often determined more by the appearance and maintenance of external spaces than by spaciousness in isolation.

The aims of systems and techniques of design ought to set out the possibilities available to designers rather than to form a 'strait-jacket' to design method. Yet, clearly rational thought and a logical philosophy are a means to the designer who may also see speculative invention as a way of achieving his aim. There has been a reaction to the framing of firm rules for designers in favour of one concerning assessment of the probability of a need or activity occurring.

Although design may be a product of a search through an order of precedence of standards that may amend design from an ideal to a compromised solution, in the design of housing in particular, this may be achieved both through study of the concept of the utilisation of space and of facilitating the functional or behavioural activity. However, rules derived from anthropometric design continue to influence the process of design, yet this approach ought not to be considered in isolation from that of an integrated approach to design.

The context of recent history

In the development of studies of environmental functions, that is of the relationship between the built environment and people's awareness of physical and climatological factors the premis on which research has been based is that social survey work upon which legislation and rules are in turn based is invariably dated and that in some cases the rules governing design have unclear origins. There was also a divergence between the way in which the recommendations or indications from research work was interpreted by designers. On the one hand legislations, whilst recognising the implications of research findings, in practice found that the traditional guidelines which had been proved economically viable were to continue to effect the design standards. On the other hand designers used research work, especially in the 1960s and 1970s resulting from the Ministry of Housing and Local Government and then the Department of the Environment to reinforce their own perceptions (Noble and Adams, 1968). Thus emphasis was given, in theory if not in practice, to the effect of space and landscaping upon notions of satisfaction in housing. The way in which the questionnaire techniques developed by the government departments were applied led, on the whole, to deductive analysis. That is of the research of social studies being presented to designers and explained by a commentary on the process of the research investigators.

Although the implications of research findings often appeared to emphasize quantitative values of satisfaction or preference as design references, designers often found the descriptive notes upon life styles and living conditions, frequently conducted by the researcher in an open ended discussion to be more stimulating. That is an inductive understanding was intrinsically preferred by designers to deductive statements often related to isolated phenomenon. This probably is why the writings of Young and Willmott (1962), of Jane Jacobs (1961), and Coates and Silburn (1970) proved to be attractive to architects with a social attitude to design. That, in part, accounts for the concern with the conservation and rehabilitation of environmental areas that occurred in the late 1960s and 1970s.

During that period some designers looked to the social sciences to provide data that could be set aside that from the physical sciences, which for a while had influenced design. To a large extent, the social sciences were concerned with empirical studies, whereas designers had need of applied research. The social sciences were keen to define the parameters of their study and to control the variables. In contrast, designers possibly sought support for preconceived ideas on the needs of people.

There was clearly a need which gained recognition at the end of the 1960s to find common ground between the social sciences and design. One way of achieving this was to consider the meaning of concepts to people and the effects of those concepts upon design decisions. Levels of satisfaction and of perceived qualities in the environment could be put into the context of design parameters. By means of open ended interview, scales of satisfaction, of spaciousness and of some of the factors of visual privacy could be statistically analysed and considered in the light of physical measures of environmental factors. Conclusions derived from such work indicated the cumulative effect of increases in environmental provision upon satisfaction. However, beyond a specified level of physical provision the determinants of satisfaction were unclear and controlled by environmental factors not included in the parameters of the study (Markus et al, 1972).

By the nature of such studies of isolating factors an integrated approach to design is arguably less easy to evolve. Also the context of the methodology of such investigations is that of analysis rather than synthesis. Then, how might designers benefit from interdisciplinary work? Legislation and recommendations to designers in practice are often assessed as unsatisfactory for the needs of people but to apply more generous standards has implications in housing for economics and densities of development which outweigh the results or implications of social studies. In reality the value of conceptual analysis and of assessments of satisfaction is that the perceptive designer may become more sensitive to the needs of people and more able to challenge the rules governing housing design.

Influence upon housing studies

Whilst the value of studies in terms of either effecting legislation or of influencing designers is not easy to define, the interdisciplinary work between the social sciences and designers had raised the level of awareness of each discipline by the other. This led to an influence upon design education, which was of some consequence in the 1970s. Also inductive experience was found in these cases to be the result of interdisciplinary studies. So that designers sought influences that could be effective in term of environmental studies. The work of Sommer (1969) and Kira (1966) on the way people use space was particularly of value.

A whole range of studies developed based upon the form and use of space. Those projects which related, or rather juxtaposed, the intentions of designers with the preferences of the occupiers held the attention of people concerned in studies of housing design. The designers notions in indicating furniture layout could be thought of at two levels. That his proposals for layout were solutions advocated as best possible solutions for the users or that he envisaged that the layout of furniture he indicated in his designs was the probable one to be adopted by the users of the space (Brierley, 1989).

Work by a number of research workers with a background of design indicated that in practice the positioning of furniture was frequently not due to functional or formal needs, which was often the basis of the designer's work but due to other factors. Sometimes the layout reflected symbolic values, at other times the cultural background and personality of the user was the critical factor. If any rule could be derived for designers, it was that people tended to be aquiescent of the space provided for them. However, once their material wealth improved the dominant motive for wanting to move was the inadequacy of the space provided and yet, spatial satisfaction appeared to be independent of the length of residence, Boalt (1970).

It is probable that the effect of environmental function studies upon legislation and design recommendations has been marginal in terms of decisions affecting design but equally it would be unfair to say that the effect of this work upon the perceived values of designers was of little consequence. Changes in government policy in the 1970s and 1980s which resulted during the 1970s to a considerable emphasis being placed upon the rehabilitation policies for dwellings and housing areas, and in the 1980s in both a reduction in the quantity of new build and a change in preferred tenancy from the rented sector to owner occupiers had implications for the way in which designers reacted to the research work of the social sciences.

In effect, these changes in policy clouded the issue for in the 1960s designers had used analytical methods of design to support reasoned argument for their perceptions of the needs of people. Not only had the social and political climate in which designers worked changed but also the conceptual appreciation of design had changed. The essence of the architectural debate was that of the contrasting values of modernism and postmodernism. Whilst modernism had allowed the designer to consider spatial ideas in a new light, postmodernism included the concepts of referential studies and precedent.

The changing nature of spatial studies

In order to understand the changing nature of the way spatial studies were appreciated it is necessary to recognise the contrasting features of modernism and postmodernism. The former conceived space as a continuum and proposed that modern spatiality allowed freedom yet frequently the effect of analytical functionalism on modernism was not duly accepted. Postmodernism had as a basic premis the idea that context or place had an essential role to play in the study of space. The postmodernists also saw their role as that of an integrated, or inclusive approach to design. Norberg-Schulz (1982) developed his theoretical stance to accept postmodernist issues.

'The traditional concept of 'place' is breaking down, that is the place as an independent universe distinguished by a particular genus loci. In the past, thus, the purpose of architecture was to 'make an ethnic domain visible', to quote Susan Langer. The general characteristic of our day, however, is the open, 'global' world, where the 'ethnic domains' loose their definition and we, so to speak, experience a 'simultaneity of places'. Physically we are in one place at a time, but every day the whole world is brought to us by the new media. This is the existential situation behind what pioneers of the Modern Movement called the 'new conception of space'(Norberg-Schulz, 1982, p20).

However, Norberg-Schulz attempts to resolve this apparent contradiction in postmodern thought between the conceptual notion of place and the lack of definition of the 'ethnic domain'. He achieves this to some extent by rejecting the implication of the modernist 'new concept of space' and suggests that the concept of place, or context, is not obsolete. One aim of place in this situation is to create an identity from which cross cultural influences may be appreciated. Yet, the social implications of how man relates to place or of the value attached to the identity of place is not fully discussed by Norberg-Schulz, who accepts the loss of clear ethnic boundaries without questioning if new definitions may not arise.

The case can be argued that the discussions on the basis of quantifiable rules for housing design and the support offered during the 1960s by the social sciences was appropriate to the time. Yet it would be incorrect to suggest that an emphasis upon an integrated approach to design and to experiential influences is a recent phenomenon. One source who may be quoted from the 1960s to support the latter case is that of Lynch (1960). On the assumption that the way aspects of the environment are perceived are a function of experience, an attempt can be made to formulate the structural components of the city. However, in keeping with the spirit of the 1960s, his work became formalized and was to an extent considered as a means to aid design rather than as an enquiry into perceptual information.

Studies such as those by Lynch and in more recent times by Alexander (1987) also brought into focus the urban context of housing research which could be applied to design. Perhaps it is more common in the 1980s, and probably also in the 1990s, to refer to the theoretical issues of Urban Design rather than to propositions for Housing Research in a design context. A contrast can be observed between the phenomenon of openness and enclosure in studies of the 1970s and 1980s. In the 1970s those designers aware of the work of social scientists could use the results of scaler analysis of satisfaction determinants to indicate parameters for enclosure. Whilst, in the 1980s Alexander's (1987) recommendations stemmed from experiential values of the quality of enclosure to provide coherent and well-shaped spaces, without it should be added the support of detailed empirical study.

The use of precedent

The implication of these developments in research has been for designers to place an emphasis upon the ideas of precedent as a basis for design decisions rather than upon empirical study. An illustration of the changing nature of housing studies is to be found in the way precedent was anlaysed in the 1960s in comparison to the more amorphous use of the term in the 1980s. Precedent or case studies derived from the design appraisals of housing areas relied upon quantifiable studies of areas of specific formal characteristics. Social survey work assessed levels of satisfaction, and in more sensitive studies awareness of spaciousness and notions of privacy, that were perceived by the residents of the areas. Correlations between the two means of assessment, those of design appraisal and of social survey could then be evaluated. The process may be considered an abstract and analytical one.

Precedent, viewed by more recent research work such as that of Jadelius (1990) emphasizes the way cultural influnces indicate the relationship of place and space. Often these studies were determined by a concern for ethnic values, frequently the concept of territory is considered in a cultural context. The implication is that to an extent the study of precedent becomes personalised and is placed in the area of experiential values. The method is clearly more concerned with subjective beliefs than analytical abstraction. Jadelius rejects the 'annihilation' of the understanding of space that was to be discovered in older cultures.

'In older cultures, both among independent peasants and in the feudal- dominated areas there existed an ethnically-tied building culture incorporating a type of cultural self-censorship. Every house or place was unique, but every single unit had the place given to it by society and in accordance with it one should build and dwell'. (Jadelius, 1990, p. 294).

This form of understanding the spatial attributes of housing holds much of interest for designers who are concerned to both search-out the potential spatial relationships and to formulate an integrated approach to design that acknowledges cultural influences. On the other hand, design guides appear too frequently to indicate the effect of controlling rules rather than to show an understanding of conceptual awareness.

An understanding of the way designers think has been central to conceptual studies during the last two decades. In the 1960s designers were controlled by physical standards such as rules for spaces inside and outside the dwelling, of recommendations for the provision of sunlight and daylight, and also of the effect of density. This clearly influenced the way in which the designers perceived the value of the social scientists. However, the designer of the 1980s may draw upon a wide range of influences particularly those of experience and of inductive attitudes.

One effect of this development is that appreciation of the design activity ought to acknowledge the way in which the wider experience of the designer may effect the design process. It has been too easy simply to view design in terms of the relationship of cause and effect or in terms of analytical data and the synthesis of the solution. Yet, throughout the twentieth century symbolic values associated with the conceptual approach of designers has proved influential. Norberg-Schulz's theory was one that accepted these symbolic values.

If architecture is an art, it has to fulfil this criterion. That architecture may symbolize cultural objects is an empirical fact, since architectural history shows that this aspect has generally formed an important part of the building task. Why architecture is used in this way, however, is a question which so far has hardly been studied', (Norberg- Schulz, 1968, p. 122).

To a large extent, symbolic and cultural values were used by designers as part of the reaction to the functional and analytical views of the pre-war years of C.I.A.M. That thinking led to an acceptance of the way observations of ethnic cultures may allow the designer to gain insights into the relationship of people to design. So that, the designers sought conceptual relationships rather than empirical rules. An effect of this form of study has been to place an emphasis on the significance of precedent in the creative process. The recent work of Rapoport (1990) in studies of urban form recognises the manner in which theory can be a product of the interaction of culture and environment. Central to this work is the notion of precedent.

Yet designers know that modern movement concepts are still present in contemporary design and indeed may be considered to reflect aspects of culture in a more thoughtful way than the transient ideas of postmodernism. That designers search for influences from culture, precedent and context rather than solely from analytical processes of design indicates a shift in emphasis rather than a reappraisal of the contribution of the social sciences to design.

References

Alexander, C. (1987), *A New Theory of Urban Design*, Oxford University Press, Oxford.

Boalt, C. (1970), 'Living habits in residential areas', *Build International*, September.

Brierley, E. S. (1974), 'Sunshine, Daylight, Visual Privacy and View in Housing', in *Proc. of the Third International Symposium on Lower-Cost Housing Problems*, Concordia University, Montreal, pp. 385-392.

Brierley, E. S. (1989), 'The Density of Dwellings in Occupancy', paper presented at The International Symposium on Home and Neighbourhood, The National Swedish Institute for Building Research, Gavle.

Coates, K. & Silburn, R. (1970), *Poverty : The Forgotten Englishmen*, Penguin Books, Harmondsworth.

Jacobs, J. (1961), *The Death and Life of Great American Cities*, Random House, New York.

Jadelius, L. (1990), 'Apartments of Spaces and Places', in Pamir, H., Imamoglu, V. & Teymur, N., (eds.) *Culture, Space, History*, METU, Ankara, vol. 2, pp. 290-299.
Kira, A. (1966), *The Bathroom: Criteria for Design*, Bantam Books, New York.
Lynch, K. (1960), *The Image of the City*, MIT Press, Cambridge, Mass.
Lynch, K. (1981), *A Theory of Good City Form*, MIT Press, Cambridge, Mass.
Markus, T. A., Brierley, E. S. & Gray, A. (1972), *Sunshine, Daylight, Visual Privacy and View in Housing*, Strathclyde University, Social Science Research Council.
Noble, J. & Adams, B. (1968), 'The Home in its Setting', *Architects' Journal*, 11 September.
Norberg-Schulz, C. (1968), *Intentions in Architecture*, MIT Press, Cambridge, Mass.
Norberg-Schulz, C. (1980), *Genus Loci: Towards a Phenmenology of Architecture*, Rizzoli International, New York.
Norberg-Schulz, C. (1982), 'The "New Tradition" today', *International Laboratory of Architecture and Urban Design Yearbook.*
Rapoport, A. (1990), *History and Precedent in Environmental Design*, Plenum, New York.
Sommer, R (1969), *Personal Space: the Behavioural Basis of Design*, Prentice-Hall, New York and London.
Young, M. & Willmott, P. (1962), *Family and Kinship in East London*, Penguin Books, Harmondsworth.

4 Homebased workers: Studies in the adaptation of space

M. Bulos and W. Chaker

Introduction

Case studies of homebased workers are used to explore the phenomenological unity constituted of people and places under the particular circumstance of employment within the home. These cases have been selected to display the rich variety of ways in which people devise, implement and sustain the use of space in what is normally regarded as the domestic domain. Constructing and using space in a manner which forces a distinction between social, familial and employment spheres such that a sense of home as essentially domestic can still be maintained. The authors also identify some of the critical incidents which rupture the established order and lead to reconstruction and change within an overall pattern of stability.

The economic and social context of homebased working

In 1979 the Department of Employment initiated a programme of research on homeworking. This programme produced a significant body of published material (Hakim, 1987, pp.1-5) which constitutes both a unique record of homeworking and a significant example of research which justifies and underpins policy inaction. The final report from the programme provides the most complete account of the nature and extent of homebased work in Britain currently available (Hakim, 1987). In 1981 7% of the labour force representing 1.7 million people either worked in their home, had their homes at their workplace or, worked from home. The total of 1.7 million was subdivided as follows:

Manufacturing homework	58,750
Other work at home	171,050
Childminders	27,650
Working from home as a base	400,000
Construction, road haulage etc.	284,000
Living at work and with live in jobs	760,000

Table 4.1 (adapted from Hakim, 1990)

Numerous researchers have demonstrated the severe problems of identifying and contacting employees who work at home. Employers may not declare their use of homeworkers, particularly if they are not paying their tax and National Insurance, many home workers themselves are reluctant to be officially identified for fear of losing their jobs, reprisals from employers and worries about breaking the law or local regulations (Allen & Wolkowitz, 1987, Birmingham City Council, 1988; West Yorkshire Homeworking Group, 1990). The existence of these problems and the reports made by councils such as Birmingham would suggest that the first two categories severely underestimate the amount of work undertaken at home.

Homebased work is diverse, being spread over all occupational categories. It is not possible to identify a 'typical' homebased worker or an occupation dominated by this type of employment. In some regions and towns there are concentrations of certain types of homework linked to specific industries and employers (Allen, 1986, Phizacklea, 1990). The diversity and type of homebased work can be illustrated by identifying specific economic sectors. Manufacturing homework involves relatively specific operations, little capital equipment, and relatively easily transportable inputs and outputs. Traditionally, certain sections of the garment industry have relied heavily on homework by sewers, machinists, tailors and dressmakers, knitters and leather workers. The boot and shoe industry also uses a diversity of homeworkers to assemble and finish footwear of all kinds. More recently the assembly of electronic components, making packing boxes, folding and filling envelopes and card making have become prevalent (West Yorkshire Homeworking Group 1990).

White collar homework jobs are even more diverse than those in manufacturing: the largest group is that of non retail clerks and cashiers with typists and secretaries making up the next most significant group. High technology jobs are numerically small with system analysts, computer programmes, punch operators and word processors. These types of employees are usually working for a single employer. There are however significant numbers of white collar workers who deal with a number of clients or employers for example telephone canvassers, sales representatives, various professionals carry out their work on a sub-contract basis architects, accountants, commerciad artists, writers and authors, translators and management consultants. Jobs done from home include: teachers, clergy, district nurses and midwives, rent and debt collectors.

There are significant qualitative distinctions between workers who operate within their home and those who use their home as a base. Work within the home is dominated by female employment much of it part time, poorly paid and predominantly carried out by women who combine such work with domestic responsibilities. For such workers:

> 'The notion that women are tied to the home by very young children emerges with important modifications homeworkers are influenced by traditional attitudes to child care and women's role in the home which makes them reluctant to go out to work even after their children reach school age and are well beyond the stage where most other mothers go out to work.' (Hakim, 1987, p.246).

These attitudes are often reinforced by men: 'Husbands exercise considerable control over home-workers conditions of work... the decision to do homework rather than go out to work is frequently made by the husband.' (Allen, 1986, p.41).

Where such homeworking exists it seems likely that there is a considerable mismatch between the supply of labour and demand, creating conditions in which homeworkers are exploited receiving extremely low pay and operating under poor conditions of employment (TUC, 1978, 1985; Phizacklea, 1990; West Yorkshire Homeworking Group, 1990).

Those who work from home rather than being confined to it show a different profile, being mainly men who have self employment status and work full time. This group also contains a minority of highly paid people. Single proprietors of small businesses, subcontracted and free-lance workers rely on their homes as both a base, a business address and a place to do much, if not all, of their work. Certain types of work which until recently were office based are becoming increasingly homebased through processes of sub contracting, franchising and casualisation of employment.

There has been much speculation about expected future trends in homebased working. Some authors have argued that there is likely to be an overall decline in the non core workforce and *ipso facto* homebased workers of all kinds (Hakim, 1985, Millward & Stevens, 1986) Hakim in particular has argued for the demise of manufacturing homework stating: 'Manufacturing homework would diminish-both in absolute terms and as proportion of the total - since it is rarely a positive choice and preference.' (Hakim, 1988, p.631).

At lease one researcher has been particularly scathing over the growth in work involving new technologies:

> 'Telework is so nebulous it can hardly be said to exist in any clearly defined and quantifiable way ... There are people working from home with their employers' agreement in order to avoid commuting (but not all that many); there are individualistic types who find large corporations so antipathetic an environment that they have set up 'electronic cottages' for themselves (but not all that many); there are women working from home with computers because they cannot find satisfactory childcare arrangements who are entirely happy with the arrangement (but not all that many); there are others in similar situations who believe they are exploited and under-paid (but not all that many); there are public and private sector organisations systematically investigating the transfer of some of their staff to homebased working ... that a majority of the population could ever become teleworkers is far-fetched. However, all these categories are growing and seem likely to continue to do so.' (Huws, 1990)

Others however have taken a much more positive view arguing that homeworking will increase. The most conservative estimate puts the number of home-based workers in 1985 at 2.2 million, one quarter of the non core work force (Hakim, 1987, p. 249). Other recent projections represent the other extreme, forecasting four million people working from home by 1955 and estimating that potentially half the working population could be involved in telecommuting (Henley Centre, 1988). Certainly, there is evidence of increases in the conversion of work from factory or office employment to homeworking in textiles and associated industries (TUC, 1991), data processing, clerical and general office work (Bisset, 1990; Dennison, 1990; CPSU, 1991) and professional work such as Training Standards Inspectors (Felix, 1989).

Support for the strength of these latter opinions comes from the debate on restructuring which suggests that a long term and permanent change is taking place in the way labour markets are organised towards a proliferation of ways of making organisations more responsive to changes in their external environment. What this means is more forms of non standard working brought about through a variety of processes: sub contracting, part time employment, franchising and reorganisation, a growth in self employment and small enterprises. All of these changes promote increases in homebased working (Kingsman 1987, Brown and Scase, 1991).

It would seem likely that the numbers of people for whom paid work is carried out in the home will increase, that the range and type of work done in this way will remain diverse. It remains to be seen if many of the characteristics of the experience of working in the home shown to be intrinsic to 'traditional' factory work become replicated amongst the growing number of new style home base workers (Huws 1984, Bulos 1990a, TUC 1991).

Homebased working, the home and the organisation of workspace

In Britain there has been a tendency in the literature on homeworking to relegate the matter of where people work as being less important than conditions of employment and other aspects of work at home such as isolation (Hakim, 1987, p. 129). Research on manufacturing homeworkers in Yorkshire found three quarters of the women used domestic space for their work noting: 'few homeworkers have a separate place for their work' (Allen, 1986, p. 40) a finding generally applicable to manufacturing homeworkers of whom only a minority had a special room in which to confine their work and storage (Hakim, 1987, p. 242). It is likely that most homebased workers do not have separate 'dedicated' space for their work although both working at home and with home as a base require the use of somewhere between 25%-100% of existing space and promote the use of extensions, barns, garages and portacabins. (Bulos, 1990b).

The consequences of this lack of separation between paid work and domestic tasks are considerable. It allows other members of the family (household) and outsiders to continue in the view that homework is in some way less demanding and less a 'real' commitment than for the person who goes out to work. Work set up in the kitchen or living room can not be left set up and has to be cleared away to make way for the preparation of meals, or for childrens play. Working at home more easily becomes linked to other tasks and responsibilities - interwoven with house work, domestic routines and child care. It is widely assumed that personal preferences, work performance and stress will be best accommodated in conditions where the homeworker is able to command separate closed off space for working purposes such assumptions are implicit in the work of Allen and Hakim (op cit) and prescriptive in guides to employers (CBI, 1988, Kingsman, 1988). However little is known about the actual experience of homeworkers over this issue and how choices are made between working separately or within the household structure of other activities. This paper examines some of these matters using case study material.

Perspective on space

The perspective on homeworkers' experience presented here is broadly phenomenological. The way in which people lay claim to spaces and fashion them into places which they feel appropriate for particular activities such as homework are viewed as the outcome of complex social processes as described by the people themselves. These social processes involve negotiations with others who may be members of the familial or domestic group or outsiders who nevertheless impinge on the domestic sphere in different and specific ways.

The 'phenomenological unity' (Sixsmith and Sixsmith, 1990, p. 20) formed by people and places changes over time, changes in people's life circumstances bring about the need for readjustments to accommodate new experiences. Recent literature on the meaning and experience of home (Sixsmith and Sixsmith 1990, Saunders, 1991) has identified marriage, the birth of a child, retirement, death and changes in tenure as marking significant changes in how people experience home life, the meanings they attach to home and their feelings about the nature of the home environment. For people who work at or from their homes these life changes become even more complex in the implications for home life. The decision to become a homebased worker is normally inextricably linked with addressing and attempting to resolve critical problems arising at key turning points in people's lives. How people decide to use space within the home to facilitate homebased work is interwoven with experiential redefinitions of personal identity and relationships with other people and can therefore only be examined by placing the practicalities of spatial definition within this context.

Approaching and describing the way people organise their space for homework purposes is both complex and difficult because of attributes of the homework experience and the contrast this has with the 'ideal' or generally perceived 'normal' experience of home. Schutz, (1964, p. 208) summarises these common expectations in the following passage:

> 'To feel 'at home' is an expression of the highest degree of familiarity and intimacy. Life at home follows an organised pattern of routine; it has its well determined goals and well-proven means to bring them about, consisting of a set of traditions, habits, institutions, timetables for activities of all kinds, etc. Most of the problems of daily life can be mastered by following this pattern ... The way of life at home governs as a scheme of expression and interpretation ... using this scheme, I shall understand what the other means and make myself understandable to him ... we not only forecast what will happen tomorrow but we also have a fair chance to plan correctly the more distant future. Of course there are new situations and unexpected events. But at home even deviations from the daily routine life are mastered in a way defined by the general style in which people at home deal with extraordinary situations. There is an approved way of meeting a crisis in business life for settling family problems for determining the attitude to adopt towards illness and even death. Paradoxically formulated, there is even a routine way for handling the novel.'

This common and routine nature of home is however endowed with different specific configurations which are culturally and historically structured, in our own contemporary and familiar society the home is first and foremost the place in which people live out their private familial and domestic lives. For the homeworker the problem arises as to how employment activities which deviate from this overall normal view of home can be contained within this context.

Firstly working in the home is perceived as deviant both by homeworkers themselves and by others and as such in need of justification and defence. The homeworker can never relax into a wholly 'taken for granted world' as the person who 'goes out to work'. The domestic non work nature of the physical conditions in which homeworkers find themselves poses a constant, tangible and in some cases intractable reminder of the perverseness of 'homework'.

Secondly the experience of place by the homeworker may be constrained or facilitated by the nature of the physical attributes of buildings and the external environment. Resolving the contradictions which arise from cultural definitions of what constitutes a proper home and the demands for an appropriate working environment constitutes a major problem which all homeworkers have to resolve. How that resolution should occur arises from the individual's definition of self which is deeply embedded in broader ideas about specific roles in society. These issues are strongly evoked by the following crie de coeur:

> 'I had my photograph taken in my 'office' where I do my writing. The photo journalist was a staunch feminist, and was so angry that my 'office' was my kitchen and that packets of breakfast cereals were in the background. I was letting the women's movement down by allowing such a photograph to be taken.
> But that was where I worked, because it was warmer, because it was convenient for me to be able to see my family when I put my typewriter to one side. I tried in vain to tell her that in my kitchen I felt I was doing more for peace in the world than the nuclear scientist ... In our kitchens we wash for them and cook for them. In our kitchens they learn to love and hate. And we send them out of our kitchens to be grown men and women.' (Emetcheter, 1988).

The phenomena of homebased work activity quite clearly disrupts and reveals the generalised patterns of subjective orientation and perception. This draws into sharp focus for the actor(s) issues that particularly refer to space and use which have otherwise been merely a taken for granted set of relevance and understandings. This tension provides for the sociological enquirer an access point to the given structures and processes of subjective action that constitutes notions of home. Sustaining the personal (subjective) and interpersonal (intersubjective) credibility and stability of notions of home in relation to others therefore becomes an essential part of the homeworkers strategy in which how space is organised and occupied becomes of central importance.

Approach

The case studies presented here were selected from possible contacts across a broad spectrum of homeworkers. Access to different categories of homeworkers was established in a number of different ways of which the most important here:

1. Through a process of networking starting with friends, family, neighbours and colleagues.
2. By contact with a Tenants' Association on an Inner London council estate.
3. From the published membership list and quarterly newsletter of OwnBase, a nationally based voluntary organisation of homebased workers.
4. Through the local trade union official at a local authority employing data processing and central office staff at home.
5. Through the National Association of Homeworkers based in Birmingham.

Information about the list of homeworkers used to select the case studies was obtained from: direct contact with individual homeworkers interviewed and photographed for previous research, phone interviews with key people who acted as mediators to access homeworkers for example the secretary of the Tenants' Association, and articles in the OwnBase newsletter.

The cases used were selected by a process of filtering existing information. Firstly we wanted people for whom homebased working has already become established, who saw themselves continuing to operate in this way over the long term, and where homebased work was their main or only occupation. Secondly we wished to display the variety of occupations and hence equipment and space requirements. If possible, we wanted to include an example of each main type of homebased work: industrial, personal and other services and commercial. Beyond this we sought to capture the experience of homeworking for people at different stages of their occupational careers. Finally of course we needed people prepared to give up a considerable amount of their time to us for a preliminary interview, visit and second interview including a demonstration of the person at work. In addition to the materials used in this paper a photographic record of the person at work has (made). Thus, the particular cases chosen provide an opportunity to examine the special and unique configurations of homeworkers' use of space in the context of a variety of life circumstances but at the same time with some overt characteristics held 'constant'. All participants shared a commitment to homework as a permanent and main way of earning their livings and undertook work which required the use of quite sophisticated equipment and supplies.

The researchers used a 'triangulation of methods' (Cook and Fonow, 1991). Data was generated for each person through a number of 'conversations with a purpose' (Webb and Webb, 1932, p.130) before, during and after visits to their homes. Essential parts of these conversations were recorded using a structured questionnaire schedule, field notes were kept to record other parts of their accounts and our observations, photographs of the main areas used for homework were taken, each 'photocall' lasted for about an hour and a half although the actual time spent with each person varied from a day to 2 hours. The participants regarded the visits as providing them with a unique opportunity to talk about circumstances which were important to them but which most other people either did not take seriously or from whom these activities were largely hidden. Although the research was clearly carried out in a quite tightly controlled manner we felt that we had achieved entre into their natural world of work where they felt at ease. We particularly asked that they should not make any kind of special arrangements for us. During all the visits opportunities arose to talk to family members, clients and friends.

We started with people's own descriptions and interpretations on which of course we subsequently placed our own understanding. The status of our interpretation or the roles of transformation deployed in analysing our qualitative data were governed by a number of criteria established prior to the field work. These criteria derived from a set of traditional concerns in the analysis of qualitative data and the authors identification of specific factors relating to the situations studied.

The latter considerations detailed our personal interest in those being researched and, the fact that we were visitors to their directly constituted home worlds. Many informal and everyday interactions took place between us which were critically and reflexively linked to the homework experience. Although these interactions were not fully recorded they contributed a resource which influenced our subsequent interpretations. We used this resource in de-briefing sessions to cross reference the formally collated data. This took the form of recounting our commentaries with the respondents and checking the content against the formal replies in the questionnaire. Disparities and contradictions were then discarded in terms of what the respondent stated they actually meant.

In terms of the former considerations we established a number of factors which would enable a check to be made on the correctness of interpretation. Firstly, recorded accounts were scrutinised for internal consistency, secondly the specific context in which the interviews took place, were recognised as being constitutive of the homework experience itself; and thirdly the status of utterances were verified by asking the same questions using different forms of words and connotations. Finally, in line with established practice we 'bracketed off' our own common and personally held assumptions and took account of the interviews in terms of the respondents own frame of reference and context of relevance.

Some kind of check on our understanding of their situations came from other sources such as direct observation and comments by other household members or friends and subsidiary written materials such as promotional literature or short articles written by our respondents.

People and their places

> 'Max: is A DRUMMER ON YOUR WORK-NEEDING NO MICS, GATES OR EVEN TAPE ... who uses 'DRUM' digital drums - these can be DI's to your desk for recording and midi connected to your sequencer or computer thus avoiding tape altogether. I can play from the wealth of superb sampled drum sounds offered by 'drum' or I can play your own drum sounds via MIDI - with all the dynamics, feel and drive of real drums.' (Francis, 1990).

What this entails is a single owner business established through an initial investment of £5,500 which paid for all the gear for recording and live performance, computing and transmission facilities, publicity and materials for soundproofing. He practices and records for about five hours a day using a room at the back of the house. Upstairs, an adjacent room and the corridor and landing provide storage space.

Age 20, self employed, Max has been running his business for 6 months on the basis of the Business Enterprise Scheme. He lives in the parental home which is a five bedroom detached house shared with his mother, a busy JP and his father, a self employed business man selling computer/office equipment. A sister visits frequently, staying at the house for short periods of time.

Ken (and Alan): combined skills acquired from studies at St. Martin's School of Art, the London College of Printing and Southampton Art College to set up their graphic design and promotions business in 1987. Named Total Re-Think they won the 'Muscle Person of the Year' award in the British Telecom Muscle Business Competition of 1989. They run their business from a basement flat in a converted semi-detached house.

Their equipment includes two DTP computers, drawing boards, a fax, photocopier, desks, chairs and storage. This occupies half the space in the flat, the 'open plan' room being divided by a bench type settee.

Marni: who describes herself as a seamstress and clothes designer works full time from her council flat where she lives with her daughter. She has worked in this way for over five years and regards both her location and mode of working as permanent.

Leslie: makes leather goods such as bags, pouches and belts which she sells each week from her rented stall at a weekend market. Her workroom for the last six years has been a small extension behind the garage of her small semi detached house in a small coastal town. The most important piece of equipment she uses is a heavy industrial leather sewing machine which will cost her £4,000 to replace when her existing old machine wears out. She currently lives alone although her only child returns to stay during college holidays. Originally working as a secretary she changed her career after attending a leather craft course. She also does part time teaching.

Elise: has worked from home as an architect for 23 years and is at the moment considering retirement. Her workroom was originally shared with her husband when they first set up a joint practice but he has long since moved out into leased premises and they work on quite separate contracts. Originally the workroom was the back room of a small 'semi' but the house next door was inherited on the death of his parents to provide on conversion a detached house with self contained flat in half of the second floor. In addition to the workroom, storage for drawing boards and plans is found in the hallway and outside shed; clients and contractors meet Elise for business 'over the kitchen table'.

Paul: middle aged and starting a new career, Paul had started to practice as a surgical chiropodist four years ago. Initially part of his three bedroomed family house had been used without it being possible to use anywhere exclusively for this purpose. In his second year of practice he commissioned an extension to the house part of which provided a separate and properly equipped surgery containing not only specialist chiropody furniture and instruments but also storage for patient records and supplies. The sitting room continues to be used for 'waiting space' and the downstairs cloakroom is also used by patients.

Claiming their space

Negotiating and claiming space and the outcome of that process is vital to the stability of homeworking. Being able to use space in order to get work completed on time and to the standard required is a major question for anyone who works in their home. In distinction to the normal workplace, the nature of management of work requires that the individual can retain notions of a 'proper' home. Where space is organised such that there is a visual and functional overlap between activities, retaining an adequate sense of home is perceived as hard to achieve and creates conditions where the dividing line between public and private spheres is constantly in need of defence and redefinition. As the following account by Ken shows.

> 'We actually work from my bedroom. We employ one trainee - number two is on her way - and apart from my bed, a sofa, armchair, TV & video recorder and my record collection we have two DTP computers, a fax, photocopier, drawing board, my desk etc.
>
> The major problems with the present arrangement is that when clients come to the work place because they see it as home rather than a place of work they tend to treat it as such and are always sitting down and socialising ... you know stopping for a chat and even bringing friends ... mind you I am as much to blame ... because I am in the home it is difficult to treat people the way I would if it was the workplace ... I'm always asking people if they want a cup of coffee and chatting informally.
>
> Inevitably late clients meet early friends and the daytime part leads on to the evening lot.'

The complexity of looking after children, home and work concurrently can lead to complex overlapping use of space, work becomes a 'moveable feast' as exemplified in Marni's description of her normal work pattern:

> 'Although I don't have a specific work area apart from the machine in the bedroom... I tend to organise my living space to accommodate work... space to lay out patterns and to cut material and so I move the dummy around ... sometimes I work in the kitchen sometimes in the front room or bedroom it all depends what else is going on or where I feel like doing the work... I've been working from home a long time now and like work to be accommodated rather than have it all round the house... I like the space for family life and socialising and other work (every day work) that are to do with running the home.'

Her experience of bring up a small child must echo that of many homeworkers when she comments that:
'It's difficult with a small child in the house because they get into everything... this place wasn't really intended for work so there isn't appropriate storage or space for work it is certainly not practical.'

Both Ken and Marni are severely restricted in terms of space: both businesses are carried out in flats where there is very little possibility of altering or adding to their space, in neither case did their work requirements enter into their choice of accommodation which in both cases was severely constrained by the processes of obtaining rented places. Neither of them have plans to move or further alter their space although Ken would ideally like 'proper business premises'. And indeed, even though Ken and Alan have made a clear distinction between work space and living space, the problems and frustrations of their present situation are sometimes quite acute:

> 'It's difficult to forget work or to feel as if I've left work ... it's a bit like staying over at the office every night ... We started with a phone... but it just grew and grew we had to adapt our living space to cope with demand, we use every room including the kitchen and the hallway areas, now it seems the work takes priority over the home: everywhere home now seems a functional minimum. It's difficult to have people round to entertain visitors, it's difficult for one of us to relax and another work in the same room, it's difficult to just take a break and relax as one would at home... and sometimes you just need to get out of the place. It's handy that my flatmate and my business partner are one and the same, and that our other flatmate is understanding and sociable!' (Ken)

Where potentially more space is available, negotiations between other household members can be crucial in establishing the location and outlook of the main work area. Elise reconciled the need to be available over the day for domestic and child care activities, meetings with clients and contractors and her desire for a quiet permanent work space by occupying a room on the ground floor at the back of the house. A room hidden from general view from inside the house but with an open aspect through French windows opening onto the secluded back garden and in a part of the house which allows her to hear most of what is going on elsewhere. Although a permanent workplace not in use for 23 years, all members of the family regard the 'office' as separate and hidden although Elise hinted that the arrangement had been the result of compromise:

'Work is definitely for that room... I personally like the kitchen, but it's impractical because it is busy... and my husband prefers me to go into the office.'

Faced with critical problems of overlapping activities and conflicting demands on time and attention the homeworker may seek a resolution through significant changes in location and organisation of space. These changes can take a considerable period of time to effect during which significant experiential redefinitions in personal identity occur.

Leslie's account of her family and work history illustrate the complexity of such processes.

Working as a secretary she sought out a course in leather craft as offering a route into a new area of employment. The course which was directed at 'the assembly line worker' 'taught (her) to make a bag with cheap leather and foam, cutting, patterns and dying' thus providing sufficient knowledge on all the process of leather craft required to set up a part time craft business from home. 'I could have taken a job as an assembly line worker doing one part of the work only ... this is what the course was designed for... (but) I would go mad (because the work would be boring and undemanding) not I do the whole job using good leather and my own designs'. Working from home using the dining table as a work bench proved to be a 'lucrative hobby' although the experience of working form home was 'a bloody nightmare in the dining room, the dog, rabbit and child in amongst the leather.

Moving house provided an opportunity to choose and plan around the demand of work as well as family life. Moving away from London enabled the purchase of a three bedroomed house with enough room at the back and side for a workroom to be built which now contains an industrial sewing machine, tools, hides an made up goods:

> 'I deliberately built this extension, small as it is, for work... it separates work from the home and provides a permanent work and storage area that is specifically organised to accommodate work, otherwise it just disrupts home life... and I feel as though I'm never away from work ...'

But she still:

> 'did not think it would become a full time job... when the teaching packed up I decided to make to go of it and taught myself all the new skills I needed for commercial work... of course it's cheaper but what I love is working from home it's great because you can do it when you want, it's your own place and you can do what the hell you want.'

Where many of the constraints which characterise the cases already cited are absent it allows the functional requirement of the work activity itself to establish a dominance in decisions of what space to use. In the case of Max the drummer the need to achieve noise isolation from neighbours, passers-by and within the house itself proved critical. Drum practice had always taken place in the dining room - a large room downstairs at the back of the house:

> 'this was always OK being only about 5 to 6 hours a week the... family don't mind the noise, they say they only notice when it stops and the house seem quiet! When I started all day the neighbours started to complain... one rang me up and said 'everyone is talking about it and we intend to get it stopped' so I just said OK I'll make sure it's moved. Now the only comment I have has is in the Summer when the chap at the back... they sit out round their pool... said it was a bit loud.'

Relocation to a room upstairs and in the corner of the house furthest away from neighbours plus sound insulation provided by blankets and a wall hung mattress serve a double purpose: avoiding noise nuisance from disturbing other household members or creating problems with the neighbours and passers-by and, as a secondary matter improving conditions for practice. 'Noise is no issue in actual recording because the sound system is completely sealed'.

The ideal which many homeworkers seek however establishes an extreme position in which the individual seeks to create the same conditions normally associated with work in a traditional workplace combined with the advantages of not being away from home. These are the conditions which Paul has managed to create for himself as part of a well planned strategy to work at home and which are quite clearly expressed by his description of his experience of changing from working in the 'spare bedroom' to a purpose built surgery in an extension to the side of the house:

> 'the spare room did not provide enough space and the stairs were a problem for OAP's, loss of an extra room and living space... using some sections of one's home just didn't feel right... with the extension it's more like an annex rather than part of our home, it's definitely a work place... attached to the home but clearly separate... I have total independence patients come by appointment... no hassle no questions... I decide who come and when... I agenda my time to my requirements, I can always be reached... even when I am out at work I'm in!
> The separation of domestic space and work space is very important in terms of 'going to work' when I use the surgery I feel I am doing the right thing in the right place. I am at work... not working from home as such... even though I am still in my own home.'

Strategies for social and spatial management

The transition to homebased work is an integral part of the longer term economic and social restructuring of British society which is likely to accelerate over the next few years (Henley Centre for Forecasting, 1988, Huws, 1990). The examination of that experience through individual histories of homeworkers allows an intuitive understanding of the radical disjuncture between traditional and commonly held notions of home and work and emerging redefinitions of the meanings given to both.

The case studies demonstrate individualised responses to the experience of homebased working within a dominant culture where such activities are largely hidden and unusual (Randall 1990). One homeworker commented on returning to part time work outside the home 'I'm loving it! I feel normal again, just like any one else'.

The individual responses recorded here were expressed in a context tightly bound by their personal and direct contacts. Throughout the interviews and visits there were only two references which indicated any awareness of the broader framework of comparison of their experience. Although some of them knew other homeworkers no references were made to them and only one, Ken, belonged to an organisation representing homeworkers. There are possibilities that this individualisation will alter as knowledge of the prevalence of homeworking prompts voluntary and commercial responses. Indeed during 1991 various developments took place which signal recognition of the pervasiveness of homeworking. In May a quarterly magazine *Live Wire* was launched as 'a modest introduction to the new and exciting world of home businesses, telecommuting, teleworking and remote management' (Golding, 1991, p.1). In June the TUC ran its first ever event specifically on homeworking and homeworkers (TUC 1991) and, *OwnBase* claimed a contact list of 4,000.(1)

However homework at the moment is such that the people detailed here have or are in the process of establishing a set of physical and social relationships which they and those they deal with directly in their homes accept.

The case studies show people consciously and continually engaged in what they regard as an evolving and progressive situation rather than a static given set of arrangements. This involves positive attention to two dimensions of their home environments, the physical and the social.

The number of physical factors which can be controlled and altered by homeworkers are multiple: the design, organisation and furnishing of workspace(s), restricting or facilitating access to 'dedicated' workspace by the opening or closing of doors and windows, constructing screens and other barriers to the 'outside'. Although more difficult to specify and identify but no less numerous are the non physical aspects of control which range from the timetabling of work activities to subtle (or less subtle!) interpersonal negotiated rules about what kind of interruptions are acceptable, when and by whom. One person commented on sharing her workroom with her husband as follows 'my work is on a large table and contained in bookcases; my husband also uses a large drawing desk in the same room. He has to switch the radio off if we both work at the same time.'(2)

The five people detailed in this paper adopt different strategies directed at achieving quite specific and explicit arrangements which they see as constituting an ideal expression of their preferred general modus operandi and the balance they consider desirable between work and non work activities.

Two extreme strategies exemplified by Paul on the one hand and Marni on the other portray quite distinctively different ways through which homework should and can be accommodated in the home environment.

The first seeks to replicate in the home the physical and social separation characteristic of conventional work experiences. The chiropody surgery is designed to be invisible and unnoticed once the home has been entered, the door providing the only means of communication with the main part of the house is soundproof and always closed. All materials, records, accounts and supplies are accommodated in the surgery itself. The outlook from the surgery is through a single small front window which is screened by venetian blinds natural light being facilitated by sloping roof lights which are not overlooked. Other members of the household do not enter the surgery nor is any work undertaken there interrupted except in domestic emergency. To repeat part of the quote given above " when I'm in my surgery I'm not in my home it is a different entity... when I leave the room I shut the door I am in my own home".

The second expresses the need to achieve a new configuration in which the notion of home becomes altered to encompass homework as a regular 'normal' activity integral to other activities. As Marni stressed where she works depends on "what else is going on or where I feel like doing the work...". She would even move her dressmaking dummy around and do pattern designs and cutting out in different parts of the home. Whilst not entirely unambiguous about this arrangement as is shown by her comment about the original design of the flat, nevertheless she made it quite clear that this way of working was a positive preference and that she wanted to feel that her work was part of normal every day event in the home not a special 'cut off' activity confined to a particular place of time. Other participants in this research show variations between these extremes. Leslie organises her workroom to maintain a sense of being at home and in touch with her domestic environment although she lives alone and for most of the week when she is working at home 'sees no one'. Two features of the workroom facilitate this contact and establish a sense of social openness, the workroom door which is always kept open and means that "I can see my kitchen when I am working" and a window over the garden; in tangible terms this openness consists of keeping in touch with the sight of non work objects, settings and sounds, the only animate intrusion the tame rabbit which has 'the run' of the kitchen. Leslie describes herself as a solitary person, her main social contacts are made at the weekend when she takes her goods to sell at the market, meeting friends, and customers and spending the Saturday night at her parents' home or when her daughter comes to stay.

Elise's case seems to show a certain degree of conflict between her own preferences to work where she has contact with all the other things going on in the house and that of her husband who 'prefers me to go into the office'.

Ken has used the physical arrangement and style of furniture and office equipment to mark out a clear distinction between work and non work thus the main room in the flat is functionally divided by the kind of equipment and furniture used although there are no visual barriers such as filing cabinets or bookcases between the two halves. He clearly finds a balance difficult to maintain given his expressed preference for overlapping and mixing work and social activities and contacts taking some pride in referring to work partners and clients as the 'day-time party'.

These possibilities can be formally expressed by bringing together the possible configurations of physical arrangements ad identifying the two extreme possibilities as architectural closure or openness. In an equivalent way social closure and openness represent the extreme possibilities for non physical interactional dimensions. The possible combinations of these configurations can be shown diagrammatically as set out below:

		OPEN	CLOSED
THE NATURE OF ARCHITECTURAL FORM	OPEN	1	2
THE NATURE OF SOCIAL INTERACTION	CLOSED	3	4

Table 4.2 Configurations of social and architectural forms

Where for 1 the person seeks to achieve both architectural and social openness: Marni and Elise (but not altogether successful!).

In 2 architectural closure is combined with social openness: Leslie and Ken.

In 3 social closure is sought where architectural openness prevails: non of the cases really display this possibility.

In 4 social and architectural closure prevail: Paul being a particularly good example.

Clearly in trying to work through to a stable expression of the particular set of relationships they most desire people find themselves constrained by numerous considerations of which the most critical are: the nature of their work, other household members, the expectations of requirements of their customers, clients or employer. Indeed it has been suggested by Kingsman that one of the key issues for managers employing homeworkers is to ensure that:

> 'the teleworker must have space - preferably a room - which can be set aside at home for these working purposes, there must be a definite 'contract' between him or her and other members of the family, agreeing that this mode of work and the demands it places upon everyone in the home unit are acceptable to all.' (Kingsman, 1988).

However sensitivity to personal preferences and circumstances may even lead employers to an accommodation as Stuart Dennison found when installing computer terminals and office equipment for homeworkers.

> 'Terminals were installed in living rooms, dining rooms, bedrooms and conservatories. A practical lesson learned is to supply desks in kit form, as spare bedrooms situated at the top of narrow staircases present installation problems not generally encountered in offices.' (Dennison, 1990).

What may be a preferred balance under one set of circumstances may become outmoded and inappropriate as work and domestic circumstances change. Expansion of work or changes in the composition of the household may create conditions within which strategies will be reformulated and redirected. A trade union official, pleased at having negotiated to work from home set up a room for work but also thought 'I could enjoy playing Mahler out of earshot of the rest of the family only after a while I found I only did work there it felt strange to play music for pleasure'.

Summary and conclusions

Clearly there are those who try to achieve a high degree of physical and social segregation or closure whilst others would prefer ways of organising their space and their relationships with other people to achieve a greater degree of integration between all aspects of their life within the home including homework. A useful way of approaching this is to identify the possible combinations of architectural and social closure sought.

Two clear and extreme models of how homework can and should be accommodated in the home environment emerge. The first of these seeks to replicate in the home the separateness of conventional work experiences, the second emphasises the need to achieve a new configuration in which the notion of home becomes altered to accommodate work as a regular 'normal' activity. The case of Paul exemplifies the first of these models, that of Marni the second.

Operating within the first mode the homeworker seeks to achieve 'architectural enclosure' through a variety of devices - this could involve a separate room, room partitions, allocating work to 'semi' domestic spaces such as hallways and landings. The 'other than domestic' aspect can be further enhanced by locating the work activities in back rooms, corners of the dwelling, outside in sheds or extensions and ensuring an individual outlook away from the interior. Soundproofing, decor and work equipment can all be used to emphasise the differences between the domestic sphere and the work environment. The details of distinction will be constrained by the required work facilities, client requirements and employers' conditions.

An ideological and practical emphasis on obtaining the 'best of both worlds', those of home and work, will influence the outward expression of: dress, work demeanour and time scheduling. Situations which restrict or prevent the realisation of these conditions will prevent a cognisance between the tangible surroundings and the person's internalisation of their identity creating conflicts which unresolved will lead to instability at a number of experiential levels. Clearly many factors can facilitate or constrain the realisation of this model: income capacity, domestic responsibilities, relative power within the household to command resources, as well as exterior influences of planning controls, tax structures and insurance.

The second mode is highly problematic because it is here that individuals are struggling to create alternatives for which we have no given cultural norm except maybe that of the low paid 'traditional' female homeworker or the historical 'picture' of domestic/cottage industry of previous centuries. Norms which the modern graphic designer, photographer, date processor or management consultant would find it hard to empathise with.

It is vital that these alternatives develop in all their personal variety if homeworking is to become accepted as a legitimate activity for those who perforce will increasingly have to combine responsibilities in the domestic sphere with working at home. Homeworking is ideally suited to people with disabilities and carers who may have difficulty attending a central office. Indeed it is likely that women carers in particular will become increasingly under pressure to work from home by employers in a tightening labour market trying to cut costs. As more women return to the labour force homework will provide one major way in which women can continue to care for their children and others in the absence of adequate state or private care provision.

Others for whom homework will become more important are those who run small businesses and freelance workers many of whom see current economic and social changes as holding out the possibility for homework as one of the vehicles for achieving personal integration and non alienation.

Notes

1. This figure was given in a letter sent to the author by one of officials on *OwnBase* in May 1991.
2. This quote was taken from a reply to a questionnaire survey of homeworkers undertaken in May 1991.

References

Allen, S. (1986), 'The Control of Women's Labour: The Case of Homeworking', *Feminist Review*, no. 22.

Allen, S. & Wolkowitz, C. (1987), *Homeworking Myths and Realities*, MacMillan, London.

Birmingham City Council (1988), *Homeworking in Birmingham*, Birmingham City Council.

Blisset, E. (1990), *Homeworking*, Banking Insurance and Finance Union, London.

Brown, P. & Scase, R. (1991), *Poor Work: Disadvantage and the Division of Labour*, Oxford University Press.

Bulos, M. (1990a), 'Homebased Working: New Opportunities or Old Divisions', a paper presented at the BSA Annual Conference, mimeo, South Bank Polytechnic.

Bulos, M. (1990b), 'The Use of Space and Home Adaptations by Homebased Workers', in Putnam, T. and Newton, C. (eds.), *Household Choices*, Futures Publications, London.

Civil and Public Services Union, (1991), *Homeworking in the Civil Service*, TUC, London.

Confederation of British Industry, (1988), *Tomorrow's Workplace*, Conference Proceedings, CBI, London.

Cook, J. & Fonow, M.M. (1991), 'Knowledge and Women's Interests: Issues of Epistemology and Methodology in Feminist Sociology', in McCarl Neilson, J. (ed.), *Feminist Research Methods*, Westview Press, London.

D'Cruz, K. (1990), 'More Space (age) Angles', *OwnBase*, vol. 2, no.4, July.

Dennison, S. (1990), 'Home Sweet Home'. *Public Finance and Accountancy*, 2 February, CIPFA, London.

Emetecheter, B. (1988), *The Guardian*, 21 November, p. 6.

Felix, D. (1989), *Evaluation of Remote Working*, Department of Employment, Sheffield.

Golding, G. (1991), 'Foreword', *Live Wire*, vol. 1, no. 1, Spring.

Francis, M. (1990), 'A Drummer on your Work', Publicity Pamphlet.

Hakim, C. (1988) 'Homeworking in Britain ' in Pahl, R.E. *On Work: Historical and Comparative Theoretical Approaches*, Blackwell, Oxford.

Hakim, C. (1989), *Homebased Work in Britain*, DOE, London.

Henley Centre For Forecasting, (1988), *A Cost/Benefit Analysis of Teleworking*, Henley Centre for Forecasting, London.

Huws, U. (1984), *The New Homeworkers*, Low Pay Unit, London.

Huws, U. (1991), 'Telework Projects', *Futures*, vol. 23, no. 1, Jan/Feb.

Kingsman, F. (1987), *The Telecommuters*, John Wiley & Sons, Chichester.

Kingsman, F. (1988), *Tomorrow's Workplace*, British Telecom, London.

Pahl, R.E. (d.) (1988), *On Work: Historical and Comparative Theoretical Approaches*, Blackwell, Oxford.

Pennington, S. & Westover, B. (1989), *The Hidden Workforce*, MacMillan Education, London.

Phizacklea, A. (1990), *Unpacking the Fashion Industry: Gender, Racism and Class in Production*, Routledge, London.
Randall, J. (1990), 'At Work "At Home": a boundary crossed', BSA Seminar, Nov., mimeo.
Saunders, P. (1990), *A Nation of Homeowners*, Unwin Hyman, London. Shutz, A. (1964), *Collected Papers: Studies in Social Theory*, Martinus Nihsoff, The Hague.
Sixsmith, J. & Sixsmith, A. (1990), 'Places in Transition: the Impact of Life Events on the Experience of Home', in Putnam, T. & Newman, C. *Household Choices*, Fortune Publications, London.
Trades Union Council, (1975), *Homeworking: A TUC Statement*, TUC, London.
Trades Union Council, (1987), *Homeworking: A TUC Statement*, TUC, London.
Trades Union Council, (1991), *Homeworking and Homeworkers: A TUC Seminar for Trades Unionists*, TUC, London.
Webb, S. & Webb, B. (1932), *Methods of Social Study*, Longmans Green, London.

5 Autobiographical reports of residential experience: An exploratory study

M.V. Giuliani and G. Barbey

Introduction

Literature on home environments largely emphasises the dynamic aspect of people's transactions with the domestic environment. Processes by which people are linked to homes occur in time, and are time bound (Werner *et al.*, 1985, p. 5, Giuliani, 1989, 1991). A comparison between different stages of life can highlight changes in the meaning and use of the home. However, in order to understand how people perceive the evolution of this process of change, more powerful and sensitive methodologies have to be adopted.

In the present chapter an exploratory study is presented, aimed to investigate the evolution of the intimate ties existing between a resident and his/her home through an analysis of autobiographical accounts of residential life.

The biographical approach has been extensively discussed in many areas of social research, from clinical and personality psychology to history, sociology and anthropology. Ferrarotti (1981) and Catani and Mazé (1982) argue that the use of life stories is an autonomous method, fundamental to the progress of social research. The concept of ego-history has been discussed by Chanu and Perrot (1985). In environmental literature, the phenomenological perspective has focused on the importance of subjective and personal descriptions of environmental experiences, and the autobiographical approach has been adopted in order to include the temporal dimension of residential life (Helphand, 1979, Cooper Marcus, 1979, Horwitz and Tognoli, 1982).

Method

Participants

Our interest in autobiographical accounts of residential experience was announced during the symposium on 'Affective and temporal dimensions of experiencing home' held in Ankara in 1990 at IAPS 11. In this occasion, a brief residential autobiography written by one of the authors of the present chapter was presented. After the conference, a few participants spontaneously sent their residential autobiographies. In the following, a written request was addressed to other colleagues to collaborate in our research by writing a brief text on their residential biographies.

The choice of colleagues as respondents in our research had two main purposes: i) to make explicit the cultural and personal background of people involved in people-environment research through a self-conscious examination of their residential experience (Cooper Marcus, 1978); ii) to facilitate an interactive relationship (Ferrarotti, 1981) between researchers and respondents in order to overcome the academic distinction between scientist and so-called subjects.

Procedure

Very simple instructions were given to the authors to allow them to freely report their residential experiences. They were asked to write a three page autobiographical essay focused on their residential life, and to try to convey both relevant information and reflections about their residential experience. A spontaneous and informal style was suggested, in the language they preferred out of French, English, and Italian. The expected utilisation of the texts was also explained.

Analysis

A separate and mutual analysis of the texts was carried out by the two authors. The main purpose of the analysis was to explore the potential usefulness of biographies in capturing recurring historical sequences in the process of people's appropriation of the home throughout their life span as well as the singularities of individual experiences. Informative data about living events, as well as conscious reflections on meaningful units of residential experience were considered in the analysis (Alexander, 1988). A high interpretive agreement between authors was found in particular as regards the identification of salient issues.

Results

name	sex	age	family status	country of birth	country of resid	lenght of text (in lines)
J.S.	M	40	single (sep)	U.K.	U.K.	125
M.S.	M	60	married + ch	France	France	78
J.R.	F	45	married + ch	USA	USA	250
B.B.	F	58	re-married + ch	France	Switzerland	124
M.B.	F	48	married + ch	Italy	Italy	86
P.S.	F	35	single	Italy	Italy	38
A.C.	F	53	married + ch	Canada	Israel	52
S.K.	M	42	married + ch	Japan	Japan	160
Y.B.	F	60	widow	France	France	231
V.G.	F	48	married	Italy	Italy	43
R.L.	M	41	married + ch	Australia	Switzerland	84
G.B.	M	58	re-married + ch	Switzerland	Switzerland	153
P.R.	F	33	single	Italy	Italy	130
K.D.	M	46	couple + ch	Australia (temp)	USA	227

Table 5.1 Description of respondents

The respondents

13 residential biographies were collected, including those of the authors of the present chapter. An additional life narrative - the autobiographical account of a case of house-hunting - was sent us

although not written specifically, and was considered separately. The 14 authors (8 females and 6 males) are either environmental designers or social scientists concerned with behavioural issues. The geographical origin is extremely heterogeneous, and in some cases does not coincide with current country of residence. The age ranges from 33 to 60 years. Most of the respondents are, or have been married, and own the dwelling in which they live. We did not require any specific information about respondents' characteristics, and the information given in the biographies is sometimes very scanty. The basic biographical data are reported in Table 1.

Since most, if not all, respondents are of middle class origin, they tend to consider the home as a place of freedom and enjoyment, rather than a place of constraint like the working class dwelling. We acknowledge that the population of respondents is not typical of a vast majority of urban residents spread over all the social classes. We therefore do not feel entitled to extrapolate our conclusions in order to apply them to a wider range of residents.

Nature of the texts

The texts differ greatly both in length and in nature. The total length ranges from 38 lines (P.S.) to 250 lines (J.R.) with an average length of 127 lines. A major difference among the texts can be found in the more exogenous or endogenous perspective (Jelmini, 1987) adopted by participants. Some of the texts are real life narratives (Y.B., J.S., B.B., K.D.), some others are mainly a description of the dwellings occupied during the life span (S.K., R.L., J.R., M.S., M.B., P.R.), others yet are more a personal interpretation of the meaning of the residential life (A.C., V.G., G.B., P.S.).

Furthermore, the biographies vary in the emotional involvement shown in the respondents' productions, ranging from the neutral description by S.K. to the feeling-centred narrative by J.S. and Y.B.

Home and life stages

Most biographies are arranged into a sequence of residential periods, comprising three main periods: childhood, university studies and adulthood, which usually begins with marriage. Each of these periods is characterised by specific types of relationship with the home place.

It is noteworthy that in most cases the space devoted to the childhood period is greater than to the current situation. Indeed it is in these childhood experiences that the key to subsequent residential experiences is sought by identifying a significant or recurring factor. This continuity in time is often referred to explicitly:

> '...I am rediscovering feelings for the garden and physical world which have lain dormant since my childhood...' (J.S.)
> 'Since my early childhood the space around the house has left as many traces as the interior.' (M.S.)
> 'I have always felt that my attraction for Normandy, where I have a house today, was linked to this childhood memory.' (Y.B.)
> 'That is, my early experiences of city life were accompanied by an attraction for the country. This ambiguity has remained in me until this day' (G.B.)

In other cases the whole text is written in such a way as to show up the relation between childhood residential experiences and later life. See, for instance, the autobiography of V.G., where the lack of any feeling of geographical belonging is traced back to residential mobility during childhood and that of P.S., centred entirely on the continuing search for a home following a way of life exemplified by rituals learned during childhood.

Childhood space emerges from memory mainly as a sensorial space. Childhood memories are generally associated with immediate perceptions, often related to elements of the natural environment.

> 'I even remember the little acorns, which I would find on the ground where they had fallen from the oak trees each year. I remember liking the texture of an acorn as I grasped and stroked it in my hands' (J.S.)
> '... the leafy branches of avenue Henri Martin and especially the smell of petrol from the cars or fresh bread ...' (G.B.)
> '... I can still remember the strange smell that came out when drawers and cupboards in little used rooms were opened ...' (M.B.)

It is significant that trees are sometimes mentioned in the childhood memories of persons who later make no further mention of natural elements.

The fragmentary nature of these childhood memories does not seem due to impoverishment caused by their distance in time but rather to the different way children relate to the environment. Houses, and places in general, draw their importance from the personal experiences used to build up an image of the physical world and to try out one's capacity to move around in it. Prohibitions and risk only increase the thrill of discovery:

> 'I was not allowed to go into this room, but I used to tiptoe into it, holding my breath, and constantly expecting to see the bishop's ghost jump out' (Y.B.)
> 'You had to climb to the top of a step ladder to reach the hatch, and then you could pull yourself up onto the roof [...] There you really felt to be at the top of the world. Getting back down you had to lower your body until your feet hit the top of the (unsteady) step ladder. It was a very nerve- wracking experience.' (J.R.)

In this process of discovering one's self and the world, holiday residences play a very important role. The middle class ritual of holidays is often celebrated in the grandparents' house, a large, 'family' home, which sometimes becomes a pleasant refuge in periods of life otherwise difficult, such as wartime. Regular returns to this holiday house, which is often more stable than the town house, can turn it into a place rich in symbolic meanings, the place of one's roots, to which one belongs:

> 'I was not born or brought up in St. David's. Yet I always felt that in some sense it was somewhere we spiritually belonged. In my childhood my parents regularly took us to St. David's for summer holidays...' (J.S.)

As one grows older a more active space appropriating attitude emerges: it is attempted to gain a space of one's own (R.L.) or else strategies of territorial subdivision are brought to bear, particularly in cases in which a room is shared with a brother or sister (Y.B., B.B.).

Leaving the parental home usually coincides with the period of higher studies, or that immediately following the first working experiences. Detachment from the family, particularly for those from the provinces, usually coincides with the first experience of a large city. This is also the period of the first trips abroad, living in temporary dwellings, often shared with others. The joy of freedom is often mingled with homesickness and loneliness, which are sometimes heightened by the precariousness of the dwelling. Although life in these dwellings is lived with enthusiasm, as a first experience of decorative freedom, they are unlikely to be considered real homes.

From the physic-sensorial space it used to be in childhood, the home seems to be transformed into a mental space (Barbey, 1990). Home no longer coincides automatically with the dwelling, but becomes a life project that is built up in time, in which affective relations play a primary role:

> 'Once I had a home [...] But I have (I hope temporarily) lost that home. [...] I have gone through dozens of temporary houses in temporary places looking for this home.'(P.S.)
>
> 'If one takes investment of time, effort and resources as a measure of emotional attachment, then only towards my present home in Israel do I feel that. All the other places I lived in as an adult were places I considered temporary, even when we lived there for 10 years ... The important point for me was that I wanted to return to Israel ...' (A.C.)

The meaning attributed to the home and the meaning of life in general are so closely interrelated that it is very difficult to perceive the common features shared by the various biographies as far as adulthood compared to childhood is concerned. The differences due to the time of life, the relational situation, and perhaps even to gender and cultural origin, are affected also by the willingness shown by respondents to discuss such an emotionally charged topic no longer filtered through memory, but with respect to the current situation .

In many cases the interdependence between home and the affective life that takes place in it is acknowledged explicitly:

> '...we have celebrated many family occasions there, including our eldest daughter's wedding, and each of them makes it more and more a 'family home'. Now, as a grandmother, I get enormous pleasure out of seeing how our grandchildren feel that this is their second home, and seeing how our grown-up daughters still feel a very strong attachment to it (and us).' (A.C.)
>
> 'This house, which I still love 23 years after having built it, is worth all the more to me in that I felt I possessed it truly only after my second marriage and my wife discovered the meaning of living in it that I had unconsciously developed.' (G.B.)
>
> 'In writing this account, I realise that it is in any case impossible to talk of places without relating them to the lives of those who have lived there.' (Y.B.)
>
> 'Living is not restricted to the house and its walls. It is also necessary to be in harmony with oneself, a harmony that is based

on the couple for the lucky ones, and on the individual for the others...' (B.B.)

In other cases the symbolic meaning of the home as the locus of domestic intimacy must be read between the lines:

> 'Much more can be written about my current home, which has been appropriated in diverse ways to accommodate three sons...as well as a stream of house guests from abroad.' (R.L.)

The interdependence between home and affective ties, particularly those of the couple, becomes extremely clear when these ties are broken:

> '...She had met someone else with whom she went to live. [...] The house felt unbearably empty. [...] I still live in this house... I know the house is partially an emotional trap, symbolically representing a link to a shared past which cannot be recaptured.' (J.S.)
> '...I came back to Switzerland with my three children but leaving a husband behind. Many years were to pass before I again felt capable of really 'living' in a home with love.' (B.B.)

The connotation of relational affectivity associated with the home may extend also to the extra-family relations, just as the home may take in a space which is larger than the actual house or apartment:

> 'It is even more difficult for me to say where my home is now...[whether] in Rome, where nearly all my friends are also my colleagues [...] or in Montecampano [...] where my husband lives [...] and the residents of the tiny village know me...' (V.G.)
> 'His death [i.e. the death of a neighbour]... has been symbolically disruptive; no more neighbourly talks over the garden fence about the seasons...' (J.S.)
> 'I don't think that I can separate my love and attachment to our home from my love and attachment to the land of Israel.' (A.C.)

This does not mean that the physical and material aspects of dwelling are not relevant. Several biographies describe the physical transformation of domestic space as the primary condition for being happily settled. The repetition of the same kind of action, for instance:

> 'The first thing I did was to knock down the wall between the two

rooms - actually I forgot to say that in practically all the flats I have lived in I have knocked down walls...' (Y.B.)

shows that the transformation of space is not just a function response to a particular environment in order to adapt it to one's needs, but reflects an active attitude towards space that is displayed as a constant attribute of an individual's personality.

More often than not, however, it is clear that it is not so much the physical result of the action which gives the house its value of home but rather the actual process of appropriation:

'I feel strong ties with this home which has grown with us over all these years... What with the time spent thinking about transforming it and that devoted to actually transforming it, I can say that I have invested a lot of my time and energy in it.' (M.B.)

The physical transformation of space within the home fulfils another symbolic objective which consists in the eradication of the presence of previous residents, whose memory must not interfere with the home:

'The fact that my ex-mother-in-law chose our old house in Piedmont means that I don't like it at all. I painted the whole interior with 30 gallons of white paint. I wanted to eliminate all traces of previous occupants before leaving my mark.' (B.B.)

Conversely, being forced to leave a home may be accompanied by a desire for its physical destruction, as in the case of Y.B. after the death of her husband:

'...it seemed very important to me at the time to transform this space, to break it up, to destroy it, so as to leave nothing behind me...I felt that it was very unfair that others could be happy in it after us.' (Y.B.)

The spatial dimension of home experience

It is commonly agreed that the floor plan of dwelling units tends to reflect the life styles of the residents. At the same time, while today's standard housing types follow an almost invariable pattern, this does not imply that the life styles of the residents are identical. The uniformity of the housing stock is obviously likely to inhibit the spectrum of domestic activities. Such considerations seem to be confirmed by the biographies, where the symbolic values of the past homes is often related to the morphological and qualitative aspects of the domestic spaces as experienced in childhood:

> 'A deep apartment, covered with soft carpets, with a balcony overlooking the square where the markets follow one another...' (M.S.)
> '...large sunlit kitchen, lots of rooms, marble floors ...' (P.R.)

The experience of domestic spaces gained during youth is often related to play and exploration. The various parts of the home are perceived in terms of mobility and movement, of hazards too:

> '...the long corridor where I could run...' (P.R.)
> 'The second dwelling I remember was a small detached house with a porch where I fell and got hurt...' (S.K.)
> 'There was a gate in the wall to the side alley, so that when people were coming you could either run and join them, or escape them, slamming the gate behind you.' (J.R.)

Home includes outdoor playrooms and underground hideouts. There is no clear limit between internal and external spaces, as these are interconnected by a network of paths. Nature is perceived as a means to strengthen the domestic ties, as it is characterised by a feeling of permanence, stability and continuity:

> 'Home is partly my house and to an increasing extent my small garden [...] I am rediscovering feelings for the garden and physical world which have lain dormant since my childhood' (J.S.)
> '... the pleasure of the house is enhanced by the relation with the natural elements of its garden...' (M.B.)
> 'The screened porch opens onto our garden in which we have, like at our former house, planted a perennial flower garden.' (J.R.)

As opposed to tamed nature, wild nature can act in contrast with the interior of the house and stress the corresponding feeling of domestic comfort:

> 'If my house could be magically transported to a large plot of land, in a wilder landscape, nearer to the sea, I would feel more 'alive'.' (J.S.)

Somehow, it is important that the home is self contained and at the same time, strongly related to its surroundings:

> 'This self-contained flat with 3 main rooms was the extended upper floor of a traditional English terrace house...' (R.L.)
> 'One of the joys of this house is that it is two blocks from a small lake that is perfect for taking walks around.' (J.R.)

While the physical definition of home is very precise, its abstract definition is extremely broad in scope and is limited practically only by the nation or the world. This different scale of reference is typical of domestic issues.

Another interesting question is the way in which space is described as a support of the self. In times of isolation, confinement or retirement the home is visualised as a secluded portion of space, while it is envisaged in its more open dimension in periods of socialising:

> 'The apartment was actually very badly divided up. It had a tiny entrance and all the rooms were communicating [...] The apartment too was wonderful. It was very large and all the rooms were arranged in a row with very large windows... friends were always dropping in [...] This meant deciding to live in a single room... I think that at the time this corresponded to a desire to adapt myself to a solitary life)' (Y.B.)

It is obvious that interconnected rooms can be alternatively considered as a source of trouble or enjoyment, depending on the scenario. This can be a reminder that homes should invariably consist of a combination of closed and open spaces in order to accommodate the changing circumstances of life. We demonstrated earlier that ordinary dwelling units consist of a combination of 'spatial archetypes', i.e. the correspondence of individual 'cells' to a suite of rooms.

It is interesting to note that age tends to modify the perception of spatial values. In childhood years the diversity of perceived and recorded places and spatial resources is more important than at a later age. With their increasing power of action, adults are likely to have a more instrumental (and less poetic) view of the dwelling. They view and evaluate it in terms of practicality and everyday life. If it is considered inappropriate for such activities, changes are bound to occur.

Conclusion

The conclusion of this chapter cannot be a general synthesis of such a wide area. We will try instead to establish a tentative relationship between the common themes identified in the biographies and a set of underlying values currently associated with home life. Our hypothesis is that different systems of domestic values could be identified for different people and for different stages of life.

The suggested relationship between autobiographical themes and domestic values is shown in Table 2.

Familiarity, homeliness, sensory aspects of home life	Usage/ Experiential values
Domestic roles adopted by residents	Usage value
Importance of garden and nature as complement of home	Usage/ Symbolic values
Drive to transform the internal spaces of a new home	Usage/ Artistic values
Perceived use value of specific rooms	Usage value
Importance of a study or workplace within home	Usage/ Symbolic values
Presence of others/Social relations between residents	Affective value
Poetic or metaphorical meanings of home	Symbolic value
Essence of the dwelling and emotional attachment	Symbolic/ Affective values
Temporality and timeliness of the home	Usage/ Memorial values
Cultural changes in housing design	Usage/ Cultural values

Table 5.2 Relations between autobiographical themes and values

The table above is a tentative summary of the domestic value system of respondents. The usage value is almost omnipresent and several themes are illustrated by combined values. It should be further noted that most of the values that are referred to in the biographies are positive values. The reason for such a predominantly positive attitude is the affective homology between the self and the home. The home is currently viewed as an 'image of the self' and it is therefore often characterised by positive ratings. Furthermore, the combination of the above mentioned values is a confirmation of the attachment dimensions (Giuliani, 1991). The domestic value system is congruent with intensity, quality, and duration of the attachment to the home.

Further research including empirical work should facilitate a deeper investigation and understanding of these values.

References

Alexander, I.E. (1988) 'Personality, Psychological Assessment, and Psychobiography', *Journal of Personality*, vol. 56, no. 1, pp. 265-294.

Barbey, G. (1990) *L'évasion domestique. Essai sur les rélations d'affectivité au logis*, Presses polytechnique et universitaires romandes, Lausanne.

Catani, M. & Mazé, S. (1982), *Tante Suzanne ou l'histoire de vie sociale et du devenir d'une femme* (Aunt Susanne, or the history of social life and of evolution of a woman), Librairie des Méridiens, Paris.

Chaunu, P. & Perrot, M. (1985), 'L'ego-histoire' (Ego-history), *Le débat*, no. 37, pp. 119-151.

Cooper Marcus, C. (1978), 'Remembrance of landscapes past', *Landscape*, vol. 22, no. 3, pp. 34-43.

Ferrarotti, F. (1981), *Storia e storie di vita* (History and life histories), Laterza, Bari.

Giuliani, M.V. (1989), 'La casa come sistema territoriale (The house as a territorial system)', *Edilizia Popolare*, vol. 36, no. 206-207, pp. 58-65.

Giuliani, M.V. (1991), 'Toward an analysis of mental representations of attachment to the home', *Journal of Architectural and Planning Research*, vol. 8, no. 2, pp. 133-146.

Helphand, K. (1979), *Environmental Autobiography*, mimeo, University of Surrey, U.K.

Horwitz, J. & Tognoli, J. (1982), 'Role of home in adult development: Women and men living alone describe their residential histories', *Family Relations*, vol. 31, pp. 335-341.

Jelmini, J.P. (1987), 'Le point de vue d'un historien (The point of view of an historian)', *Recherches at travaux de l'Institut d'ethnologie de Neuchtel*, no. 7.
Werner, C.M., Altman, I. & Oxley, D. (1975), 'Temporal Aspects of Homes: A Transactional Perspective', in Altman, I. and Werner, C.M. (eds.), *Home Environments*, Plenum Press, New York.

6 Home and homelessness

J. Moore and D. Canter

Introduction

The psychological significance of home has generally been assumed for homeless people. This has been reflected in the 'domestication' of institutions such as hostels. Therapeutic models such as normalisation and individual growth (Canter and Canter, 1979) become translated into design theory as 'homeliness' and designs with a 'domestic feel' (Moore and Canter, 1990). At the centre of this approach is the assumption that making somewhere more-like-home is of psychological benefit to homeless groups. In order to form policy on effective provision, it is important to explore what a home actually provides.

Existing research on homelessness has tended to ignore both the psychological implications of being without a home and the contribution psychology has to make generally in understanding this growing problem.

This paper presents the preliminary findings from a questionnaire completed by 530 homeless people in London. It argues:

1. That people in different homeless settings have different conceptions with regard to aspects of home.
2. Different groups within settings consider different aspects important.
3. These differences can help shape design theory for hostels.
4. The differences also show that the notion of 'home' is a complex one that cannot be assumed.

The meaning of home

Existing research on the meaning of home has generally focused on the perceived socio-economic and to a lesser extent phenomenological aspects of having a home. The varied perspectives of home have ranged from home as a physical structure to a social unit and an expression of self identity (Sixsmith, 1986). The exploration of the meaning of home stems from the necessary but as yet un-verified view that 'home is a place which holds meaning and significance' (Tuan, 1975).

There have been a number of attempts to break-down the concept of home into themes. Seamon (1979) ran experiential encounter groups and came up with 5 themes of 'at homeness':

1) rootedness - roots a person spatially;
2) appropriation- a) possession, b) privacy;
3) regeneration - restorative powers;
4) at-easeness - freedom to be;
5) warmth - atmosphere of friendliness, concern and support.

While these have not been tested empirically, they begin to untangle the multivariate nature of 'home'. These themes provided part of the inspiration for the distinction between personal, social and physical aspects of the experience of home, derived by Sixsmith in 1986. Sixsmith argues that these aspects of home are qualitatively distinct from one another but are equally part of the holistic environmental experience (Sixsmith, 1986). These aspects emerged from an in-depth phenomenological study of the experience of home with a small group using a sorting task and in-depth interviews.

While the homeless population cannot be said to be representative of the general population, the focus on the meaning of home to them as an extreme group help focus research on the meaning of home in general. Indeed it could be said that who better to ask what something means than the group who no longer have it in their possession?

The psychological implications of being without a home

The experience of homelessness has rarely been explored from a psychological perspective and not in any empirical way. Many studies have focused on the societal and economic causes of homelessness such as lack of affordable housing (Greve, 1964). Others have directed attention towards psychopathological issues for example, levels of psychiatric illness in the population (Lodge-Patch, 1978).

There has been little if any attempt to focus on the psychological and psychosocial experience and implications of homelessness. Furthermore, there has been little attempt to focus on the experience of homelessness with a view of the homeless person as active, purposive and goal-orientated. The view of the person on which this study was based takes as its starting point the experience of the interpretative person in his/her particular physical and social situation (Canter, 1977).

In some ways this study may be seen as a marriage of the traditional sociological method of exploration of homelessness with the uniquely social psychological. This gathering of perspectives will fill a large gap left by the perspectives which have in the past been used to explore homelessness in England and in the States: that is the sociological and the psychopathological. The further development of this approach could be of global and general value to psychologists exploring the meaning of home and to those in the field of homelessness.

The experiential approach underlies this perspective. It argues that any exploration of a place must take as its basis the users' experience of that place. Within this framework there is a focus on the conceptions of the individual within a particular role or organisational system; aspects of how the individual 'views' the world. Implicit in this approach is the view of people as purposive and goal-orientated, which suggests that people have reasons for their actions. Thus the experience of the individual and the understanding of their motivation and goals is of prime importance to the Environmental Psychology approach, and must be drawn on in the evaluation or design of a building in which that person works or lives.

The focus of this paper is therefore on the aspects of home positively evaluated and considered important by homeless people in different settings.

Methodology

The study was initiated by the Salvation Army in 1988 ago to help them address the problem of homelessness in London. The study began by focusing on the varieties and distribution of homeless people in London by conducting two surveys of people on the street, in hostels and squats (Canter *et al*, 1989).

The second phase of the research was to focus on subgroups of homelessness people in detail. 530 residents from over 30 facilities in London completed a questionnaire over a period of three months (February to April 1990). This questionnaire was piloted on a total of 43 homeless men and women from a range of settings.

A framework for sampling settings was devised which used published lists of settings and included examples of all types. A random sampling procedure was used as much as is possible targeting people to interview. Experienced interviewers visited each facility as well as observing and talking to staff, assisting anyone who needed help in the completion of the questionnaire.

The entire data collection procedure was very difficult by way of the nature of the population and required the co-operation of many of the voluntary agencies in the field of homelessness.

Sample

A random sampling procedure was used to target residents from 33 settings. The resident sample in the study consists of 414 men and 94 women from 31 hostels, squats and the street. The staff population comprises 52 men and 40 women.

The questionnaire

The questionnaire explored a range of organisational, personal and social issues of life in a homeless setting, as well as focusing on biographical details, health, self esteem and locus of control. The Meaning of Home Questionnaire was only one part of this eight-part questionnaire. It asked respondents to evaluate where they were staying in terms of aspects of home and also to consider how important other aspects of home were to them. The 14 items of the Home Questionnaire are presented in the Appendix. These items were developed from pilot work and broadly reflect the social/personal/physical distinction. The two sections of the questionnaire: the evaluation of their current place in terms of aspects of home and the importance of other aspects of home were developed to explore a complete view of home both in terms of what homeless people consider important and what they have.

Results

The meaning of home questionnaire on first examination indicates some interesting differences between homeless groups in how they conceptualise home. Firstly, this section explores these differences across three homeless settings and the overall response across the whole sample. Secondly, two subgroups of hostel residents and their responses are presented and a comparison made to illustrate that different groups of people evaluate home in different ways.

Asking respondents to evaluate the place they were staying provided some indications of which aspects of home were most salient to them at that time. Figure 6.1 presents the responses to this section of the questionnaire in percentage form. The percentage agreement is the combined percentage of those who Strongly Agreed and those who Agreed with these statements.

The aspects of home which were highly evaluated by most of the sample were to do with physical aspects such as getting a good night's sleep, feeling safe and being comfortable and highest of all being the only way they can afford to live. Less satisfactory were the personal and social aspects such as 'doing what I want' and 'the social life is good here'. This suggests that current facilities are generally providing basic shelter and little else.

There are differences across the settings which reflect both the differences between hostels, squats, hotels and the street and the differences between the people in those settings. For 75% of squatters, the social life and 'doing what I want' were evaluated positively. Few liked staying on the street, thought they could get a good night's sleep or thought that the social life was good but 75% did think they could do what they wanted. Being able to 'do what I want' was commonly used by people on the street as a positive aspect of their situation and many imagine hostels as places where this feeling of independence will be destroyed. Having this independence is an important part of the psychological character of both squatters and those on the street.

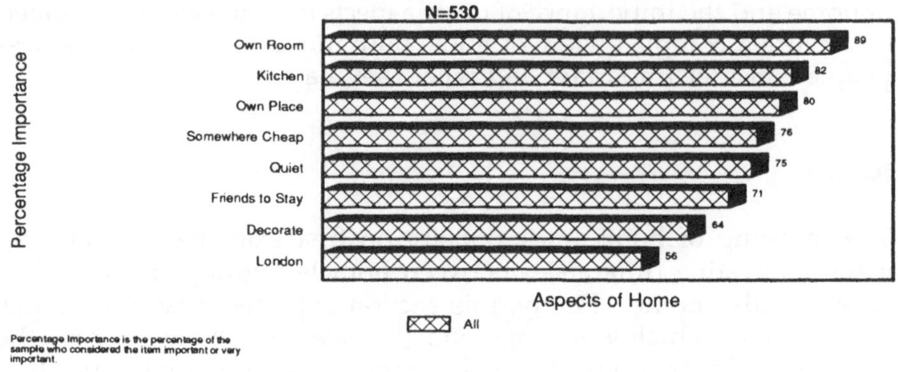

Figure 6.1 Percentage agreement to meaning of home items: all of sample

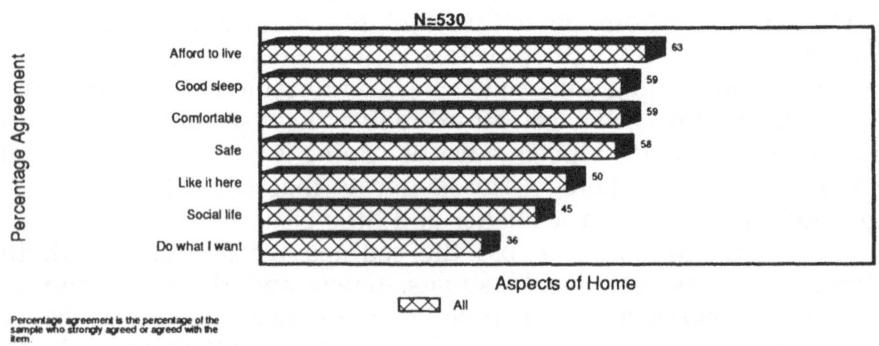

Figure 6.2 Presents the responses from the second section of this questionnaire which focuses on the importance of varied aspects of home. The percentage importance is the combined percentages of those who considered it Very Important and those who considered it Important.

In terms of aspects which homeless people in general consider important, there were high responses for having a room of one's own, having the use of a kitchen and having a place of one's own. These three aspects with 'finding somewhere cheap to live' are the central aspects of home in general to this sample of homeless people.

This would suggest that any provision should, at the very least, provide these fundamental aspects.

The differences emerge when the settings are compared. More squatters consider having the use of a kitchen important, as well as their own room and having somewhere where their friends could stay. The latter would seem to be of importance to fewer of the other settings given that more people considered the other aspects important. Thus having friends to say may be something that only squatters can actually do and therefore consider it important. Of importance to fewer squatters was living in London and living somewhere quiet. Of importance to fewer people on the street and in hostels was being able to decorate.

To explore this population further, two sub-groups of hostel residents were selected and their responses to the questionnaire are presented in Table 1. The first sub-group was made up of those residents under 50 years of age, who were working in some capacity and who had stayed less than one year. The older group was made up of those over 50 years who were retired, unemployed or invalid/ill and who had stayed for longer than one year.

Aspect of Home	Younger Group (180) F		Older Group (48) F		Chi-Square >/5.991 sign. level =0.05 df=2
Social Life	44%	(80)	66%	(30)	8.742 significant.
Like It Here	47%	(84)	71%	(34)	8.4789 significant.
Comfort	58%	(104)	79%	(36)	7.445 significant.
Safe	57%	(90)	81%	(25)	6.766 significant.
Afford	57%	(111)	75%	(36)	5.333 not signif.
Good Night's Sleep	60%	(107)	75%	(36)	3.746 not signif.
Do What I Want	36%	(64)	47%	(21)	2.548 not signif.

Table 6.1 Percentage agreement to meaning of home items

Table 1 presents the responses to the evaluation section of the questionnaire and places the items in order of their chi squared results. This illustrates those items which differed significantly between these two subgroups.

Of interest in Table 1 is the different aspects of home which are positively evaluated by the two subgroups. For the younger, working group who have stayed less than a year in the hostel, the aspects evaluated most positively were the physical aspects: getting a good night's sleep, how comfortable it was and how safe they feel. For the older group who are retired, unemployed or invalid/ill the aspect of safety is evaluated highly by more of them than any other aspect. Getting a good night's sleep was also positively evaluated as well as being the only place they could afford to live.

Overall, the hostels were evaluated positively by more of the older group than the younger. For example, 71% of this group liked staying there overall, as compared with 47% of the younger group.

Four aspects of home were found to be significantly different between the two groups: 'social life', 'like it here', comfortable and safety. These aspects were highly evaluated by more of the older group than the younger. The varied experience and goals of these groups can be illustrated by these four aspects and could form the basis of the meaning of home to older hostel residents.

Aspect of Home	Younger Group (180) F		Older Group (48) F		Chi-Square >/5.991 sign. level =0.05 df=2
Kitchen	82%	(130)	40%	(12)	32.075 significant.
Decorate	71%	(125)	32%	(15)	25.52 significant.
Own Place	86%	(152)	55%	(25)	25.409 significant.
Friends Back	75%	(134)	37%	(17)	19.9146 significant.
Cheap	76%	(137)	54%	(25)	17.472 significant.
London	52%	(82)	84%	(26)	11.06 significant.
Quiet	70%	(125)	83%	(40)	7.310 significant.
Own Room	85%	(135)	87%	(26)	.2671 not signif.

Table 6.2 Percentage agreement to importance items

Clearly there is one aspect which is agreed important by large percentages of both groups, which is having a room of one's own. However, after that there is little similarity in emphasis. Important to more of the younger group was to have a place of their own, own room, the use of a kitchen and having friends back. Of importance to fewer of this group was living in London. Many of the other group of older residents considered living in London, and living somewhere that's quiet, important; as well as their own room. These aspects would seem to reflect the age of this group: a concern for quiet and continuing to reside in the same place. Of importance to this group in general were being able to decorate, having friends back and having the use of a kitchen, things associated with the young, social adult. The largest significant difference was for 'having the use of a kitchen' which was important to more young people than old.

These differences in both evaluation and aspects which are considered important can and have been developed into more concrete models of provision. By focusing on the meaning of home in this way, and exploring the views of the variety of homeless people, the complexities of home can be made more explicit.

Discussion

The starting point for this paper was that home is multivariate with many constituents. Using Sixsmith's three basic aspects of home, a questionnaire was devised to explore these with homeless people. From a preliminary examination of the results, it seems that different sub-groups of homeless people evaluate their setting in different ways, and that they also differ in terms of what most of them consider important. This simple finding enables these sub-groups to be better understood. Discovering the aspects of home important to most of the hostel residents for example, helps in the design process of further facilities. Furthermore that different subgroups within this one setting evaluate it in different ways and consider different things important adds further support to this fundamental point.

That different people see their environment in different ways has been one of the basic starting points of the development of Environmental Psychology and in particular to Canter's theory of place (Canter, 1977). However it is often difficult demonstrate this in a way that can be used by an architect or designer. By focusing on home and what it means to people in a quantitative way, the views of these different subgroups can be taken into account in obvious ways. The culmination of the Salvation Army research was the development of a typology of hostels. This emerged from the views of hostel residents on these items on home and other organisational items. This typology has formed the basis of a system of provision in London (Moore et al, forthcoming).

Thus the potential contribution of focusing on home for design is enormous. The constituents of home in terms of the social, personal and physical have been explored quantitatively. Respondents evaluated their surroundings placing an emphasis on different constituents depending on their experience and their particular environment. More people sleeping rough on the street tend to evaluate the physical aspects of their surroundings positively than other groups. But in addition the personal, 'being able to do what I want' was evaluated positively by this group and those in squats more than those in other facilities. Tying this in to constituents which were considered important, a general picture emerges of these subgroups evaluation of independence as a personal constituent of home.

Different sub-groups of hostel residents conceptualise home in very different ways. Indeed the few common aspects of young, and old were that they could get a good night's sleep, that it was the only way they could afford to live and that few could do what they wanted. These common aspects are set against a background of differences which reflect the more settled outlook of the older residents. Furthermore, having a room of one's own was the only shared aspect considered important by many of both groups. This suggests that the only similarity in types of facility designed for them would be that they would each have their own room: every other aspect differs from group to group.

Using the importance of aspects as a measure is sometimes problematic as it is difficult to discover whether people consider things less important because they take it for granted or because it is less important in the overall way of things. In the present results, this may be the case with the item 'living in London' as fewer people considered this important when all of them are doing so. However, another item 'being able to decorate' was considered important by relatively more squatters than those in hostels and on the street and they are probably the only group who can decorate their surroundings. So it is something which needs further exploration.

Future work funded by the Economic and Social Research Council will address this question and will explore further the multivariate nature of home.

Notes

Meaning of home questionnaire. Derived from Sixsmith's (1986 three aspects of the meaning of home, this questionnaire allows an exploration of the meaning of home to homeless people. It focuses on the benefits of the places where people are staying as well as of the places in which they would like to live in the future. In this way it provides information on their existing situation and further explores their goals and aspirations.

1. The extent to which (X) agrees that

A	B
1. (particular	1. (social
2. (general	2. (personal aspects
	3. (physical
	4. (financial
	5. (environmental

of the place where he/she stays provides

C

1. (present
2. (future

benefits, by stating whether he/she very strongly agrees to very strongly disagrees, where (X) is a resident of squats, hostels and bed and breakfast hotels.

Questionnaire items

How much do you agree with the following?

1 = Strongly Agree, 2 = Agree, 3 = Neither, 4 = Disagree, 5 = Strongly Disagree

1. The social life is good here.
2. I can do what I want here.
3. I think this is a comfortable place to be in.
4. I can get a good night's sleep here.
5. Being here is the only way I can afford to live.
6. I feel safe here.

How important are the following to you?

1 = Very Important, 2 = Important, 3 = Neither, 4 = Unimportant, 5 = Very Unimportant

7. To be able to decorate where I live in a style that suits me.
8. To live somewhere that's quiet.

9. To have a place of my own.
10. To be in a place where my friends could stay overnight.
11. To find somewhere cheap to live.
12. To have the use of a kitchen.
13. To have a room of my own.
14. To live in London.

References

Canter, D.V. (1977), *The Psychology of Place*, Architectural Press, London.

Canter, D.V. (ed), (1985), *Facet Theory, Approaches to Social Research*, Springer-Verlag, London and New York.

Canter, D.V. & Canter, S. (1979), 'Building For Therapy', in Canter D.V. & Canter, (eds.), *Designing for Therapeutic Environments, A Review of Research*, Wiley, Chichester.

Canter, D., Moore, J., Drake, M. & Stockley, D. (1989), 'The Faces of Homelessness', Interim Report to the Salvation Army, University of Surrey.

Greve, J. (1964), *London's Homeless: Occasional Papers on Social Administration*, no. 1, The Social Administration Research Trust.

Lodge Patch, P. (1978), 'Homeless Men - A London Survey', Royal Society of Medicine, 63, pp. 441 - 445.

Moore, J. & Canter, D.V. (1990), 'Designing for Therapy: Testing A Design Theory, in Pamir, H., Imamoglu, V. & Teymur, N. (eds.), *Culture, Space, History*, METU, Ankara.

Moore, J., Canter, D.V., Stockley, D.J. & Drake, M. (forthcoming), *The Faces of Homelessness in London*, Dartmouth Publishing, Aldershot.

Seamon, D. (1979), *A Geography of the Lifeworld*, Croom Helm, London.

Sixsmith, J. (1986), 'The Meaning of Home: An Exploratory Study of Environmental Experience', *Journal of Environmental Psychology*, no. 6, pp. 281-298.

Tuan, Y. (1977), *Space and Place: The Perspective of Experience*, University of Minnesota Press, Minneapolis.

7 ‘At home’, ‘at work’: A boundary crossed

J. Randall

Introduction

People have always worked at or from home. But in the seventies what was identified as ‘homeworking’ (perhaps more correctly out-work, done by women) was apparently rediscovered, although it had never gone away. Research specifically focusing on this type of homework followed (for example, Hakim, 1982; Allen & Wolkowitz, 1987; Pennington & Westover, 1989).

At roughly the same time, however, a group of ‘homeworkers’ consisting of neither out-workers nor contracted-out workers was discovered by Cragg and Dawson (1981) in their ‘Qualitative research among homeworkers’. This indicated that there was much greater variation than had been thought amongst this group; the work represented included: manufacturing, clerical work, and what they called ‘other professional people’.

Then, in 1984 Ursula Huws identified the ‘new home workers’; like the out-workers they were predominantly women and employed, but using computers. This development in the use of technology in the home generated a great deal of interest, especially amongst employers; British Telecom, for example, got the Henley Centre to forecast future trends and possibilities. The numbers involved have however remained relatively small (a point taken up by John and Celia Stanworth, 1989).

On the other hand the overall number of people using their home as a place of work was increasing. The Department of Employment commissioned a large survey and in 1987 the report, ‘Homebased work in Britain’, was published (Hakim, 1987). It reinforced Cragg and Dawson's earlier conclusions concerning the variety of work involved. But, in addition, it was found that home-based workers were in general particularly well-educated. One in four had a degree or other higher educational qualification compared with one in seven in the population as a whole. This contrasted with the stereotype of the 'homeworker'.

The term 'homeworker' is rejected by the members of OwnBase - an organisation of predominantly self-employed people, working from home - who form the basis of the research drawn on in this chapter. Interviews and a survey showed that they identified with the terms 'professional', 'freelance' and 'independent'. There is a parallel here with earlier research into women providing Bed and Breakfast in the South East; women who firmly rejected the term 'landlady' (Randall, 1984).

The group represented by the OwnBase members, being neither homeworkers in the traditional sense, nor teleworkers, has not so far been well researched; only perhaps in the literature that sees it as an alternative way of working, even an alternative life-style (see for example, Postgate, 1984; Handy, 1985; Robertson, 1985). But Ray Pahl has said that many 'future-orientated' books are 'embarrassingly ethnocentric and obsessed with the imputed consequences of new technology' (Pahl, 1988;750).

Against this background, which amounts to deep divisions in emphasis, perspective and agenda, the distinctive feature shared by all those who use their home as a place of work is, nevertheless, that they have crossed the boundary between 'home' and 'work', making them a deviant group in terms of the prevailing norms or the 'legitimate order' (Weber, 1947;124-126). It is for this reason that their situation emphasises the extent to which these concepts have become taken-for-granted, almost reified.

It is argued in this chapter that terms such as 'home', 'work', 'at home', 'from home', 'at work' - and 'homeworker' - cannot, and should not, be treated as anything other than concepts with socially created meanings (Berger and Luckmann, 1976).

Historical background - the separation of home and work

Before the Industrial Revolution work for most people was centered on their homes in the form of domestic industry. The household could be seen as a unit of production in an 'industrious home' (Quiney, 1986).

The process of transition seems to have been fairly complex. Perkin (1969) cites the work of Neil Smelser as having shown that in the cotton industry the segregation of activities 'was a long-drawn-out, syncopated process, proceeding in different ways and at different speeds' (Perkin, *ibid*, p. 155). In spinning, for example, the 'cottage' jenny served to keep the woman in the home.

Joyce warns against 'propagandistic accounts' that:

> 'tend to exaggerate the novelty of recent developments, such as homeworking. This is so in large measure because they deal with very crude 2 stage model notions of industrialization' (Joyce, 1987: p.5).

Quoting Maxine Berg's 'assault on the notion of a "great divide" between home and work in early industrialization' he concludes that:

> 'A more complex and satisfying picture emerges which notes marked differentiation earlier, considerable continuity, but also elements of integration later on' (*ibid*, p. 23).

It seems, therefore, that although by 1840 the factory system had become well established (Perkin, 1969, p. 114), too simplistic a model is not appropriate.

But if the changes have sometimes been overstated, or misinterpreted, it is argued here that it was the idea of 'home' that became a separate entity from the idea of 'work'; it was an ideological divide that essentially resulted from the developments associated with the Industrial Revolution.

Home

There are a number of popular sayings that sum up an idealistic picture of home; for example, 'an Englishman's home is his castle' and 'home, sweet home'. On the other hand, terms such as 'homely' conjure up a mundane, even banal, image; it is this kind of image of the home that is frequently associated with women. The home became a place of rest for the 'worker', usually the man; a private place separated from the public world of work.

In Victorian times, and earlier this century, a wife who did not have to 'work' was available to run the house and entertain guests. These women, mainly from the middle and upper classes, were generally given a housekeeping allowance, emphasising their dependence - a custom that has continued well into this century (Pahl, 1983). While the men were 'at work', the women were 'at home' and therefore available to run the household to expected standards (Muthesius, 1982) and to socialise; indeed the 'At Home' card is still used as a formal invitation. Activities in the home came to be seen as 'hobbies', 'pastimes', and 'leisure', but not 'work'. In the 1960 edition of *Mrs Beeton's Cookery and Household Management*, we find the following advice:

> 'A satisfying meal served promptly and without fuss to "the world's workers" (and that, of course, includes school children) can go far to remove the tensions and tiredness of the day' (*ibid*, p. 77).

It is the legacy of these values and beliefs that can be seen to constitute a specific image of the home. The meanings created have been reflected in the law regarding 'homemakers' and 'breadwinners' (Atkins & Hoggett, 1984); and can be seen to have reinforced, and been reinforced by, planning and other regulations and constraints that upheld the segregation of the home (Walsh *et al*, 1986). 'Residential' areas as opposed to 'industrial'/'commercial' areas, and a general trends towards zoning became prevalent. Commenting from an architect's point of view, Allsopp had in 1974 regretted the move towards mass commuting which isolated and marginalised the home and completely neglected its importance and potential. A home had come to be seen as just accommodation - hence 'dormitory towns'.

Another architectural perspective has been provided by a group of women architects, MATRIX (1985). They make the link between the perceived roles of men and women and the divisions within and around the home. It is their contention that the constraints, created by the needs of men and a predominantly male workforce, fell most heavily on women; the result being a separation not only of home and work, but of public and private, 'production' and 'consumption'. This has been on top of 'stereotypical ideas about "proper" home environments' (*ibid*, p. 39). These ideas include cultural assumptions as to the designation of rooms for specific purposes: dining room, sitting room, bathroom, bedroom. Relatively few houses have a 'study' or 'office', a room in the recent past associated almost exclusively with men (MATRIX, *ibid*). Account needs to be taken of this the 'symbolic meaning' of the 'architecture and the internal arrangements of the home, of patterns of consumption, of language and of imagination' (Joyce, *op cit*, p. 28).

When estate agents and property developers sell 'homes', it is just such an image or idea that is on offer; although strictly speaking they can only sell bricks, mortar, land. Davidoff et al have suggested that this idea is, furthermore, modelled on village-like rural settings - emulating, that is, a 'rural idyll' (Davidoff, L'Espere and Newby, 1976); the attraction of 'vernacular' architecture (though not perhaps to architects)?

Without an appreciation of these meanings attached to 'home', it is not possible to appreciate fully the meaning of 'work'; and the reverse is also true.

Work

Like 'home', 'work' is not without ambiguity; 'there is a revulsion from work, but also a continuing obsession with it' (Joyce, 1987, p. 24). In the nineteenth century Thomas Carlyle referred to the 'nobleness, even sacredness, in work'; and Karl Marx to the potential for 'self-realization' - or alienation - in work (Clayre, 1977). Weber's 'Protestant work ethic' identified the moral dimension of work; and Samuel Smiles' emphasis on 'self-help' evoked notions of the virtue of industriousness.

Again the influence of the Industrial Revolution can be overstated; and it is easy to be seduced into technological determinism as an explanation for all subsequent developments. But, nevertheless, the focus of attention settled firmly on industry, and organisations; and organisations, as Weber pointed out, have legitimacy, which involves the ability to justify. The legitimacy is passed on to those who work in the organisations:

> 'The basis of legitimacy is never specified in personal terms, even in business organisations of an entrepreneurial type. Instead, authority is perceived as an impersonal set of claims' (Giddens, 1987, p. 164).

The bulk of the workforce now 'went out to work' in organisations or industry; and between 9 a.m. and 5 p.m. they were 'at work'; distinct - socially created - boundaries were established in terms of time and space. 'Work' occurred away from home, and became synomymous with 'full-time' paid employment. As Kumar put it:

> 'To be "at work" was henceforward to be "in work", to be employed as a "worker" in the formal economy ... all activities outside the formal work setting were devalued as non-work, as "unproductive"' (Kumar, 1979/80, p. 8).

This became the 'natural' state of affairs. It became part of a dominant ideology, an ideology that, with the work ethic, ideally served the needs of industry and capitalism. An ideology such as this can create a powerful reality:

> 'the central symbols of a society (not least those to do with "work") may be so overwhelming that they sometimes mislead us about what actually happens, because of our assumptions associating work with formal, full-time paid employment' (Finnegan, 1985, p. 151).

In their study of *The Concept of Organisation,* Bradley and Wilkie make a similar point:

> 'The behaviour is not, first of all, observed and then evaluated; our values, in fact, allow us to describe the behaviour' (Bradley & Wilkie, 1974, p. 108).

Values or ideas, that is, influence what is 'seen', blinding the observer to an alternative interpretation. So, certain activities are associated with an organisational or industrial setting; 'administration', 'management', 'education' - and 'work' for example; as though they cannot take place elsewhere. Work in organisations is legitimate work. Kumar refers to the 'dominant ideology and institutions of the industrial mode' (Kumar, *op cit,* p. 306).

Academics have colluded with this state of affairs. The psychology of work - or lack of it - has focused on employment in organisations. In sociology, the dominance of labour process theory - together with aspects of technological determinism - has meant a tendency towards 'avoidance of cultural and ideological aspects' (Joyce, *op cit,* p. 11), which would question the taken-for-granted.

The terms 'at home' and 'at work' have, in this way, come to have very specific meanings and associations. For a person working from home their meanings cannot be ignored, but are 'given', producing a contradictory context.

The interviews with members of OwnBase revealed the problem of being seen as 'at home' (and therefore available and/or accessible) as a common theme:

> 'They (family) expect, because I'm here, that I'm here to do anything they need doing. I think I have gradually got it through their heads over the last two years that I am really working.' (Publisher)

Another woman found that:

> 'I don't think she (the cleaning lady) always appreciates that when I'm in the surgery or in my back room massaging, I don't want to be disturbed. And I don't think she always appreciates that just because I'm working at home that it's not just being at home ... it's work.' (Chiropodist and relaxation therapist)

But it was not only the women who felt that they were seen as available to others' needs because they were at home:

> '(Wife) expects me to be instantly interruptible, at all times - reasonably enough. Most times it's an interesting break, and I'll go and do it. Sometimes it's a real pain because I'm just in the flow and it's all going then I've got to stop and fix whatever it is.' (Technical writer)

In some cases the person was warned of the problem by others:

'I was warned by the guy who's the guitar player in the band. He gets up at the same time every day, sits down at this desk at the same time every day - with his guitar - and writes songs. And his phone happens to be on his desk, as is mine; and he said to me, "you'll find that people will phone you up just because you're at home, and they won't have any sensitivity to the fact that you're actually in your office, or in your place of work; and that they'll expect to be able to drop round and take your time, as if it were a weekend or whatever". And I have found that exactly to be the case.' (Manager of a band)

Some can be seen to be negotiating a different meaning of the situation by introducing the term 'at work':

'To family and friends, when I started out, I said "you must realise that during the day I'm not at home, I'm at work", because I **am** at work - I wanted to avoid, especially at the beginning, family ringing up to find out how I was. If I were at work, employed, they wouldn't ring me up during the day at work to find out how I was getting on because they would know I was at work. So I emphasised that at the beginning - "I am at work" - I'm not tinkering around at home.' (Computer consultant/medical journalist -male)

'I think people have got used to me working at home. Initially you found that people phoned up for chatty phonecalls and that sort of thing, and not realise you were "at work". ... (Husband) would tend to come in for a chat and I'd say, "well, I'm sorry but I'm at work. I'm as annoyed when you come in to talk to me as you are if I phone up with a daft phone call to your office, you know". I think, after eight years, he's beginning to get the idea ... I have to try and get it across.' (Scientific editor)

More often, however, the term 'at work' was given the meaning generally associated with it, for example:

'To me when people use the term "at work" it usually means not what they're doing - it tends to mean the place they're in ... They frequently aren't (working), especially if they're in an office in London.' (Patent agent)

The association of 'work' with being 'at work' outside the home was evident:

> 'People really don't think you have a job to do unless you go out and work for somebody. I had a relative say to me a couple of years ago, "I don't understand why you don't go out and get a job".' (Researcher/report writer)
>
> 'People I meet socially quite often haven't a clue what it is I'm doing, even when I've told them. Partly because they don't understand computers, partly because even if they did they wouldn't understand technical writing - and partly because they don't see how any normal man could possibly spend all day at home. ... Or why aren't I going out like everyone else, because "out" is the operative word, to work.'

He admitted that his own perception was previously the same:

> 'As far as I was concerned, work was always something you go out for - until I found an alternative to going out to work ...' (Technical writer)

The tendency to acknowledge that a person is working only if they have physically left home and gone out to work, is illustrated here:

> 'If I have to go out to three or four meetings in a day - then that's a working day, to people who see you. They don't recognise that you being at home is working.' (Manager of a band)
>
> 'I think particularly the school has the attitude that if you're at home you're available ... I don't think they really twigged that although I'm at home, I'm not available to do a lot of extra things. ... When they begin to realise is when I come in and give them a whole string of phone numbers of places where I might be contacted. That sort of got it across to them.' (Scientific editor)

The term 'at work' can cause confusion, apparently because its taken-for-granted meaning can no longer be taken for granted:

> 'I am "at work", as we said earlier, by definition, because I'm making the money. So I am at work, I'm working; but I'm not "at work" - er, it's funny that. I hadn't thought about it. There's a subtlety there. I am at work, because this is where it's at.' (Technical writer)

These extracts from the interviews indicate that there is an apparent contradiction between being 'at home' and being 'at work'. The one tends to negate the other, and the basis of this would be difficult to explain other than by reference to created meanings.

The group of people represented here - an articulate, middle-class group of independent professionals - can be seen to be making an attempt to renegotiate these meanings, although the confusions, constraints and frustrations are still evident.

Conclusion - towards a theoretical framework

> 'In order for one meaning to be regularly produced, it had to win a kind of credibility, legitimacy or taken-for-grantedness for itself' (Beechey & Donald, 1985, p. 34).

It can be argued that this is what happened to the concept of 'home' and to that of 'work'; exclusive and rather insular meanings have been given legitimacy - variations, such as combining the two, seem to lack legitimacy. Where Weber wrote of the 'legitimate order', Berger and Luckmann found that:

> 'Legitimation justifies the institutional order by giving a normative dignity to its practical imperatives' (Berger and Luckmann, 1976, p. 111).

Those who work from home lack 'normative dignity' - they deviate from the norm. What this implies is a cultural context that cannot be ignored. A cultural system is at its most powerful when it takes the form of an ideology, made up of 'symbols and meaning' (Clifford Geertz, quoted in Wuthnow et al, 1984, p. 223).

In recent years there has been a move towards cultural analysis in the social sciences; there is again an interest in symbolism and meaning, ideology and legitimacy.

In social psychology, the work of theorists such as Irving Goffman, G. H. Mead and Lev Vygotsky has received attention and acknowledgement; and Jerome Bruner believes that there is 'a renewed cognitive revolution - a more interpretive approach to cognition concerned with "meaning-making"'. Then, because it is part of a culture, the meaning is 'rendered *public* and *shared*' (Bruner, 1990:12-13). A similarly active role is assigned to language in discourse analysis - an account can have 'a particular kind of ideological effect in the sense of legitimating the power of one group in a society' (Wetherell and Potter, 1988, p. 169).

In sociology, it was Max Weber who emphasised the importance of meaning and the influence of ideas, rejecting Marx's economic determinism; although within Marxism, Althusser and Gramsci gave ideology a central, cultural, role. More recently the interest in cultural analysis has grown noticeably since Wuthnow's 1984 publication (for example, Archer, 1988; Alexander, 1990). An emphasis on culture and language is to be found in post-modernism, for example. David Harvey defines culture from a post-modernist position as:

> 'that complex of signs and significations (including language) that mesh into codes of transmission of social values and meanings' (Harvey, 1989, p. 299).

It is also from post-modernism that we get the notion of 'transgression' of boundaries, in the light of the increasing fragmentation of society (Lash and Urry, 1987, p. 14). In this case the boundary - between home and work - is ideological. Those who work from home have transgressed such boundaries.

But in 1968 the unfashionable but respected social theorist, Robert Merton, had made the point that:

> 'Men are not permanently imprisoned in the framework of the (often inherited) concepts they use; they can not only break out of this framework but can create a new one, better suited to the needs of the occasion. Yet, at any particular time, one should be prepared to find that the governing concepts can, and often do, lag behind the behavioural requirements of the case' (Merton, 1968:146).

During such times, Merton believed, 'misapplied concepts do their damage', and it is necessary therefore to identify conceptual lag (ibid).

The meaning of concepts has sometimes altered fairly swiftly in a transition towards legitimacy. This can be seen, for example, in the case of 'fringe medicine', which became 'alternative medicine', and finally 'complementary medicine'. As with people working from home, this is not just a question of semantics; greater legitimacy is likely to improve the market situation and lessen the insecurity of those involved.

So, finally, the interesting question is: who gains and who loses as a result of the existing - or the changed - 'reality', and who is instrumental in the change coming about?

> '"When *I* use a word," Humpty Dumpty said in rather a scornful tone, "it means just what I choose it to mean - neither more nor less....The question is," said Alice, "whether you *can* make words mean so many different things....The question is," said Humpty Dumpty, "which is to be master - that's all."' (Lewis Carroll)

References

Alexander, J.C. (1990), *Culture and Society*, Cambridge University.(

Allen, S. & Wolkowitz, C. (1987), *Homeworking: Myths and Realities*, MacMillan, London.

Allsopp, B. (1974), *Towards a Humane Architecture*, Frederick Muller, London.

Althusser, L. (1971), 'Ideology and ideological state apparatuses' in *Lenin and Philosophy and Other Essays*, New Left Books, London.

Atkins, S. & Hoggett, B. (1984), *Women and the Law*, Basil Blackwell, Oxford.

Beechey, V. & Donald, J. (1985), (eds.), *Subjectivity and Social Relations*, Open University Press, Milton Keynes.

Beeton, Isabel. (1960), *Mrs. Beeton's Cookery and Household Management*, Ward, Lock & Co., London.

Berg, Maxine. (1987), 'Women's work, mechanisation and the early phases of industrialisation in England,' in Joyce, *op cit*.

Berger, P. & Luckmann, T. (1976), *The Social Construction of Reality*, Penguin Books, London.

Bradley, D. & Wilkie, R. (1974), *The Concept of Organization*, Blackie, London.

Brown, R. (1984), 'Work: past, present and future' in Thompson, K. (ed.), *Work, Employment and Unemployment: Perspectives on Work and Society*, Open University, Milton Keynes.

Carroll, L. (1872), *Through the looking glass and what Alice found there*, MacMillan, London.

Clayre, A. (ed.), (1977), *Nature and Industrialization*, Oxford University Press with The Open University Press, Oxford.

Cragg, A. & Dawson, T. (1981), *Qualitative Research Among Homeworkers*, Department of Employment Research Paper, No. 21.

Davidoff, L., L'Espere, J. & Newby, H. (1976), 'Landscape with Figures: Home and Community in English Society', in *The Rights and Wrongs of Women*, by J. Mitchell and A. Oakley, Penguin Books, Harmondsworth.

Douglas, M. (1978), *Cultural Bias*, Royal Anthropological Institute Occasional Papers, No. 35.

Finnegan, R., 'Working Outside Formal Employment', in Deem, R. and Salaman, G. (eds.), *Work, Culture and Society*, Open University Press, Milton Keynes.

Giddens, A. (1984), *The Constitution of Society*, Polity Press, Cambridge.

Giddens, A. (1987), *Social Theory and Modern Sociology*, Polity Press, Cambridge.

Goffman, E. (1959), *The Presentation of Self in Everyday Life*, Penguin Books, Harmondsworth.

Hakim, C. (1982), 'Homeworking in the London Clothing Industry', *Employment Gazette*, September, pp. 369-376.

Hakim, C. (1987), *Home-based work in Britain: a Report on the 1981 National Homeworking Survey and the DE Research Programme on Homework*, Department of Employment, Research Paper No. 60.

Handy, C. (1985), *The Future of Work*, Basil Blackwell, Oxford.

Harvey, D. (1989), *The Condition of Postmodernity*, Basil Blackwell, Oxford.

Huws, U. (1984), 'The New Home Workers', *New Society*, 22 March, pp. 454-455.

Joyce, P. (1987), *The Historical Meanings of Work*, Cambridge University Press.

Kumar, K. (1978), *Prophecy and Progress: the Sociology of Industrial and Post-industrial Society*, Penguin Books, Harmondsworth.

Kumar, K. (1979/80), 'The Social Culture of Work: Work, Employment and Unemployment as Ways of Life, in Thompson, Kenneth (ed.), *Work, Employment and Unemployment*, (1984), Open University Press, Milton Keynes.

Lash, W. & Urry, J. (1987), *The End of Organized Capitalism*, Polity Press, Cambridge.

Luckmann, B. (1970), 'The Small Life-worlds of Modern Man', in Brown, H. and Stevens, R. (eds.), *Social Behaviour and Experience*, (1978), Open University Press, Milton Keynes.

Matrix (1985), *Making Space: Women and the Man Made Environment*, Pluto Press, London.

Mead, G. H. (1964), *On Social Psychology: Selected Papers*, University of Chicago Press.

Merton, R. K. (1968), *Social Theory and Social Structure*, The Free Press, New York.

Muthesius, S. (1982), *The English Terraced House*, Yale University Press.

Pahl, J. (1983), 'The Allocation of Money and the Structuring of Inequality within Marriage', *The Sociological Review*, vol. 31, pp. 237-259.

Pahl, R. (ed.), (1988), Editor. *On Work: Historical, Comparative and Theoretical Approaches*, Basis Blackwell, Oxford.

Pennington, S. & Westover, B. (1989), *A Hidden Workforce: Homeworkers in England, 1850-1985*, MacMillan, London.

Perkin, H. (1969), *The Origins of Modern English Society 1780-1880*, Routledge & Kegan Paul, London.

Postgate, R. (1984), *Home: a Place for Work?*, Calouste Gulbenkian Foundation, London.

Quiney, A. (1986), *House and Home: a History of the Small English House*, BBC, London.

Randall, J. M. (1984), *Bed and Breakfast in the Rural South East: an Exploratory Study*, unpublished M.Sc. thesis, Surrey Univeristy.

Robertson, J. (1985), *Future Work: Jobs, Self-employment and Leisure after the Industrial Age*, Gower, Aldershot.

Stanworth, J. & Stanworth, C. (1989), 'Home Truths about Teleworking', *Personnel Management*, November, pp. 48-52.

Walsh, P., Thomas, K. & Porter, J. (1986), *Home Based Economic Activity: the Legal and Town Planning Implications*, Oxford Polytechnic Department of Town Planning, Working Paper, No. 94.

Weber, Max (1947), *The Theory of Social and Economic Organization*, (edited with an Introduction by Talcott Parsons), Oxford University Press, New York.

Weber, M. (1958), *The Protestant Ethic and the Spirit of Capitalism*, Charles Scribner's Sons, New York.

Wetherell, M. & Potter, J. (1988), 'Rhetoric and Ideology' in Antaki, Charles (ed.), *Analysing Everyday Explanation: a Casebook of Methods*, Sage, London.

Wuthnow, R. et al (1984), *Cultural Analysis: the Work of Peter Berger, Mary Douglas, Michel Foucault, and Jurgen Habermas*, Routledge and Kegan Paul, London.

Acknowledgement

I would like to thank Mike Hornsby-Smith and Angela Dale for support and encouragement over the last few years.

8 A bridge over a gap between living and design

I. Aravot

Introduction

Since the late seventies official policies of population dispersal encouraged settling in the empty areas of the Galilee mountainous regions of northern Israel.[1]

As a result dozens of new places varying in socio-economic organization, (e.g. Kibbutz, Moshav, etc.,), have been set up. Among them the Communal Villages are outstandingly numerous and successful.

A 'Communal Village' consists of few dozens to few hundred families, sharing self authority and supporting common services such as education, health, community centre, shop. Each family is financially independent, most bread winners having technical professions and working outside the village. However, partnerships and cooperations providing local sources of employment are constantly being initiated and practically encouraged. The new firms vary from high tech. research and production to semi artistic crafts and to different services.

Every member of the village has an equal vote in the assembly which is called to discuss and to decide matters concerning all facets of everyday life. The assembly elects a village committee, representatives in the regional council and members of various specific subcommittees for education, cultural activities, development etc. Almost every member of the Communal Village is practically engaged in one or several public activities.

Seen from an architectural point of view, the Communal Villages are aggregations of private houses, each on its own plot of 500- 1000 sq.m., usually in bare areas, previously never developed.

This housing pattern, while being a major source of attraction for the new comers, has been criticized by professionals and by inhabitants for aesthetic and symbolic deficiencies. It has been argued that the private houses are vulgar expressions of the nouveau-rich, poor examples of inappropriate and incoherent eclecticism.

In 1986 a design competition aiming to offer solutions to the above and other related problems, concentrated on presentation of alternative house-types and plot clusters. Also the concept of 'place' has been praised by most participants, they failed to realize that no local image could be created by an abstract approach. As could be foreseen, the competition had very little actual influence and any regional architectural language has not been produced.

It is this essay's aim to show that focussing on private-houses' so called inferior formal characteristics is a misplacement of the problem's origin. Lack of 'style' and heterogeneity of appearance though aesthetically disturbing, are indeed demonstrations of genuine cultural inclinations. The visual dissatisfaction felt by many does not originate so much in formal redundancy or congestion of individual houses as in the insufficient expression of their counterpart - the aspect of sharing, of being a community.

This unbalanced situation arises from outdated planning and design approaches which, on the one hand, imply abstraction and fragmentation and, on the other hand, prevent physical expression of the public realm.

Industrial and post industrial tendencies

One possibility to discuss the gap between the applied planning principles and the actual ways of living in the Communal Village is by relating both to the concepts of 'Industrial Era' and 'Post Industrial Era', first popularized by A. Toffler in his book *The Third Wave* (Toffler, 1980).

According to Toffler, Civilization may be roughly divided into three major eras or waves:

1) The Agricultural Wave, which lasted thousands of years;
2) The Industrial Wave, which started approximately three hundred years ago; and
3) The Post Industrial Wave , whose first manifestations date back to the late forties in the U.S.A.

Each wave is generated by a latent code, consisting of principles or tendencies that channel all patterns and scales of everyday life. Since their emergence, clashes are witnessed between Third Wave tendencies and individual and systematic conservative forces which strive to maintain various Second Wave patterns.

The Communal Villages phenomenon, although local and limited, embodies such clashes, since the villages are realizations of latent codes belonging both to the Second and the Third Waves.

The Second Wave code consists of six principles:

1) standardization;
2) specialization;
3) synchronization;
4) concentration;
5) maximization; and
6) centralization.

As opposed to that, the Third Wave is a full challenging and an assault to the Second Wave principles. For the individual it entails a transition from standardized and synchronized patterns of life to the practice of creative and influential functions within frameworks of his own design and responsibility.

Of all Third Wave principles the following seven have special relevance to the present discussion: de-standardization, de-concentration and de-synchronization (as principles of negation), and responsibility + individual influence, high tech. production, communal life and harmony with nature (as affirmative principles). Communal Village characteristics connected to housing may now be examined in relation to the above mentioned principles.

Planning and design principles

The physical reality of the villages is usually the consequence of two phases:

a) a planning process, yielding a general plan (1:2550 or 1:1250 in scale); and
b) a design process wherein houses are designed and located. As will be shown, both phases are directed by approaches pertaining mostly to Second Wave principles.

The essence of the planning phase is a systematic and reductionist standardization of a given surrounding:

- the approach towards the terrain is solely dichotomous (a piece of land is regarded as either appropriate or inappropriate for housing by measure of standardized acceptable slope);
- efforts are made to allocate plots of equal form and size. (usually rectangles 20-25 m' by 25-35 m');
- repetitive arrangement of plots, usually along roads, with very poor sensitiveness to special or unique natural features;
- formulation of general building regulations as negative instructions (not closer than...., not higher than...).

Specialization is expressed as functional zoning. This principle, consecrated by C.I.A.M. in the thirties and continuously criticized since the sixties, was adopted in the Communal Village planning as something obvious. It resulted in differentiation between residential areas, service areas, working areas, leisure areas.

The logic of both separation and aggregation of various functions according to the zoning principle is questionable. (e.g. separation of housing from work according to the plan and their eventual re-integration in actual everyday life).

Concentration is another consequence of zoning. (e.g. all non residential functions in the 'centre' area, all kindergartens in one 'educational' area within the 'centre').

Maximization is another facet of standardization. (e.g. maximum number of plots in a given area or along a road).

The design phase may take several forms: a prolonged period wherein each family separately sees for the design of its own house, a defined period wherein standardized houses are designed as final houses or a defined period wherein standardized houses are designed as nuclei to be further enlarged during a prolonged period.

As such, standardization is the clearest principle when a number of houses are built together, as a group, involving the location of standardized residential units in a similar position, on every plot, standardized pathways , equal intervals etc.

Some critical remarks

A well accepted assumption links Second Wave principles applied to planning and design with advantages in terms of cost and efficiency.

While questionable in itself (e.g. recent experience in Communal Villages showed that in the existing condition standardized houses were not necessarily cheaper to build than non standardized houses), this attitude has three major negative imprints on the physical aspects of the Communal Village:

a) suppression of a structural expression of communal life;
b) prevention of basic de-standardization;
c) negation of the principle of harmony with nature.

All three manifestations represent oppressions of Third Wave principles. Leaning on the presumption that planning or architectural patterns and modes of living must go well together, this article assigns those tendencies as negative first, because they create a gap between actual ways of life and correspondent physical expressions, and secondly, because they are responsible for the unsatisfactory aesthetical reality of the village. These two factors, as could be seen from an aesthetical examination, are mutually connected.

From an aesthetical point of view an object, a scene or a sequence is satisfactory when giving the impression of an entity, rather than of an aggregation of random parts. Such unity is the outcome of

a) coherence and of;
b) constancy within diversity;

— two concepts separable for the sake of discussion only.

Visual coherence is attained when every compound of the scene or object is essential and sufficient, i.e. when the concealing of a part arises a feeling of imperfection and the addition of a part arises the feeling of redundancy. The smaller the part of observable manipulation - the greater the coherence of the object or scene. Regarding sequences - memory is a vital factor.

As for constancy within diversity: any parts or compounds may be characterized according to their location on a scale which describes their similarities: 'uniformity' - the simplest form of constancy within diversity, is achieved when every part is repeated with the change of location alone, according to a given rule. The second extreme, 'change', is achieved when every part is completely different in shape from any other and located in a random way. None of these situations support unity. Between the extremes there are different degrees of constancy within diversity which yield different modes and degrees of unity. Regarding sequences - the aspect of rhythm is very important.

Regarding the Communal Village as an object or as a sequence of scenes - it lacks both coherence and constancy within diversity.

Lack in coherence is an attribute of the village as a whole , either from a perspective which focuses on a sequential perception of the village itself, or from a further remote perspective which examines the village as a manmade object on a natural background.

The sequential perception is vastly influenced by the zoning principle. According to this principle the village is divided into three to four completely detached parts, each of a uniform function: residence, centre, work, and sports or leisure (the above specialization principle). Between every two parts there is an interval of 'public open space' of no definite use, which may eventually be cultivated, but which prevents any part from being structurally (not functionally) indispensable.

When uncultivated, these open spaces look like 'left overs' because they are too small and too casually outlined to form perceptible links with the surroundings.

Thus, functional zoning implies structural fragmentation which prevents a perception of coherence.

When the village is related to as an object, the problem is slightly different. Today, natural elements such as a steep hill or a deep wadi are excluded for inappropriate slope and form no integral part of the village (the above standardization principle). On the other hand, efforts to standardize plots as flat rectangles bring about piles of earth and dust around the sloped boundaries of the village.

So, besides disintegration within itself the village is disintegrated from its natural surroundings as well (negation of the principle of harmony with nature).

Planning indifference to wider natural surroundings, (possibly as a consequence of considering restricted local topographic maps only), sometimes produce very grotesque situations, which can hardly be corrected. The problematic of continuity within versatility relates more to the parts of the village than to the village as a whole. The most extensive parts are the residential areas.

Here one of two extremes is to be found: either 'uniformity' or 'change'. Both situations are characterized by houses placed on plots according to some unchanging building regulations, forming equal intervals between the houses themselves and between houses and roads or pathways. Not unlike the general plan, this scale too undergoes geometrical simplification and abstraction: unique features, climatic factors, wind directions etc., hardly play any part in the process of planning and design.

On this background 'uniformity' is perceived when a standardized type of house is repeatedly placed on the standardized plots. If the houses are relatively large or if the building regulations allow no additions - this situation is to last until vegetation is grown enough to conceal the houses and to introduce significant variations.

As opposed to that, aesthetic 'change' is perceived when the standardized nuclei are enlarged or when each family builds its own house. In such incidents exhibition like diversity is erected even without violating the existing building regulations. The reason for this oddity is, that apart from the above mentioned intervals' determination, the building regulations only define quantitative geometrical boundaries practically far from being reached. (e.g. the legitimate floor expanse in some villages is about 250 sq.m. + outbuildings per house, a size beyond the intentions of most families).

In both situations the observable alienation between the village and its surroundings is transferred to the smaller scale of the house and its plot.

Building and close surrounding are not approached as one unified entity but more as an object and a background. Sometimes the plot is reshaped so as to meet the attributes of the house. When compared to another possible approach, that of mutual conditioning, such an effort can hardly assure house and plot integration. On the other hand, reshaping of a plot is likely to amplify fragmentation and discontinuity with adjoining plots.

One very important generator of this scene is the building regulation concerning side setbacks: every house has to be 3-5 m from the plot contour. Such a margin is too small to be a yard or a garden and is used either as a parking lot, eventually covered by a shed, or not used at all. Since every house has two margins, one at each side, most side setbacks are joined in pairs to form 'left overs'. Given the plots' size, the side setback regulation has an enormous influence on the general appearance: it defines the location of the house, the length of the front elevation, and the uniform repetitive rhythm of building and open space (each circa 10 m in length). It is also an important cause of the introvert plans of the houses - another aspect of the disintegration with the plots.

Still, introverted plans, side setback regulations and similar front and rear setback regulations not only influence the relation of a house to its own plot, but what is even more regrettable, they actually impose the relation of house to house, of house to pathway and of house to street.

They entail that houses are isolated elements, prevented by law from mutual formal contribution and from joined formal and symbolic contribution to public and shared counterparts.

However, these public elements could be more than that, they could create the integrating spatial and symbolic 'backbone' of the Communal Village, thus providing for coherence as well as for a unifying framework for diversity.

So, while the mere founding of the Communal Village was channelled by the principle of communal life, the applied planning approach excludes creation and accumulating development of shared elements beyond functional necessity. Manmade and potential natural components of the village are kept in isolation, yielding agglomerations rather than unified compositions.

Therefore inventions of new house types, even sophisticated and providing for variations, fail to address the origin of the problem. Deficiencies are caused not so much by what has been accomplished but by what is prevente$ from being initiated, namely the realization of physical elements that express the communal life and harmony with nature.

An outline for an alternative approach

The aim of the proposed approach is to ofercome the above mentioned deficiencies by replacing 'Second Wave' principdes of planning and design by what could be regarded as more appropriate planning according to 'Third Wave' principles.

On the background of present emigration to Israel such a proposition is more than a theoretical exercise. Although more than three dozen of Communal Villages already exist, considerable growth and foundation of new villages is to be expected.

Essentially, the alternative approach may be labelled as 'organic' (to follow C. Alexander, 1977, for example) or 'phenomenological' (to follow C. Norberg-Schulz, 1980).

It is not intended to abolish general, rational and efficient planning but to adjust it to the social and cultural reality of the Communal Village. Therefore it is directed toward; 1) de-standardization, 2) physical expression of the communal facet of life, and 3) harmony with nature.

1. General outline based on ecological and perceptional analyses

The ageneral outline and the basic organizational scheme (place, boundaries, entrance, main lines of movement) should result from a thorough examination of surroundings both from an ecological and a perceptional perspective.

The ecological examination is to contribute the scientific and objective information (climate, topography, geology, hydrology, vegetation, archaeology, etc.).

The perceptional examination is to clarify intersubjective information: perceptions and evaluations (what is perceived as one area and its natural boundaries, what is seen from that area, wherefrom is it seen, does it carry a meaning, does it arouse an emotional responce.

The general plan of a village should be based on a synthesis of both analyses.

2. Integration with natural surroundings: designation of public open and built space

The proposed approach regards integration with the surroundings and maximum preservation of natural patterns as the major formal (plastic) objectives.

As such two types of public spaces should be considered:

a) programmatic functionally defined public spaces; and
b) significant natural units that are to create spatial continuity with the surroundings.

Both types are to be defined and located according to the above mentioned analyses results. Unfortunately, conventional approaches tend to overlook perceptional and ecological factors in favor of abstract two dimensional compositions which presume future embellishment according to standardized patterns (a grass surface, rose shrubs, several trees). Concerning recent climatic and hydrologic changes in the Middle East such patterns are an absurd. Preservation and cultivation of local greenery, terrain formations etc., is not only easier and more efficient, but will provide for the now generally desired sense of place.

3. *A structural 'backbone'*

The structural 'backbone' which ties the whole village together and which provides for unity and coherence is to be formed by the main ways (paragraph 1) and the programmatic and non programmatic public areas (paragraph 2). For this purpose some affirmative principles and some design patterns must be defined according to a desired image of the structure. These must include obligatory forms and materials of built elements, the rhythm and proportion of open versus built spaces, road sections and greenery. Special attention must be paid to the location and definition of nodes that will enable connection of the structural 'backbone' with secondary parts of the village. Hierarchical continuation of the structure toward any such secondary part will be defined according to the characteristics of the specific areas and the preferences of the inhabitants. Still, mutual preconditioning between any part of the binding structure and near elements (houses, open spaces) must be assured even when concerning most remote parts of the village.

4. *Renouncement of functional zoning*

The zoning principle should be restricted to situations of actual hindrance and disturbance. Otherwise, heterogeneity of land and building use should be encouraged.

5. *Adjustment of road standards*

In the light of the low traffic amount in the villages, conventional road standards should be reconsidered. For example, it should be examined whether a 6-7 m' right of way could not suffice instead of the usual width of 15 m', and if road vertical angles could not reach 15% instead of the 12% limitation in use. Safety requirements could be met by adopting a 'Voonerf' like model instead of segregating between pedestrians and vehicles. This could save investments in road building and maintenance as well as minimize damages of the environment.

6. *Plot boundaries and house location*

In the present situation housing density is constant (about 1 residential unit per 1000 sq.m.). This , however, is not a necessary condition for the general image of the village, and may vary for different phases and groups within some predetermined limits.

A residential area (as a result of ecological and perceptional factors), may have several housing capacities, according to preferences and financial abilities of future inhabitants. As soon as this is clarified, the group of new inhabitants could spend a while in the area and actually mark the plots' boundaries according to very local attributes of the terrain. There is no need that all plots be equal in size or form, or that only single family houses be built.

The location of the house could also be defined in the same manner and with much attention to preferable views, prevailing wind directions etc. The process must also assure a clarification of mutual relations among houses and between houses and minor or major parts of the 'backbone' structure.

It is very possible that such a process should demand preliminary informative sessions and a balanced dynamic of forces within the group. In the light of intended life in close vicinity such efforts could have only beneficial results.

7. *The design of the house*

Had the process been followed so far , any house would already have been defined in what regards location on the plot, location and levels of outdoor private spaces, directions of entrance and main windows, contributions to shared elements such as pathways or open spaces, etc. The group could also have been encouraged to define a common denominator of forms, but this is not strictly necessary because a sufficient common denominator is already implied by the requirement of mutual conditioning.

The inhabitants active participation would have assured a thorough understanding of the potentiality as well as of the restrictions of their future houses. In such a situation they could probably define their brief and act as critical clients in relation to any designer.

Despite total absence of setback regulations neither 'left overs' nor privacy violations are to be expected. Therefore it is according to practical considerations how the process is continued from this phase onwards.

Summary

The aesthetic deficiencies of the Communal Village are expressions of an existing planning and design approach failure to express both counterparts of life in the village: the individualistic aspects as well as the common and shared ones.

This approach is directed by now outdated principles, which, after being identified, may be replaced by more appropriate ones.

Besides leaning on adequate objective and intersubjective analyses, and besides allowing more flexibility and mutual contribution, the proposed approach is to yield a sense of place and a local architectural language.

Notes

1. In order to clarify possible obscurity I would like to emphasize that the Galilee is not an occupied territory but an area of Israeli sovereignty since 1948. Therefore, a political context, although relevant to the present issue in a very generalized sense, has no direct connection to the subject under consideration.

References

Alexander, C. (1977), *A Pattern Language*, Oxford University Press.

Bentolila, D. & Bar-el, R. (1986), 'The Industrial Village', Settlement Study Centre, Rehovot.

Norberg Schulz, C. (1980), *Genius Loci*, Rizzoli, New-York.

Rokach, A. (1982), *The Galilee: Development and Settlement*, The Jewish Agency for Israel, Department of Rural Settlement, Jerusalem.

Toffler, A. (1980), *The Third Wave*, Penguin Books, New York.

Various publications in Hebrew, The Klutznick Center for Urban and Regional Studies, Technion, Haifa.

9 Things don't need (designing and talking)

R.K. Jarvis

In design discussions someone will often say 'this () needs to be ()'. But it isn't the things that need, its ourselves. Those needs are result, the projection of all that talk, all those daydreams, all those imaginings that precede action. Sometimes these are rational, sometimes they're a little bewitched.

What follows explores the poetics and the rhetoric of design practice. Its primary sources are local authority files and documents and my own notebooks. Personal and professional eposides run into one another. Gardens always mean something else.

Laundering the data

I'm looking for the flat words,/ the ones that/ won't upset/ won't spill (the beans), / the ones that always seem okay/ that always just get by; that you can always rely on/ (not to cause a scene)/ that turn up easy in talk/ don't cause problems/ don't point fingers/ don't wear their heart out/ (on your sleeve)/ that say/ just so much/ (and leave the rest unsaid/ but understood/ (you understand).

I'm looking for the words that seem/ to be saying one thing/ when they mean another/ (but you know and I know).

Words that won't:/ embarrass/ deny/ confuse/ talk back/ get quoted/ get misconstrued/ get beguiled/ or leave me wondering/ and dreaming (the words have different meanings)/ leave me lost/ for words.

Almost true

There have been meetings, there have been studies, there have been site visits, there have been reports, archive searches, structural engineers' investigations, draft policy statements, a restoration plan, and then one winter afternoon they are standing in snow, near sunset, near thawing and he turns to her and he says:

'These saplings need to be cleared and the terraces around the pond levelled again, the whole vista needs to be properly aligned with the column and the Banqueting House.'

But there is no reason inherent in the growth of conifers, the gradual slipping of earth, or silting of ponds or in the history of neglect, inheritance and afforestation, the patterns of cultivation over two hundred years, that gives rise to any of these needs.

Things don't need

Ideas of a kind of restoration, of rebuilding, a kind of overgrown formality, of the opportunities afforded by conservation projects, of countryside access programmes, of potential grant aid, of fragments of Switzer, of Castells ...... these he might need to express, and these might be combined, formulated projected into the world as needs.

As needs must.

Talking about special places

Exposed to the patterns of everyday office word work after researching the ways in which planning briefs could approximate to everyday life and place, listening to poets while the Royal Town Planning Institute attacks gobbledegook, notions of planning as a language system were gradually transformed into a research proposal 'communicating environmental quality in the planning process'. Professional calls from the (then) RTPI President that 'Actions speak louder than words', rejection of applications to attend conferences on the grounds that:

> 'theory is for 19 year olds. If you do not know what it was about by now you are in the wrong game. You do not need theory to know what is the right way to get things done you can tell that by horse sense, by experience'.

occur while reading about *media logic*, the idea that any social or technical device or procedure that is used for selection, transmission and reception of information has its own construction and celebration of reality, its own formats (Althiede and Snow, 1979). Communication in planning shifts to planning as communication. All planners do is talk. Tell stories (Krieger, 1975).

And while I'm on the phone, at site visits, sitting in public enquiries, arguing with architects, I'm making notes, I'm collecting scraps, keeping records (Jarvis, 1984).

Talking in my case, about special places, about old buildings, abandoned parklands, the site of the gasworks and trying to make sense of it all. Three times.

Of the present. Of the future. And of the process.

Dealing in dreams

Someone/ asked me the other day/ over a cup of social introduction what do you think about the backyard what sort of thing would you do with it I've brought this it might give a few ideas coffee/ "what do you do/ for a living?"/ and I paused,/ thought of the official title, the job description./ And of the legislation, the administration, the implementation, the file references and the memoranda, the Committee Reports and the progress chasing/ and said/ I dealt in dreams.

Then I wondered what I meant,/ exactly?/ How the idea came to mind?

Afternoons wandering the coal yards,/ mornings visiting the ruins,/ scribbles on the back of xeroses,/ forgotten memoranda/ what kind of sensible profession is that?/ what is the qualification?/ where is the years of training?/ (Except in the telling)/ it's only day dreams./ It's nothing, much./ It's everything that isn't.

Dissertation (Jarvis, 1990b)

The communication of environmental quality in local authorities planning and control of historic buildings and conservation areas seems more like a endless and complex debate sometimes savage, sometimes futile, sometimes humorous, than the matter of facts of implementation, the precision of interpretation and enforcement of sections of the Town and Country Planning Act and the Local Authorities (Historic Buildings) Act.

Conservation easily slips in the pen to conversation. Deciding which buildings are to be protected, which areas to be declared conservable can seem like deciding what may be spoken, each has its own patterns of speech, uses of words. Controlling development is a reply, a response, advising and persuading, reconstruing, finding other means for, before granting permission. But it is possible to have the first word, to make a plan, or issue a brief, to have an idea and shame it whether based on precise local architectural research or fantasy projections of imaginary histories. Or you can put your money where your mouth is, offer grants, commission projects, plant trees, renew railings, repair bridges.

This research draws from the three strands of environmental and design literature which continue to develop.

Talking places

Communication and its media have received varying attention.

Different analyses often reveal the bias of the analyst. Donald Appleyard's studies of professional media theoretically for a variety of practices focused on the benefits of the Berkeley Simulation laboratory and its true to life models (Appleyard 1978, 1979), but remain a valuable charting of the possibilities.

Recent work has pointed to the need and the varied possibilities for more public talking about the quality of places. The most potentially far reaching of these, implying changes not only in content but also in approach, has been the research into open space by Burgess and Harrison (1988). They used techniques of group analysis to reach beyond instant responses and professionally dominated discourse to explore deeply held values and meanings of places. Punter (1991) points to public pressures for more discussion on the design of what is now dubbed 'the public realm', at a time when it is less and less public, but he warns that such techniques as RUDATS (Regional Urban Design Assistance Teams) intensive, often elitist, brainstorming workshops can be manipulated, and that developers are used to sophisticated opinion shaping polls and other devices. (Just as group analysis has transferred as easily to advertising and product development (and is more used!) as to urban design and planning, from its psychoanalytic origins).

At a broader scale Healey and Gilroy (1990) draw similar sources to argue for the need for a 'people sensitive planning' which would eventually develop understanding and communication. Though their paper concludes at a level of social and political goals, it develops through case studies, conversations, planners talking.

Scratching at the face of the reason

They say:/ that necromancy's out of style these days./ that rock 'n' roll's the shamanism of today/ and planning,/ that supremely rational art is now a science of muddling through./ But long ago and far away/ this midnight madness/ conjured out of May time air/ spoken, almost shared,/ seemed real enough (Jarvis 1990a).

City of dreams

The spark that links dreams and madness, love and imagination has had a bad press for a few years; dressed up rational as the Art of Conjecture, (de Jouvenal, 1964) psycho analysed as the Act of Creation (Koestler, 1964) its never quite recovered as a respectable professional.

Though there are some optimistic pointers.

The rationalism of the cardinal geometry of Roman planning now seems based as much myth and religion as the rule of order, drawn up as much by priest as surveyor. Reported as an anthropological interpretation of archaeology by a respected Professor of Art History it doesn't shock as much as it should (Rykwert, 1989).

The subconscious of garden design has revived. Even Rousham, classical gem of English revision of Italian groves, has been given new potency, sexually and politically in Pugh's reading (Pugh, 1989). The themes of fantasy and symbol, of meaning and hidden purpose rise to challenge the orthodoxies of naturalism and formalism of landscape design (Riley, 1987, 1989).

The utilitarian blinkers, the dead hand of planning as factual problem solving, have been naggingly and persistently challenged from experience and reflection by King (1989) opening up some of Patrick Geddes' less familiar triads ('folk-work-place and 'survey-analysis-plan' which are embedded in so much of planning). King has repeatedly and at the forfront of his profession (King, various dates), explored Geddes chords of sense-experience-feeling, and of inner life (which boxes 'design' between 'imagination' and 'poesy').

Office procedure

'You know,/ I never give up'./ Once said, twice meant./ Lost cascades, secret grottoes, crumbling icework,/ clearing the debris,/ revealing the structure of things,/ their intersecting paths.

Only traces of the reconstruction are left./ Careful interpretation of plans for the pleasure grounds reveals/ conjectural elevations./ 'To say"you got my note"/ does not mean"you got my message" '.

Photographs, histories, sketches,/ even this,/ referenced bundled, tied, logged,/ vaulted in archives available to scholars/ and lovers/ of ephemera.

True stories

The notion that organisations were some how mechanical chains of command, flows of information, even nerves of government has gradually been disabused. Maybe the men who managed always knew. Scholarly Mr Jones' took a little longer.

Organisations can be seen less as their formal and material reality, more as their cultures of shared jokes and fantasies, rites and rituals, as 'material communities' through which flow a number of sagas - part myth part anecdote part truth with heroes and villains, (Borman, 1983), interpreted and presented with all the vicarious experience of fiction (Pacanowsky, 1983).

Designs' no different.

Hack and Canto (1984) reveal the process as a series of tentative grapplings with metaphors, examples and incomplete ideas in language that shows experts have no claim to clarity. Bucciarelli (1984) suggests that (even) engineering design is no more precise, that design theory must be developed to include the social and informal.

Some planning theorists are focusing on 'the phenomenology of the professional episode' (Bolan, 1980), to study 'the politics of storytelling in planning practice' (Forester, 1990) with detailed accounts of a world not so much of rational sober judgments but also of the experience, messiness and emotion that somehow makes sense and produces plans.

Puzzlin' evidence

Looking now at eight and a half years work, at five conservation areas, at four volumes of notebooks, at the case studies in *Talking About Special Places* (Jarvis, 1990b), this is what comes to mind.

CWS Soap Works aka ca' Ekin, Dunston

> 'Neglected and unsightly ... casts a depressing light'/ 'Looks like a Venetian palazzo to me'. (Jarvis, 1990, b, p.154).

The public, formal statement a committee report, a planning permission, the inclusion of a historic building on a list of those protected by statute, the designation of an area for conservation) are small fragments of a continuing process. Preceding these formulaic episodes may be a large number of unrecorded or (eventually) unimportant sequences. Sometimes different individuals or groups within an organisation will describe a building in a wholly different way. Judgements based on architectural, historical values may often be at odds with decisions made programmatically. Conversational, informal contacts may be used to find ways to challenge official decisions.

The Whickham local plan

> 'Held together by the bells of the clock, bird song across the valley and a few low walls' (Jarvis, 1990, b, p.184).

The picturesque tradition that underlies conservation is rooted in the poetics of the eighteenth century and expressed in the romantic townscape tradition (Smith, 1976; Cullen 1962), but its current expression is tidied into the phrasing of local government and the vocabulary of architectural history, whatever impulses underlie individual experience and response to place.

But persistence, acceptance, sympathetic editors, production competence in the sub clauses of drafts for public consultation, eventually wear down some resistance. The appendix to the Whickham local plan on conservation begins with a description of two doorways. One is handmade, abandoned, crumbling, ivy twined, the other is modern, machined, steel lintelled. In that glance the plan's conservation proposals are rooted. At the meeting to discuss the draft the Chairman of Planning Committee comes over and says now he understands what conservation is about it seems 'almost like poetry' (Jarvis, 1990, b, p.184).

Broom Lane, Whickham

> 'Andrew, half joking, mentions the idea of a formal group, as if an earlier owner had extended his stables'. (Jarvis, 1990, b, p.218)

Written briefs with, all the stuff about drains and road widths, is not the only way that ideas for development come from property speculation, through planning control to architectural commissions.

All kinds of references, visual and verbal citations, fragments, copies can also be used. They might be woven together in a note that is photocopied, passed across the table at meetings, never endorsed by managers, never shown to councillors. They might be adapted, translated into architects own conventions, styles and details. Eventually they might even satisfy government inspectors; Andrew's joke, developed and designed by David and Jane Darbyshire, 'has considerable architectural merit, and would fit in well with the conservation area' (Jarvis, 1990, b, p.233).

Axwell Park

> 'What was the brief? Did it come from the Trust? How did we get into this? Where do we stand with Committee?' (Jarvis, 1990b, p.268).

Sometimes the only way through the impasse of disputing planning teams, between the strictures of Green Belt and Local Plan, is to take a long walk around the site, to sit in the woods, to stare at the old engravings, to shuffle through the histories of gardens, and to cut and paste and sketch together what is variously seen as fanciful, utopian, unrealistic, even 'pure Disneyland'. But the architects liked it, the agents like it, only the Trustees were unconvinced and unable to speculate.

A singular fantasy seemed to make statutory planning, briefly, irrelevant. The brief for Axwell Park has a clear vision that outlined in an open manner an interpretation that invited response: its wobbly sketches, juxtaposed collages were literally unbuildable, but they could be given shapes that were: 'thrown caution and economics to the wind ... yet produced a scheme that was not as unviable as seemed at first' (Jarvis, 1990b, p.269).

Saltwell Towers

> 'Mr Jarvis's proposals, in the name of the Joint Conservation Team, appear to have been made without regard to the authority's decision to dispose of the building' (Jarvis, 1990b, p.346).

Killing an idea is difficult. The idea that Saltwell Towers, a Victorian merchant's medieval fantasy house, once a museum, then a derelict shell, could be returned to public use as just that a shell, an empty box that could contain ...... almost anything, from scaffold propping to ghost trains, first emerged in evidence at a public enquiry - even then challenging demolition - and were upheld. Attempts to sell, to demolish, to do nothing, to lease for offices by the local authority continually foundered for want of access, money, properly vetted private lids.

Chief officers sometimes don't think it worth fighting difficult cases, won't pick up the phone and when individuals come face to face there is anger and rage, that reasonable proposals are suppressed. Eventually in sympathetic officers in other departments, through the issue of formal instructions, innocuous committee reports 'to re-examine alternative options' those ideas, once sketched in dayglo markers and silver pens take shape albeit in sober schedules of delapidations and training schemes.

Gibside Estate

> 'There had been no work carried out. The legacy of the years of meetings, hours of research, sheafs of photographs, prints off old maps, long walks around the woods were two documents' (Jarvis, 1990b, p. 319).

Maybe, after all is said and little done, when the crayonned perspectives are lost, when documents are destroyed in office moves, when officers have moved post, when authorities have been abolished, all that is left is possibility to start over again.

Out of discussions with civil servants, meetings with the National Trust, establishing a building preservation trust, schedules of works on site, visits by experts, inspections by engineers, visiting by inspectors, registering by historians, all that is the possibility of speaking.

The ancestry of ruined landscapes is respectable, the symbolism acknowledged. Their cycles run deep. But they aren't on the files of local authorities.

On the necessity for ruins

In the park lie fallen columns, forgotten memorials,/ lost inscriptions, moss stained dampscented/ follies./ Relics, where at the silent night edge,/ bordering the communication zone/ scribbled graffiti, obliterated initials/ spatter half truths,/ etch the walls of lost mansions.

In collapsed cellars of hope/ speech is set to the limits of tolerance. Among the fragments of language/ among the abandoned shrubberies/ among the chords of sentences,/ among the overgrown topiaries,/ among the undergrowth of sense/ at midnight,/ lost, in the maze of possibilities:/ phantoms, recollections, imaginings.

Astrologies circle endlessly. All message and no meaning./ Alphabetic stars fade; erase, rub out dead words./ Distortion enters: roots undermine the rubble;/ scrub covers the revetments. By chance/ weeds slur the ponds. Geometries loose focus, blur./ Larch widens the terraces. Only ruins stand./ Silence seems like truth. (Jarvis, 1983).

Oppositions

Underneath all this seem to lie three paired oppositions.

Between *People and Organisations* fall attempts to structure and regulate styles and channels of communication, to lay out proforma for reports, to manage attendance at meetings, to monitor the progress of projects, to feedback information from committees. They fail because officers are human, because people feel uncomfortable when challenged in a small meeting with their peers, because people meet on site or over lunch; because the world is not all facts; because whatever the orthodoxy of officers being the servants of members, individuals need to feel valued, to have a response to their efforts of caring for places when they have - as planners do - no defined role other than to talk.

Between *Organisation and Place* are stretched individual loyalties. At the heart of conservation still resides the spirit of the place; much of a conservation officers time is spent on site, visiting house or gardens, looking at walls or trees or pavements or street furniture, persuading owners to consider this way of building a garage, or extending a dormer, tiling a roof; their professional jargon includes words like 'context', or 'townscape' or 'appropriate to its setting' or 'maintaining the character of the area'. Their working environment is surrounded by old maps, photographs, records of demolished buildings, street length elevations and models. Small wonder then that against the intricacies of local government administration they seem like a conscience, a flickering remnant of that spirit.

This instinctive response to place, the potential wildness of the creative leap is one side of *Poetics and Power*. On the other stands regulation and control of the development of land and buildings as defined by statute, delegated variously to advisers and committees, ministers and civil servants. What is a material consideration, what may be required, what may be financed are defined. Individually managers delete evocative adjectives from reports; officers learn to write in the third person passive: 'The Committee will recall ....'. Yet the inspector still visits the site of an appeal alone, after all is said, after all the evidence has been heard, alone.

Conclusions

Conclusion 1: powers of speech

There is evidence here to suggest a positive role for planning and urban design as a way of talking, or a process of opening and admitting debate, of exploring, mutually and publicly, possible futures, dreams and visions of how places might be shaped, might be used. The present powers and their use are too often limited, regulated to instrumental views of implementation. My research focused on a few motivated, committed individuals in a particular geographical and organisational context, with only limited scope for action. They cultivated imagination, description, the evocation of possibility. If the scope to imagine, the capacity to develop and discuss possibilities that seem at first fantastic were extended what shape would planning take?

Conclusion 2: poems and memoranda

My enduring impression of the casework is of the continual and gradual impoverishment of the language and media of topographical description, analysis and the evocation of possibility in local authority practice.

There is a richness that is continually filtered out in drafting and redrafting in presenting to committee, in writing formal notices, that has been lost from the language of the memoranda.

Speculation on the conundrum whether the perfect poem is a memorandum, or whether the perfect memorandum is a poem recurs.

Conclusion 3: reading

These ideas suggest some revitalisation, some re-emphasising of areas of the professional curriculum. They suggest a greater importance of the cultivation of a sense of place, of reading the clues of a landscape and its use, of empathy with its users to broaden and draw attention outwards to place rather than procedure. They suggest a cultivation of skills of expression and communication - learning to listen and share and develop ideas about the future, to express them openly to permit their development. It would be a school of environmental eloquence, a rhetoric of possibilities.

Postscript

One response to this at the conference was to liken it to Adrain Henri and the other Liverpool poets. Certainly there is something here that is searching for a poetic kind of truth, that might be different from a scientific or sociological truth. If that seems odd, remember: many of the key texts in the history of (garden) design are poems; Mayakovsky celebrated the plans of the Russian Revolution; even Thomas Sharp was a poet (Stansfield 1982); Gordon Cullen's *Nostalgia* and the *White Peacock* in *Townscape* (Cullen, 1962) show vestiges of surrealism. These days we put 'poetry' in a special culture box.

But if design is talking, if all planners do is talk, and deal in dreams, shouldn't that box of talking about dreams be opened? Even a little?

References

Althiede, D.C. & Snow, R.P. (1979), *Media Logic*, Sage, Beverley Hills and London.

Borman, E.G. (1983), 'Symbolic Convergence: Organisational Theory and Culture' in Putnam, L.L. & Pacanowsky, M.E. (eds.), *Communication and Organisations, an Interpretive Approach*, Sage, Beverley Hills and London.

Bucciarelli, M. (1984), 'Reflective Practice in Engineering Design', *Design Studies*, vol. 5, no. 3, July, pp. 185-190.

Bolan, R.S. (1990), 'The Practitioner as Theorist', *American Planners Association Journal*, July, pp. 261-274.

Cullen, G. (1962), *Townscape*, Architectural Press, London.

Forrester, J. (1990), The Politics of Storytelling in Planning Practice, unpublished, Cornell University, October.

Hack, G. & Canto, M. (1984), 'Collaboration and Context in Urban Design', *Design Studies*, vol. 5, no. 3, July, pp. 178-184.

Harrison, C. & Burgess, J. (1988), 'Qualitative Research and Open Space Policy', *The Planner*, November, pp. 16-18 (and other publication pages).

Healey, P. & Gilroy, R. (1990), 'Towards People Sensitive Planning', *Planning Policy and Research*, vol. 5, no. 2, pp. 21-29.

Jarvis, R. (1983), 'A Garden Path', unpublished lecture, Laing Art Gallery, Newcastle Upon Tyne.

Jarvis, R. (1984), 'Every Once in a While (For Liz France)', *Urban Design Quarterly*, 16, December, p.9.

Jarvis, R. (1990a), 'Scratching at the Face of Reason: A Fable of our Time', *Landscape Research*, vol. 15, no. 1, pp. 23-26.

Jarvis, R. (1990b), *Talking About Special Places: A Covert Participant Observation Study of the Communication of Environmental Quality in Local Authority Planning and Control of Historic Buildings and Conservation Areas 1974-1986*, unpublished dissertations, submitted to Open University, Milton Keynes, (under review: pagination may change).

De Jouvenal, B. (1964), *The Art of Conjecture*, (translated 1967), Weidenfeld and Nicholson, London.

King, G.A.D. (1989), *Town Planning, Information, Technology, and the Art of Memory: A Re-assessment of Patrick Geddess*, RTPI 75 Anniversary conference, Birmingham Polytechnic.

King, G.A.D. (Various dates), 'Philosophically Speaking' (series), The Planner.

Koestler, A. (1964), *The Act of Creation*, Hutchinson, London.
Kreiger, M. (1975), 'What Do Planners Do?' *American Institute of Planners Journal*, September, pp. 437-9.
Pacanowsky, M.E. (1983), 'Small Town Cop', in Putnam, L.L. & Pacanowsky, M.E., *Communication and Organisations: An Interpretive Approach*, Sage, Beverley Hills & London.
Pugh, S. (1989), *Garden - Nature - Language*, University of Manchester Press, Manchester.
Riley, R.B. (1987), *From Sacred Grove to Disney World: The Search for Garden Meaning*, unpublished, Department of Landscape Architecture, University of Illinois.
Riley, R.B. (1989), *Flowers, Power and Sex: Some Themes from the Literature of Garden Meaning*, unpublished draft, Department of Landscape Architecture, University of Illinois.
Rykwert, J. (1989), *The Idea of a Town*, MIT, Cambridge & London.
Smith, C.G. (1976), *The Picturesque in Conservation*, unpublished MSc Thesis, Heriot Watt University, Edinburgh.
Stansfield, C. (1982), *The Poetry of Planning: a Biography of Thomas Sharp*, unpublished MA Thesis, University of Manchester.

10 Research on the concept of home in ancient Scandinavia: A case study example

D.N. Benjamin

Introduction

This paper will try to give a short presentation of an ongoing research project at the Norwegian Institute of Technology. The project will attempt to investigate the nature and conditions of the home by looking at the presently available material on ancient wooden buildings from Scandinavia.

The importance of older wooden buildings has already been championed by the likes of Mies Van der Rohe and Frank Lloyd Wright. Their texts are worth quoting:

> 'The true basis for any serious study of the art of Architecture still lies in those indigenous, more humble buildings everywhere that are to architecture what folklore is to literature or folk song to music and with which academic architects were seldom concerned ... these many folk structures are of the soil, natural. Though often slight, their virtue is intimately related to environment and to the heart-life of the people. Functions are usually truthfully concieved and rendered invariably with natural feeling. Results are often beautiful and always instructive.' (Lloyd-Wright, 1986, p.8).

> 'Where can we find greater structural clarity than in the wooden buildings of old?
> Where else can we find such unity of material, construction and form?
> What warmth and beauty they have! They seem to be echoes of old songs.

What better examples could there be for young architects?' (Van der Rohe, 1969, p.5).

The main emphasis of this research project can be stated as the following question:

What were the architectural and landscape conditions that contributed to the nature and use of the home among the pre-christian peoples of Scandinavia, in particular the area now known as Denmark?

To formulate the question in this way gives us the possibility to, on the one hand, use the theoretical work of social anthropologists who have written about related concepts such as feeling at home, (Bror Westman), and on the other hand, connects this home feeling to two more or less measurable easily identifiable factors: The landscape through the study of historical geography and the ancient buildings themselves through the study of ancient archaeology. Even though the task of reconstructing houses from the iron and bronze ages is risky at best and the literature sparse, the amount of literature that covers the two kinds of knowledge mentioned above is enormous, and therefore limits have to be set from the beginning. I have therefore chosen to address subjects such as the aesthetic development of ancient architecture and the influence of architecture on our connection to human spiritual capacities in a cursory way.

Where can this line of research lead? Generally, I would propose that this concept can be used to better understand how the home changes for a given geographical area and why, and how, people in a given place use the concept of the home. More specifically, it can help us to understand how architecture and the home affect each other. For example; is the home a fundamental aspect of vernacular domestic architecture? Is the home altered by a transition between a rural and town environment?

The goal of this project is to interpret the relationships that constitute the space of domestic daily life by using museum reconstructions of ancient and historical houses.

Theoretical basis of the study

Bror Westman, at the laboratory for house building at the Art Academy of Copenhagen has written about feeling-at-home. For him, architectural anthropology is the study of the constructing human, and therefore we should study houses in order to learn about feeling-at-home, and the home concept itself.

Westman's model is dependent upon the assumption of these hypotheses: That we reveal things to ourselves with the help of our bodies and their movements in a literal way by going to and fro and using things for our culture. In addition, the understanding of things is dependent upon the anchoring of thought and imagination in our bodies. This placement of importance on the body is a recognition of the fundamental nature of the to and fro movement of people in relation to their surroundings.

This model defines the object of research by examining and comparing the most important thresholds in our lives: the grave, the prison, and the house.

Inside the house are three important turning points: the bed, the fireplace and the threshold. The bed is important because of the fundamental nature of sleep for humans, the fireplace because it is often the place to gather and share food, and the threshold because this is where we become aware of choice.

The movement back and forth between these turning points creates a weave of time and place that take on meaning for us, whether it be personal or, more often, ritualistic. These places are symbols, binding the meaning to the place.

Along with feeling-at-home being an abstract concept, so also is the home itself. It is an image, or a feeling that we can perhaps get a better grasp of by investigating physical remains through the framework of the following factors: placement, orientation, form, color, material and activity patterns, (which are sex and age conditional). The above factors are all subject to the forces of stability and change. A study that can make the interaction of these factors clearer within stability and change will then give a basis for understanding where and how the abstract 'home' resided in ancient houses and what sort of expression it probably had in three dimensions.

Cultures do not live in a place only according to their wishes or ideals. Especially indigenous or ancient cultures lived in places that had specific economic/resource capacities. The concept of a biozone, or ecological niche can be described as that, 'particular complex of land and resources in a habitat exploited by a population and that population's manner of exploitation.' (Vivelo, 1978, p. 244). This concept can be particularly helpful for those studying rural peoples as opposed to urban situations.

Reconstructions are the point of departure

I have chosen archeological reconstructions as the major source material against two other possible sources. There is an abundance of excavation reports on ancient houses, and there still exist a certain number of old wooden houses from the middles ages in Norway, but with the reconstructed houses we can go to the archeologists's goals, theory, methodology, and data base. Therefore it is possible to falsify his general theories or his particular reconstructions. In addition, reconstructions give the most information in three dimensions about materials, structure, order, craftsmanship, and placement in one complete image. This is the nearest one comes to architecture in archeology. However, reconstructions can be either idiographical or nomothetical. The first type indicates an object or action that we see as unique in time and space, whereas the second means that we study an object or an action in such a way that we can deduce general conclusions from it. (Egerbladh, 1982, p. 164).

A case study example of the reconstructed houses

Figures 10.1 through 10.2 show a relatively nomothetic house reconstruction from the iron-age west coast of Jutland. The Lejre Historical-Archaeological Research Center on Zeeland has reconstructed the house as the home of a typical farmer with domestic animals from Gröntoft Village A. The shrine in the western end of the house is from an excavation of Gudmund Hatt from Nörre Fjand, Jutland. This house should be read as an image of a particular group of archaeologists theory of what the tradition of iron-age house building could produce in Jutland by using a house plan excavated by C.J. Becker. (Becker, 1987, p. 82).

scale: 1: 5000

Figure 10.1 Topographic survey map: Gröntoft, Denmark, from Becker, 1982.

Preliminary results

To produce some concrete knowledge about the possible patterned movements of these ancient scandinavian villagers, we will seek information about placement, orientation, form and color at the settlement and individual house level. The to and fro activity patterns, we can investigate through the study of either normal archaeology or experimental ethno-archaeology, in addition to the basic knowledge to be gained from reconstructing the way in which the climate and resources of the region affected the villager's production apparatus, their attitude toward the land, where and when and with what cycles they moved to and fro, and the organization they used to achieve these movements, etc. The results mentioned below are therefore the result of investigations into these two primary physical factors affecting daily life in ancient Denmark: climate and resources.

For reasons of brevity the one case study presented here is the lejre house reconstruction no.2 from the years 300-200 B.C. (See Fig. 1-5). Even though this house is a nomothetical reconstruction its plan is based on a particular excavation at Gröntoft in Jutland peninsula by C.J. Becker. (Becker, 1987, p. 82).

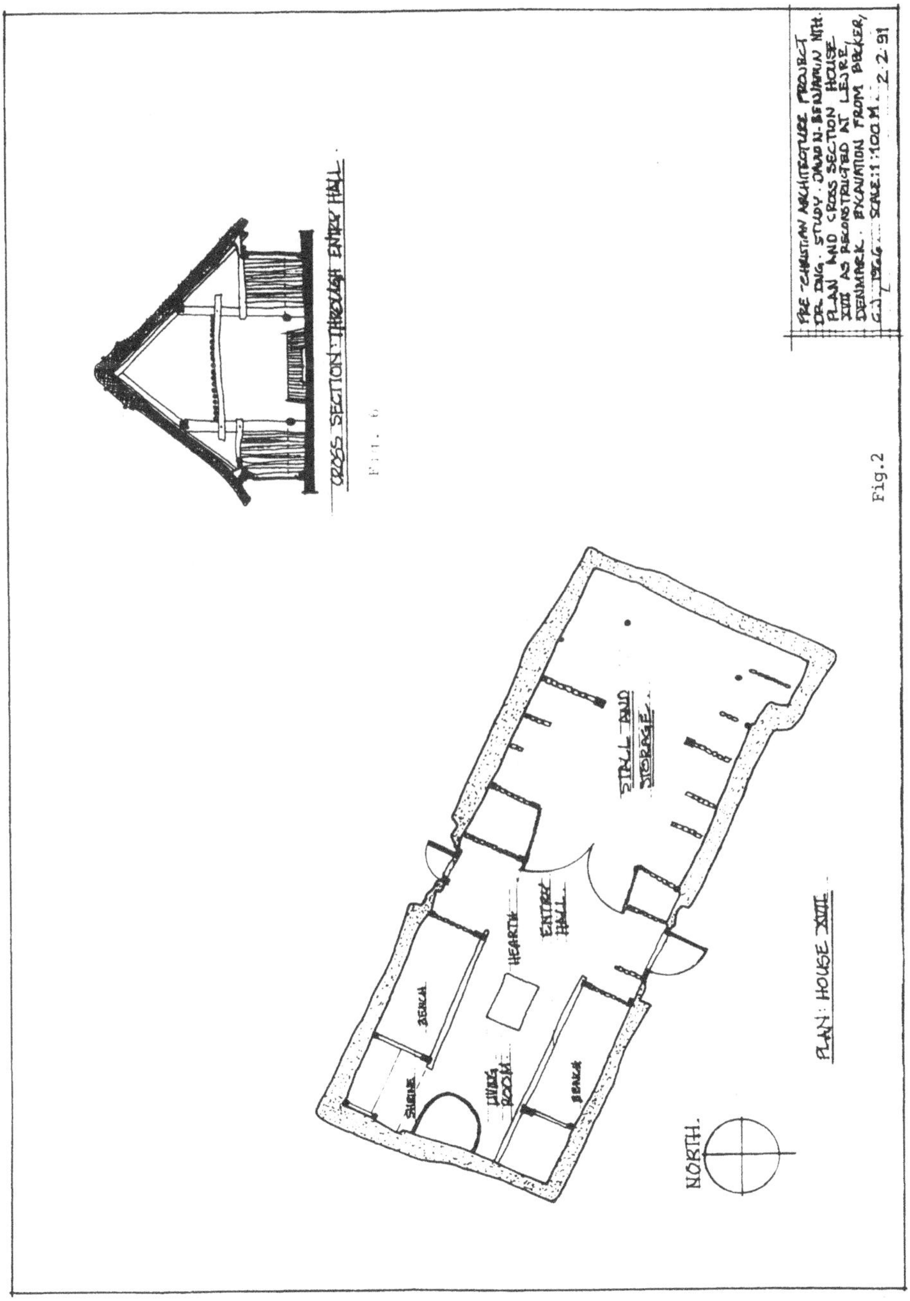

Figure 10.2 Plan and Section of the Gröntoft House

Reconstruction of the basic conditions

The 3 basic areas reconstructed in this settlement are the house itself, the terrain, and the climate.

The house was reconstructed based on an excavation of Village A Gröntoft, undertaken by C.J. Becker as reported in Becker, 1966. (pp. 39-50).

The terrain was reconstructed from the oldest surviving contour maps from Denmark, this one drawn in 1872, obtained from the Danish Matrikelstyrelsen in Copenhagen. For the purpose of constructing a model for testing the general wind conditions of the site, this map was then blown up to a scale of 1:500 from the original 1:20000, and the building placement and form was thereafter transposed to this 1:500 blow-up from Beckers published drawings. (Becker, 1966, p. 40). This terrain map appears as fig. 5.

The site itself is situated about halfway between Ringköbing and Holstebro in the western half of the Jutland peninsula. The landscape is made up of pre-glacial moraine hills, some of the highest in all of Jutland. The contemporary soil condition was that of a light sandy humus laden clay at the top of a podzol profile, a podzol profile being a specific type of acidic soil where the lime nutrients of the soil have been washed away and where the only natural vegetation, in this case, was mushrooms and heather.For an explanation of these profiles see Odgaard, 1985. (pp. 121-27).

The climate was reconstructed based on recent literature covering the climatic history of Europe. (Iversen, 1967, p. 419; Lysgaard, 1968, p. 154; and Lamb, 1977).

This period of the iron-age was colder and wetter than the preceding bronze-age, but probably had warmer winters, (by about 0.5 C.), than the present Denmark. Nonetheless, archaeologists believe that there was snow during the Danish winter in the iron-age.

The effect of wind and precipitation

Wind first became a serious problem that ancient Danes had to contend with during the late bronze-age with the felling of large portions of the original thick forest cover in Denmark. This condition intensified in the iron-age with the creation of an open landscape made up of fields, grassland, and smaller patches of forest. Without the former thick forest cover the average wind speed over the landscape near the ground level increased markedly. (Glaumann, 1988).

The iron-age Danish houses were placed and oriented in such a way as to deal with wind and snow, either because of long-standing tradition or because of the people's individual ingenuity. By looking at other archeological sites in Denmark we can confirm that other settlements used similiar techniques and used them over a period of approximately 1500 years from about 500 B.C. to 1000 A.D. making it more likely that it was the cultural tradition that determined the basic form of these settlements.

These techniques included such things as the size of the houses being relatively small, (4.5 x 10 meters), which thereby reduced the average wind speed among the houses. Also the orientation of all the houses east-west with respect to the long-axis with a slight tilt of the south facade toward the west seems to have been a traditional feature of village 'planning' from ancient Denmark.

These, and other conclusions about the wind conditions of the Gröntoft village are the result of a model study of wind using a terrain model at a scale of 1:500, with a technique for seeing the areas of wind stillness, windiness and turbulence developed by Prof. Harald Höyem at the Norwegian Institute of Technology. (See figs.10.4 and 10.5 for this where the presence of snow indicates either still areas or drifting, and the absence of snow indicates windy or turbulent areas).

A glance at village A in figure 3, will show that the areas near the houses themselves experience relative wind stillness, whereas areas of open ground between the houses experience relatively more wind, especially on the southern side of the houses. In comparison to this village, an earlier village from the same site, see fig. 4, seems to have protected the areas around the houses while seeking to blow the snow away from the entrances, at least those situated on the south side long wall.

Perhaps the inhabitants of village A experienced less precipitation in the weather and at the same time saw the necessity of protecting the house's openings from cold winds in order to reduce energy losses due to infiltration.

Figure 3 also shows that the presence of a low wall or fence around the village perimeter did not markedly increase drifting and turbulence. This may have had something to do with the fact that it was constructed so that there were small vertical openings in the fence for its entire height.

The figure shows the snow pattern when the fan was at maximum power, this is in order to produce a wind pattern in the snow over the entire village, even though it is likely that the village would never

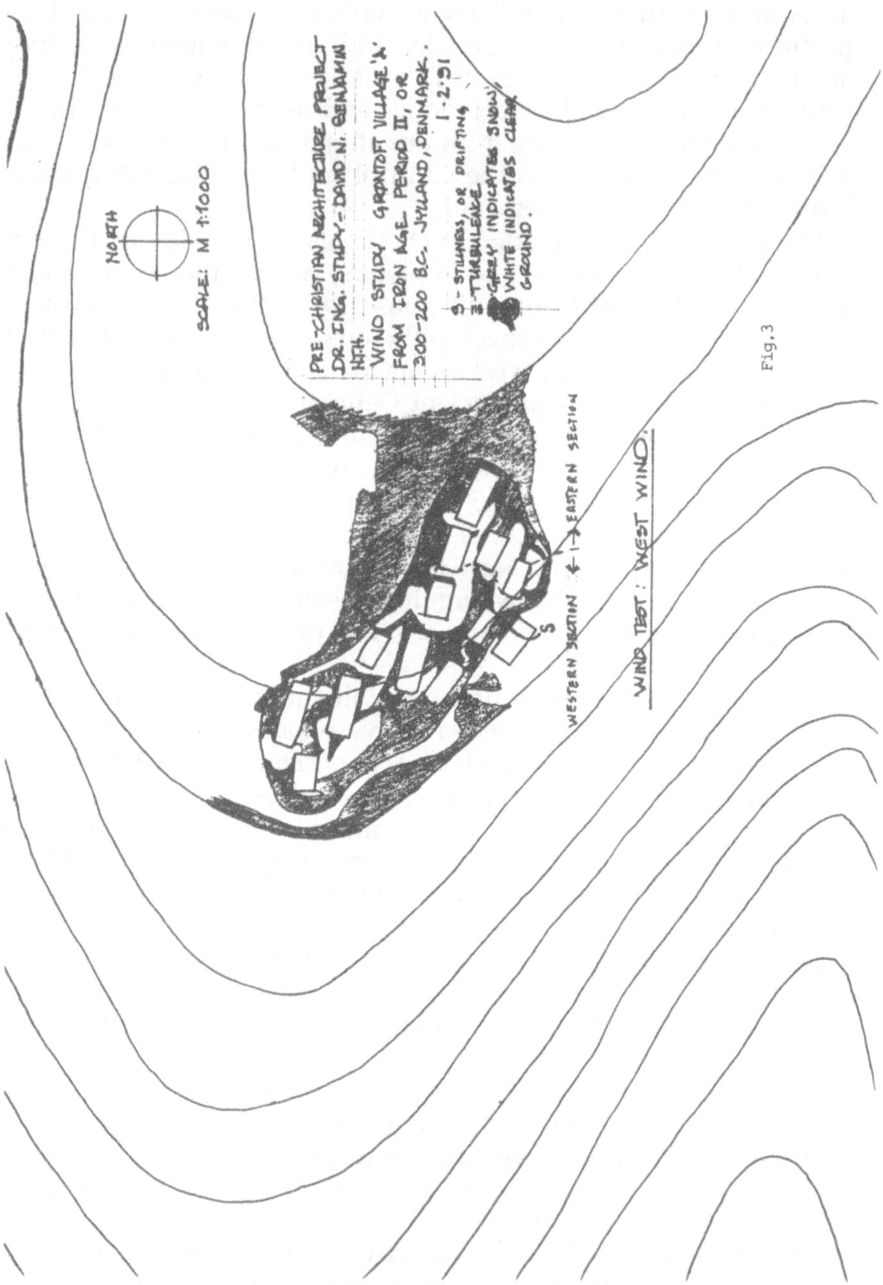

Figure 10.3 Wind test: Gröntoft Village A

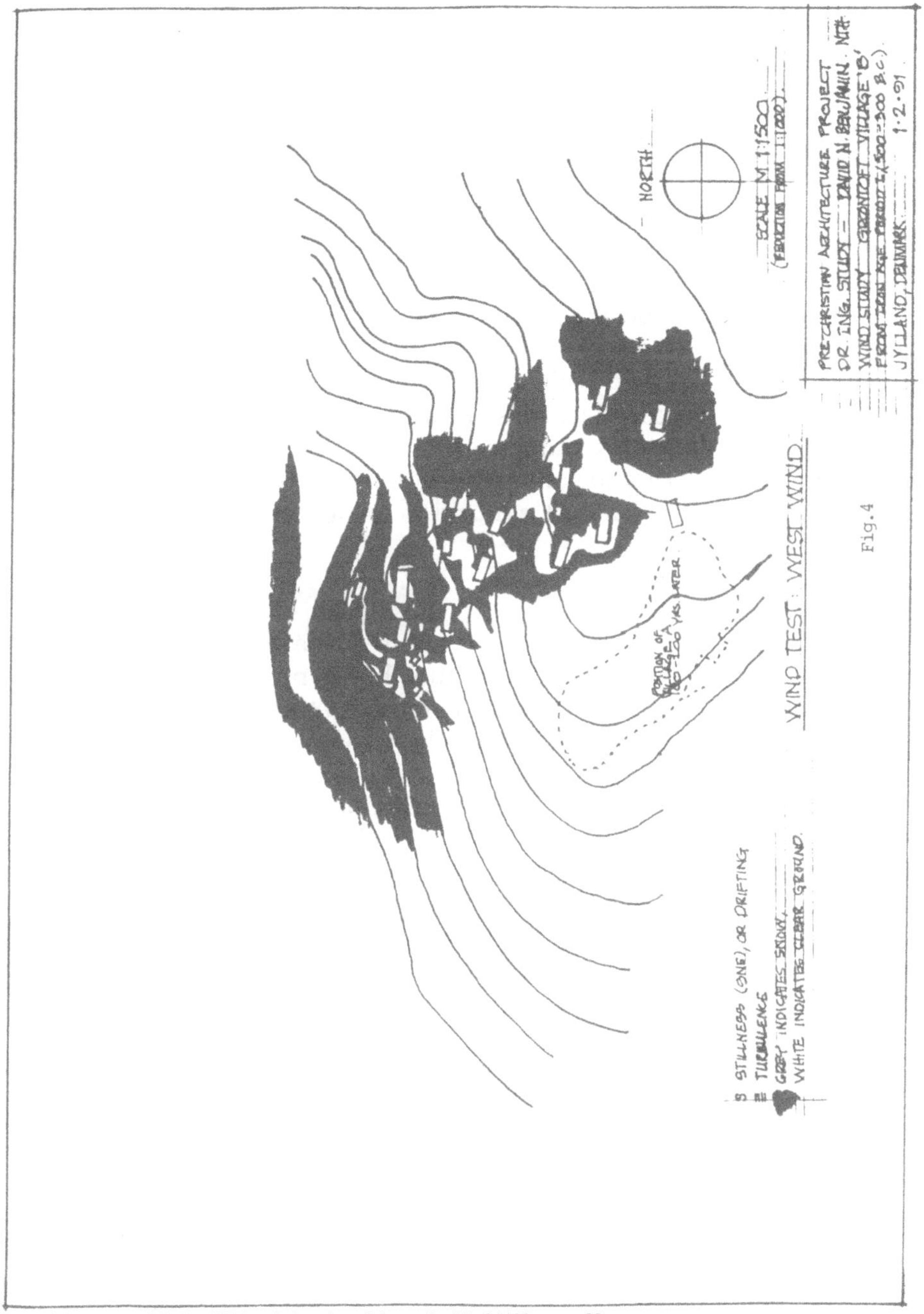

Figure 10.4 Wind test: Grontoft Village B

have experienced such winds. At a more reasonable fan power representing a more normal wind speed the eastern section of the village, (to the right of the dotted line in the illustration), experienced almost complete wind stillness and no turbulence. This indicates that the ancient 'plan' of the village resulted in some houses experiencing almost total wind stillness while others experienced only moderate protection from the wind. In compensation for those houses situated in the western part of the village, here the villagers had an easier time getting to the front door after snow storms, as most of the snow would have been blown away by the relative windiness.

It seems that the specific placement of the houses within a low fence has produced a wind environment that was especially suitable for cold temperatures and little precipitation in the form of snow. We should then try to correlate these findings with a more detailed study of paleoclimatological research to see if the ancient village 'planners' actually were reacting to some environmental factors or their villages were more an expression of cultural developments.

The effects of resources

We can assume that this village required the following resources: fresh water, corn fields, grassland, fuel, house building materials and other coincidental resources for their production apparatus. Two of these factors were problematic for the Gröntoft Village: fresh water and corn fields.

The archeologist, C.J. Becker, (from personal communication), found an ancient well near the village but could not confirm it's dating to this particular part of the iron-age. There are two still existing creeks to the east and the west of the village within about 4 kilometers distance of each other, but this is still very problematic for a society without irrigation, pumps, and the like. We still do not know what technological and organizational means allowed these people to utilize these water resources.

Concerning the fields used for cultivation, it seems that these people chose to cultivate this light, sandy ground rather than the nutrient rich, heavy clay of eastern Jutland probably because as some archeologists suggest, it required less effort to plow. On the other hand, this sandy soil required a great deal of fertilizer which the society produced in the form of cow dung. This fertilization system involved a good deal of work to collect and distribute the dung along with the inconvenience of having it in your house along with all the flies. But producing fertilizer seems to have been a matter of survival

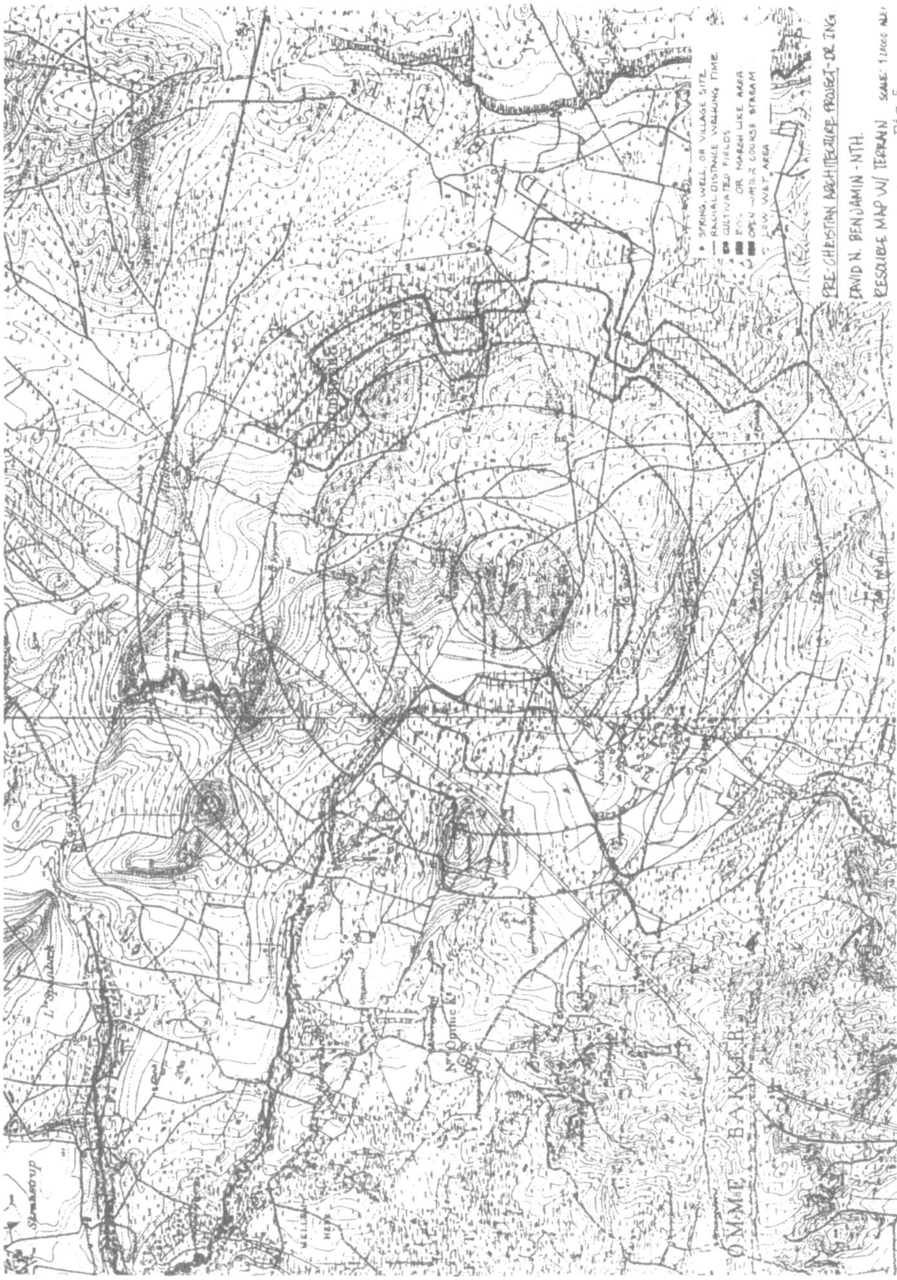

Figure 10.5 **Resource terrain map of the Gröntoft area**

for these people and an enclosed house where the dung could be collected and the cows cared for seems to have been society's answer to the short term problem of growing grain crops season to season, on the same fields with short fallow periods.

This society seems to have also had ways of enriching the soil over the longer term. C.J. Becker, 1966, (p. 50), has remarked that these people moved their village every second or third generation a short distance away. They simply tore down or burned down all the old houses of the village and plowed them into the ground thereby giving the earth whatever nutrients were contained in the house, which were many as these houses were made only of organic materials, and earth. They literally exchanged grandfathers' village for new grain fields.

Conclusions

It appears that because of certain traditions that were apparently common to many iron-age villages in Denmark, there existed a technology and an organizational structure or attitude among these people to adapt their settlement to the climate and to utilize to the maximum the available resources. Because of the relatively awesome nature of these physical tasks it seems reasonable that people in this society did many of these tasks in organized or traditional groups as rituals or habits. This village can therefore be seen, (at a primitive hypothetical level), as a complex totality that organized the ritualistic movement of individuals and groups in time and space with respect to how they utilized the land's resources and how they dealt with given climatic conditions.

We can get a grasp of the time cycles by thinking of the resource utilization according to the day, season, year and generation. Their space divisions are problematic for us since we have little in common with their concept of territory but here we should intensify our comparative studies of the placement of archaeological artifacts with where the various resources were found at the time. A graphical comparison of these two factors will hopefully show some correlations that we can deduce a hypothesis from concerning group movement to and fro in space and time, and it's meaning.

As an example of their utilization of space we notice that this village, over it's entire duration of successive villages of about 300 years, was placed between two large water courses about 4 kilometers from each other. Viggo Hansen, 1970, (p. 134), has proposed a correlation between the sites of Danish villages in historical times and places where two water sources come near to one another. This also seems to be the case with Gröntoft in the iron-age. The nearness of these water sources determined the availability of not only fresh water but also the presence of low lying grass meadows that were essential sources of food for the farm animals as well as providing building materials for the houses. The siting of Gröntoft meant a measure of control over these water sources along with the prestige that control gives. See fig. 5 where the red radial lines indicate five minute intervals of walking time from the village, the green areas indicate bogs and wetlands, while the blue areas indicate water courses.

This control of the water and grassland resources certainly exerted some effect on the villager's errands back and forth as opposed to contemporary villages by the coast, or inland villages that did not have large bodies of open water at hand. This siting near water courses was not uncommon for ancient Denmark and we can therefore hypothesize that it could have been the result of a traditional way of looking at, or responding to natural resources.

We should therefore be able to summarize our results in order to provide a basis for further study thus: the movement patterns of these people involved going back and forth in groups to control the resources that gave them their livelihood and their social status, moving the village as a group from place to place in order to renew the fields, bringing the cows in to the house for the winter and shovelling the dung out to the fields for the spring, all within a fixed structure of cyclical time of day, season and generation, and territorial boundaries.

The placing of the settlement we can read is then an image of a traditional-ritual resource control system. Even though this 'system' did eventually mean the eventual impoverishment of the nutrient standard of the soil, the Gröntoft villagers were able to survive in their biozone for approximately 300 years, a remarkable feat taking into account their level of technology.

The use of anthropological concepts

We can see the home as a concept for thinking about an abstract anthropological concept concerning the physical environment by citing Levi-Strauss: 'When the person is confronted with a given ecological and techno-economic situation, the person's consciousness is not inactive. Consciousness does not only register the situation, but reacts to it and transforms it into a system.' (Levi-Strauss, 1972, pp. 15,16). I would propose that by living in a place, people order a world around them, not only in their minds subconsciously or consciously, but also on the physical plane so that their economic and meaning production systems can carry on working in the specific biozone chosen by the specific society. We concieve of this place as significant in relation to all others, and the permanent location of our being.

Final notes on methodology

By especially concentrating on the comparison between how modern people and ancient society's used the hearth, table, bed and threshold we can begin to get a grip on the ancient peoples traditional ordering of life spatially and temporally, both as regards the use of the interior and the use of the external environment.

The conclusions from such research should be especially interesting for us since it seems that these ancient societies had a much more intimate relationship with the surrounding environment, at least economically, if not spiritually. We might then conjecture that there was a greater amount of agreement between inhabitants of these villages concerning their ordering of the physical-spiritual world through rational and affective relationships, there was more agreement among the inhabitants concerning the way they felt about their 'home'.

I would propose that research that has the potential of bringing to light the traditions of our cognitive relationships to the house and the landscape is both an important field for housing research, and more generally, for the study of cultural geography.

References

Becker, C.J. (1966), 'To Landsbyer fra Tidlige Jernalder ...' *Nationalmuseets Arbejdsmark*, (Copenhagen).

Becker, C.J. (1987), 'Farms and Villages in Denmark from the Late Bronze Age to the Viking Period', *Proceedings of the British Academy, LXXIII*, fig. 5, in English.

Egerbladh, I. (1982), 'The Significance of Time for Rural Settlement Patterns', in Baker, Alan R.H., *Period and Place*, Cambridge University Press, Cambridge.

Glaumann, Mauritz (1988), *Klimatplanering Vind*, Stockholm.

Hansen, Viggo (1970),'Hedens Historie', in Nörrevang, A. (ed.), *Danmarks Natur*, Copenhagen, vol. 7.
Iverson, Johannes (1967), 'Naturens Udvikling Siden Sidste Istid', in Nörrevang, A. (ed.), *Danmarks Natur*, Copenhagen, vol. 1.
Lamb, H.H. (1977), 'Climatic History and the Future', Vol. 2, in *Climate Present, Past and Future*, Methuen, London.
Levi-Strauss, C. (1972), 'Structuralism and Ecology', *Social Science Information*, 12^1, February, (Paris).
Lloyd Wright, Frank (1986), *Studies and Executed Buildings By Frank Lloyd Wright*, copyright Verlag Ernst Wasmuth, Tubingen, Rizzoli International, New York.
Lysgaard, Leo (1968), 'Vejr og Klima', in Nörrevang, A. (ed.), *Danmarks Natur*, Copenhagen, vol. 2.
Odgaard, Bent V. (1985), 'A Pollen Analytical Investigation of a Bronze Age ...', *Journal of Danish Archeology*, vol. 4.
Van der Rohe, Mies (1969), quoted in *Stav og Laft*, Bugge, Gunnar, Buggekunst, Oslo.
Vivelo, F.R. (1978), *Cultural Anthropology Handbook*, McGraw Hill, New York.

11 Flexibility in the usage of dwelling

Y. Bernard

Introduction

Before the 18th century, housing architecture, at least the one that we know best the one belonging to the most well-off inhabitants was founded on principles and aesthetic rules. The differences in rooms had very little or no relation at all with regard to its purported usage. As M. Vidal stated in her work; *Architecture of Private Life* (1989), it was only in the 18th century, largely on account of architect François Blondel's work that architecture has become practical and that distribution has become an object of architecture.

If the interest in usage has become prevalent only recently, it is due to the fact that functions are defined badly, and also to the fact that space does not correspond to a precise function. Furniture is moved from one room to another, tables are mobile, dining rooms are varied, bedrooms are open to one another transforming them into living rooms. With the advent of conjugal rooms in the 19th century, emphasis was placed on specialization, in the sense that dining rooms were consacrated as a ritual place where bourgeois meals are held. At the beginning of the 20th century, the functionnalist style started to develop and, for a long time, clearly fixed the relation between space and function. Each room has a designation corresponding to the usage attributed to it. The shape of the room itself is conceived in relation to this usage.

In the Seventies some architects and sociologists began to question the rigidity of this system, the subject of flexibility was back in fashion. Indeed, one of the questions concerns the conception of construction or the transformation of dwelling which we know should last a sufficient amount of time, long enough so that life styles would have greater chances to undergo important modifications. The flexibility in usage appears to be the right answer to this question.

This would enable the change in usage of rooms in relation to life cycle, allow for new choices, new settings, give the occupant the possibility to move around on the spot[2] 'that is if the same occupant does not possess the means to change homes'are still the arguments advanced today by suporters of flexibility. The checking of the veracity and the weight of these arguments consitute an interesting point to elucidate in an investigation on the usage of dwelling.

Presentation of the investigation

The investigation was made on behalf of the INSEE in 1988 by a team of 500 investigators on 12,500 homes drawn by lottery based on a poll which ensured the representation of the French population. The investigation comprised two meetings about the home in question. During these meetings, five themes were presented.

1) Description of the composition of the characteristics of the home including: type of family, matrimonial situation, number and sex of the children, age, profession, educational attainment and geographical origin.
2) Detailed description of dwelling to cover: type of housing, date of construction, elements of comfort on the surface and dwelling status.
3) Exhaustive inventory of electrical applicance equipments.
4) Total inventory of the pieces of furniture and their placement in each room.
5) Housing usage: the object of this section of the questionnaire was to analyze the frequency and the area wherein the main activities of the family are held.

    - Daily activities: sleeping, dining, performing repairs at home, childrens games.
    - Non-routine activities: professional work done on the house, repairs, sewing.
    - Leisure activities: watching television and listening to music, receiving and housing of friends and their families, etc.

The purpose of a number of questions asked was to analyze the manner in a more profound way, some behavioral patterns which interpret space relations: management of space, satisfaction criterias, desires, flexibility in usage of dwelling.

The results which we will present here are derived from the last point.

The flexibility in usage inside the dwelling may be defined through compartments situated at different levels. The most general level is that which consists of modifying the usage of rooms in terms of time. The most particular level is the one which concerns the usage of objects and the more or less rigid character of the function which is attributed to it. Between these two extremes, a set of behaviors may be situated, which allows the dweller to change decors, to transform the interior arrangements by moving the elements already in place to another place. These three levels have been analyzed through the results of a series of questions asked during the investigation.

Change in usage of rooms

The change in usage of a room may occur on two occassions: the designation of a room in accordance to its function is put in question through experience. This is how we notice that it is more practical to put dining room and kitchen closer to each other, or to set living room far from the childrens' bedroom. The most frequent situation arises, however, when a room loses the value of its function at one point during a life cycle, which generally coincides with the modification of a family group. The departure of grown-up children may lead to the redesignation of space as in the case of a bedroom being transformed into an office or into a laundry room.

The questions asked originally, focused on the behavior of the family at some point in its residential history to the one which concerns housing at the present.

Have you modified the destination of some rooms since you occupied this house? 1) Never. 2) Once. 3) Several times.

The subject to whom the question is asked may be relatively young, but has occupied the house for a few years, but he/she could also be older and has only occupied the house for only a few months. In other words, the duration of the occupation of the house as a test variable could probably have permitted the release of the effect of other variables. As we u ,rtunately do not have the means at the moment to control such information, we can only state that there is a general tendency towards conservatism.

The most striking point indeed, was the high proportion of subjects (78%) who declared that they never have modified or effected any changes in the function of the rooms. Farmers were the only ones who slightly differ from the average and this is undoubtedly due to spatial modifications which have often accompanied the modernizations of farms.

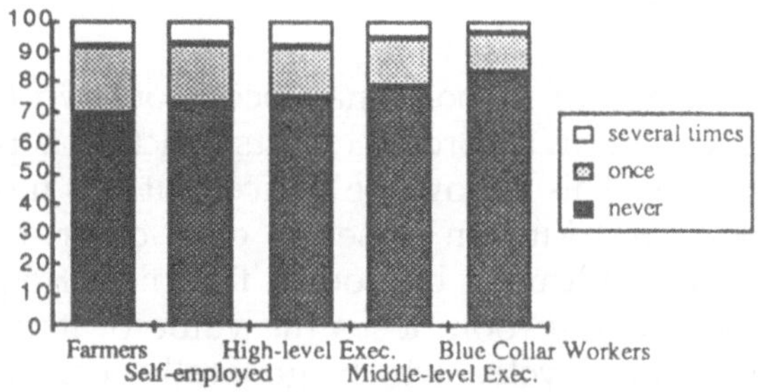

Figure 11.1 Change in the destination of rooms x SPC

If we exclude this category of subjects and those who are less than 30 years of age, whom we may fairly suppose to have settled down recently, the degrees of percentage shown are remarkably stable. Faced with this observation, we may ask whether this conservatism is a matter of choice or is forced. Technical constraints, particularly with the arrival of running water and telephone installations, TV set plugs imposing certain configurations, the allocation of and the connection between some rooms suggest certain solutions which seem better than others. It is therefore highly difficult to make a conclusion on the basis of the fact of knowing whether these constraints are factors against the desire for an eventual change. The analysis of the mobility of the pieces of furniture will permit us to measure this kind of aspiration better.

The mobility of the pieces of furniture

The area wherein a piece of furniture is situated is determined by the function of the room and by the role it plays within the framework of usage. The dining table is set up in such a way that people may turn around it. Moreover, each piece of furniture is integrated in a system which links it to others in the same room. Chairs are generally gathered in proximity to the table. Existence of spatial constraints: the way doors and windows are disposed of, size and height of walls, location of TV antenna may induce certain arrangements. However, the dweller generally has the possibility to effect modifications should these be desired so, either all of it or a part of it.

Two questions will allow us to evaluate this mobility and to know the reasons why it arises or why it does not.

The first question is purely informative;

> Do you ever change the place of your furniture?
>
> 1) Never.
> 2) Only rarely.
> 3) Quite often.

A majority of the subjects (58%) declare that they have never changed the place of their furniture, 13% declare that they do it quite often while 29% declared that they do it rarely.

As may be expected, age has a great bearing on the fixity of the installations. The older one becomes, the more importance is given on routine usage, the less one becomes inclined to effect any change. The following chart shows that this attitude develops more particularly from the age of fifty. However, there is still a part of this age group that continues to make space changes often, and is not negligible (11%), rarely does but does it just the same (31%).

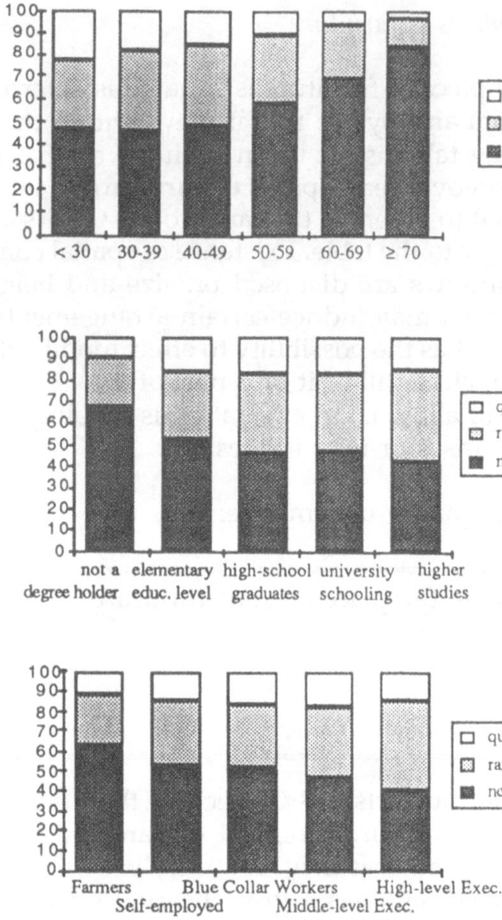

Figure 11.2 Cross-sections of age and socio-professional categories

A cross-section of age and socio-professional category enables us to test the effect of age on the socio-cultural level factor. Is this effect general or does it work in a different manner according to the socio-professional category?

In all categories, the answer count never increases in terms of age but the gap widens more or less. The higher the rigidness from the very start, meaning in the case of the younger ones of the category, the lower the effect. Thus the score, with blue collar workers comprising 54% of the youngest subjects, answer that they never change the place of their furniture reach 57% in subjects aged between 50 and 60. While among high-level where executives only 34% of the young subjects answer never and the effect of age is more noticeable since the score attained becomes 46% for subjects in the 50 to 60 age bracket.

Moreover, the chart below confirms, age bracket considered, the significant effects of the differenciation observed in the Socio-Professional Category. The behavior of middle and high-level executives becomes more distinct from others particularly in younger subjects. Age has very little bearing on the behaviour of office employees or of blue collar workers in whom we find a relatively stable proportion of subjects who never change the place of their furniture.

SPC Age	Farmers	handcraft. shopkeep.	mid/high exec.	in between type of prof.	office empl.	blue collar w.
25 - 40	49	52	34	40	51	54
40 - 50	59	49	40	44	51	53
50 - 60	76	58	46	50	52	57

Table 11.1 Never modifies the place of furniture x age x SPC

The existence of differences, which have been observed may be interpreted in several ways. We may advance a hypothesis denoting cultural determinism in terms of flexibility, one that corresponds to a dynamic attitude, to a desire to make changes in the environment in relation to circumstances and the evolution of life styles, but we may also think that it simply indicates the possibility or the impossibility of adopting this type of attitude. It is in effect among the more modest bracket that we find people who are badly housed, due to environmental constraints, room size, space standardizations, factors which halt all inclination towards any change.

A second question enables us to verify this second hypothesis. It also enables us to confirm the results expressed in the preceeding question through a more precise verification of the transofrmations which have affected the distribution of the furniture;

Have you changed the disposition of the pieces of furniture in the place of origin?

1) No, it isn't possible.
2) No, we don't feel like doing it.
3) Yes, but only chairs, armchairs, center tables.
4) Yes, including big pieces of furniture in the place of origin.

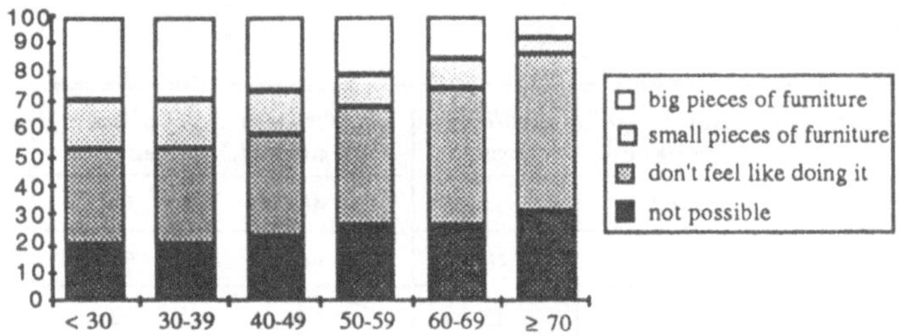

Figure 11.3 Change in the disposition of furniture x age

The above chart confirms the effect of age on the desire for stability in the habitat. The answer 'I don't feel like doing it' increases in a regular manner with age and again, we find the inflexion already observed when the fifties is reached. The chart below shows us that the hypothesis of forced conservatism in terms of behavior in the lower income bracket, i.e., blue collar workers, those that are not degree holders is perfectly plausible. The percentage of response 'don't feel like doing it or don't feel the need to do it' by blue collar workers differs only by three points from those that give the same answer among executives (36-33) whereas the answer 'not possible' differs by nine points (24-15).

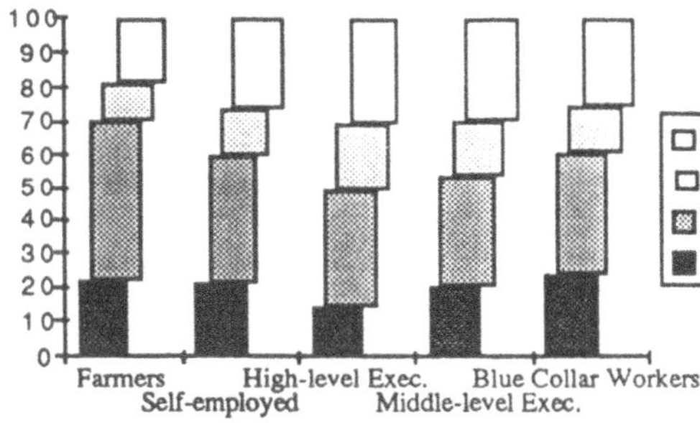

Figure 11.4 Change in disposition of furniture x SPC

The gap observed based on educational attainment (see following chart) confirms a decrease in the constraints in relation to attainment level, but we also observe a difference of 14 points in the category of subjects that gave the answer 'I don't feel like doing it' those who are not degree holders (46) and those who possess a high school degree or those who hold a high school degree plus two years of higher studies (32). This last category of subjects, which globally represent the middle-level executive category seems to be the most dynamic. The most static category is undoubtedly that of farmers who, in 48% of the case don't feel that there is a need to modify the condition of the place. If, as we have seen, they are led to effect modifications more than others, probably for reasons of modernizations made on the farm, they however, don't wish to effect any changes once they are done. With regard to traditions, the peasant milieu is undoubtedly the one where the way of living or life style has had very little changes and where relation between the organization of space and use is highly determined, in other words, the least flexible.

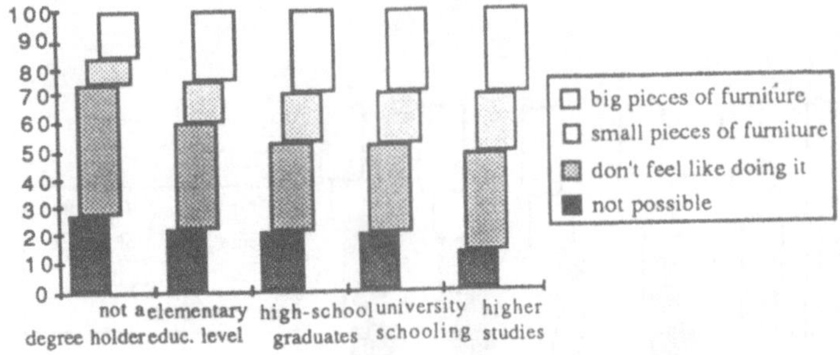

Figure 11.5 Change in the disposition of furniture x educational attainment

The attitude of farmers differs more significantly when considering age. About 50% of the youngest subjects declare that they feel like moving their furniture, a percentage which is much higher than what we find among subjects in the fifties age bracket of any category. The lowest figures in the said age bracket is found in the higher-level executive level (27%) closely followed by young middle-level executives (29%).

SPC Age	Farmers	handcraft. shopkeep.	mid/high exec.	in between type of prof.	office empl.	blue collar w.
25 - 40	49	36	27	29	33	35
40 - 50	48	36	33	31	34	35
50 - 60	56	43	41	39	34	40

Table 11.2 Answer: I dont feel like doing it x SPC and age

Again, we find in each category, the age effect which has a more or less strong influence according to the average score of the category, and may be determined wholly or partly as we have seen by the degree of liberty with which change may be effected.

Multiple usage of the same object

The function of the rooms in the dwelling is reinforced by the presence of pieces of furniture which are themselves designated for a precise purpose. For some of them, shape determines one distinct function. We, evidently cannot use a chair other than for sitting. For others, on the contrary, there is a multiple function as in the case of a table. In the main room of each home, whether in the living or the dining room, we find a table designated generally by the dwellers to be the dining table. Indeed, this table has for main purpose that of uniting the family or guests for a meal in the room, but it may also have other functions: for writing, for doing repairs, for playing.....The purpose of two questions asked is to verify the manner in which the table may be used.

Has it ever occured to you to use the table in the dining room other than for meals or for drinks? 1) Yes, often. 2) Sometimes. 3) Never.	If yes, for 1) Writing. 2) Ironing or doing repairs. 3) Playing.

The following chart shows us that if on the whole, only 27% of subjects interviewed declare that they have never used the table other than for eating as opposed to 43% who declare that they, on the other hand, use it often in other circumstances, while 30% do it sometimes (chart 417-418), usage and frequency of usage vary according to age and the socio-cultural circle to which the subjects belong.

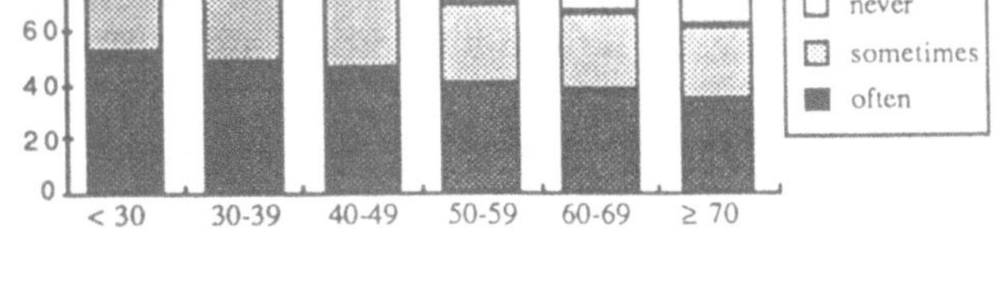

Figure 11.6 Use of table in the dining room for other purposes x age

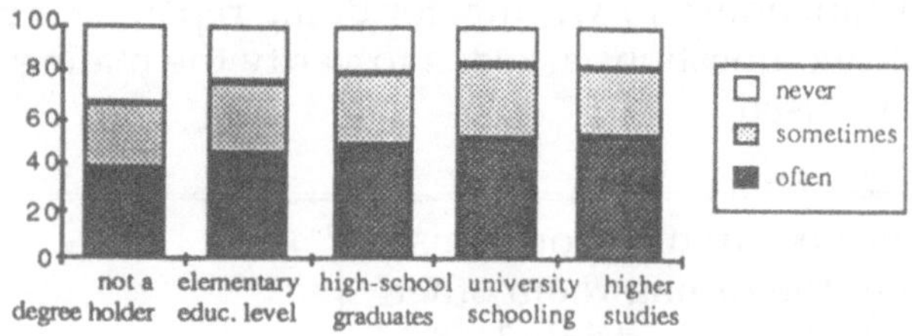

Figure 11.7 Use of table in the dining room for other purposes x educational attainment

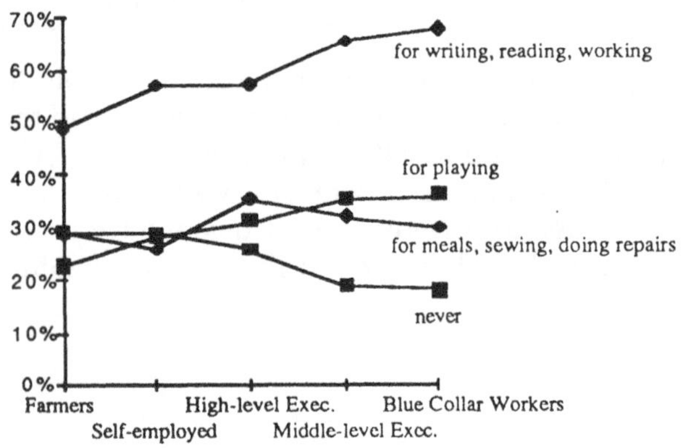

Figure 11.8 Other uses of table in the dining room x SPC

We notice that the flexibility in usage diminishes with age and increases with educational attainment. The age effect may be interpreted as the strengthening of habits, and also as a factor that affects the decrease of activities especially in the older than 60 years age bracket.

Relation to educational attainment may be justified by the type of activities in the house. As we can see in the SPC chart, 70% of higher-level executives declare that they use the table for writing or for working, but we may also believe-and effect is found concerning the mobility of furniture-that the higher one goes on the socio-cultural scale, the less rigid the behavior becomes towards usage. As we have shown in a comparative research on the living room, the flexible use of space and furniture is a behavioral trait found in artists, in the intellectual class and in the higher-level executive class.

Conclusion

The desire to effect changes with regard to space is not as widespread as we might believe it to be. If 78% of the French population have never modified the designated function of the pieces in their present dwelling, it is perhaps because they do not have the possibility to do so. This reason is less obvious with regard to pieces of furniture, where we find once more 58% of the subjects interviewed declaring that they never had to modify the organization of the living room ever since they settled down in their particular dwelling. Environmental constraints were given as the obstacle to any change by 24% of them, however, this figure is very low compared to those who simply declare that they do not feel like doing it and who represent 40% of the total population of subjects asked. The desire or the will to change is therefore obstructed by housing constraints, but in the majority of cases, this reflects rather on the attitude towards any change what ever. This attitude varies considerably when considering the age and cultural level factors.

References

Bernard, Y. *et al*, (1987), 'Pratiques de l'habitat et mondes sociaux', (Housing Practices and the Social World), *Revue Française de Psychologie*, no. 32.

Blanc, J.N., Vasselon, R. & Bellet, M. (1987), *Vers le logement pluriel*, (Towards Pluralized Lodging), Collection Recherches Plan Construction.

Eleb-Vidal, M. (1989), *Architecture de la vie privée*, (Architecture of Private Life), AAM Editions.

This research has been supported by the French Ministry of Equipment and the National Institute of Statistic and Economic Studies (INSEE).

12 Home as expression of identity

J.H. Jin

Introductory summary

The purpose of this research is to examine the meaning and relationship of home environments and identity through a study of changes which people make in their home environments. This study also explores the sociocultural differences that influence how people perceive and modify their home environments.

The research approach provides a better understanding of how people use and perceive their home environments in the inner-city neighbourhood by employing comparative methods and observational techniques to document home personalization activity. Four neighbourhoods were selected to be representative of a wide range of sociocultural groups. The initial phase of the study involved observation of housing fronts and informal discussions with residents. Subsequently, a structured questionnaire was used and residents were interviewed about their images, perceptions, their meaningful objects, and the changes they made in their homes.

Major findings are:

1) home environment is used as a symbol of identity;
2) different socio-cultural groups show different taste, perception, and use of space;
3) home environment corresponds to social class, values and ethnicity as much as it does to personal preferences; and

4) thus, home environment is integral to and reflects a variety of social and cultural values regarding individual and family identities.

Introduction

During the past few decades, many theorists have emphasized that the home environment is the central aspect of human experience and provides a unique experience of dwelling, or a person's intimate interaction with objects, spaces, and persons in the home. The home environment and its contents have been described as objects that symbolically express the social class, personality traits, and aesthetic preferences of their occupants. Duncan (1973, 1976), who has analyzed the role of residential landscape in a variety of social context, shows empirically that the dwelling is one of the principal symbols of social status. Cooper (1982) argues that humans have a natural propensity to symbolize the self through the house. Csikszentmihalyi and Rochberg-Halton (1981) argue that the house represents social background as well as the personal world of the resident. They argue that household objects are endowed with meanings and that people cherish household objects especially because they are symbols of the self and one's connection to others. Despite considerable consensus that home environments and their associated objects are related to characteristics of the self and social world, there are few empirical studies that document the characteristics of the identity that are expressed in the home environment. This study will further explore the issue of home environment and identity and provide further empirical evidence of this relationship.

This study specifically deals with the relationships between identity and physical form of the home environment. A primary objective of this study is to examine how people experience and modify their home environments as a way of expressing their personal and sociocultural identity. I will analyze the ways that home environments are mechanisms for defining and communicating identity.

A second objective is to examine the sociocultural variations in the symbolic use of home environments for the presentation of identity. This research attempts to demonstrate that residents varying in sociocultural backgrounds would respond differently toward their home environments. I will compare perceptions and use of domestic space across sociocultural groups.

This study combines social interactionism and cultural analysis to provide a theoretical perspective on the question of identity, social world, and the role of home environments in establishing identity. Both theories provide a theoretical background for an understanding of how people interpret social situations from the environment and then adjust behavior afterwards. I focus on the concepts of identity as a social construction. In this study, the home environment is viewed as a tool used in self-presentational performances.

This study provides a conceptual framework for understanding sociocultural meaning of home environments and identity. This work contributes theoretically and empirically to how people use their home environments for the presentation of personal and socio-cultural identity.

Research method

This study presents a cross-cultural analysis of the use of domestic space based on the completion of ethnographic research in four neighbourhoods. Three methods (observation, questionnaire, and interview) were conducted sequentially in Center City Philadelphia from May through August, 1987. I began with descriptive observations of the neighborhoods to get an overview of social and physical situations. Emphasis was given to the direct observation, and photographs and sketches were used to record those changes which have been made to the home environment. This observational period helped to develop an understanding of the setting and provide a broad range of evidence. Then, after recording and analyzing initial data, I conducted a survey using a structured questionnaire and focused observations. The questionnaire was designed to collect residents' perceptions, attitudes and preferences of their housing. Finally, after more analysis and repeated observations, I narrowed my investigation still further to selective observations and interviews, which were used to elicit information about residents' images of home environments.

Four inner-city neighbourhoods in Philadelphia were selected for this study in order to develop the comparison of different social and cultural contexts. The first goal in the selection of neighbourhoods for this study was to choose different class and ethnic groups. These neighbourhoods were also chosen because they initially contained the same row house type. In order to develop the comparison of class and ethnic differences, four types of neighborhoods were selected as follows:

Class Differences		
1. Case Study 1	Professional-Class	(Society Hill)
2. Case Study 2	Working-Class	(Fairmount)
Ethnic Differences		
3. Case Study 3	Irish	(Irish Neighbourhood)
4. Case Study 4	Italian	(Italian Neighbourhood)

The following chart outlines the research procedures, methods, measures and number of respondents.

Procedure	Method	Measure	Data
Descriptive	**Observation**	Housing Characteristics	Total: 503
(May 10 - June 10)	Photographs Physical Trace Sketching Designer Plans	Decoration Condition	Soc = 140 Fai = 135 Iri = 96 Ita = 132
Focused	**Questionnaire**	Perception	Total = 132
(June 1 - July 15)		Personalization Viewpoints	Soc = 37 Fai = 36 Iri = 26 Ita = 33
Selective	**Interview**	Images	Total = 23
(July 1 - July 31)		Special Objects	Soc = 6 Fai = 5 Iri = 5 Ita = 7

Analysis

Using the SPSSX CROSSTABS statistical analysis computer program, contingency table analyses were made of the relationship between the social groups and home environment. CROSSTABS program produces tables that are the joint distribution of four neighbourhoods. The frequency distribution of one variable is subdivided according to the values of each neighborhood.

Observation: home exteriors for expression

Home occupies a psychologically central role and is used to display aspects of identity. People enjoy the opportunity for self-expression. They attribute meanings to domestic space and show their values and creativity in decorating the front of their houses. Four distinct neighbourhood groups use different symbols in decorating their homes.

Society Hill is something of a synonym for upper-class status. Living in this neighbourhood, in itself, symbolizes power and wealth for the individual. Society Hill residents decorate their homes in typical ways. Their homes reflect their values and identities. They think of taste as an individually defined matter. They feel that the home represents themselves, their personalities and values. Consequently, they like a variety of home environment and prefer to insert individual and family values into their home environments. The houses are elaborately decorated and well-maintained. The house signifies the wealth and inclination of the residents. Professionals have given more thought to the problem of establishing a home that adequately reinforces the status images they wish to project. The facades are used as opportunities to show variety and individuality in Society Hill. Society Hill facades have lots of variation in door color, pediment, fanlight, shutter, dormer, tree/flower, and street numbers. All the diverse elements are really well-maintained. Shutters and ornate detailing on old, historically important buildings enhance the identification with social class. A colonial door with fanlight and pediment, and colonial type 6/6 window are most popular in Society Hill. People try to achieve variety in various ways: by painting different colors on door, windows, and shutters; by planting flowers and putting out flower pots; by installing a street number and light. Potted plants and flowers embellish this neighbourhood.

Even though houses in the Fairmount neighbourhood are not elaborately decorated like those in Society Hill, the houses are well-kept by the residents. Everybody feels comfortable. To a working-class people, 'home' means shelter. Even though working-class people are as concerned about the maintenance and appearance of their homes as the professionals, they are more concerned that the house be comfortable and neat. It should not present them as showing off. They do not like the extreme deviation from group standards.

Regardless of geographic origin and status within a particular society at any particular time, ethnic groups are associated with distinct subcultures - with values, norms, beliefs, customs, and skills - that distinguish these groups in certain respects, from other ethnic groups in a society. The social networks are largely closed, and social standing is homogeneous and well-established by intimate knowledge of one another. The social status of the Irish and Italians would be classified as lower-middle class in Philadelphia. Group membership becomes an important motivator, influencing the perceptions of Italian- and Irish-Americans. Although there are many similarities in socio-economic status and religion, the Italians differ from the Irish in a number of ways. The Irish express introverted attitudes and appreciation of traditional, formal, and modest arrangements, while the Italians are more expressive and communicative than the Irish. The way they manipulate their homes and perceive that manipulation is quite different. The Irish prefer uniformity and simplicity whereas the Italians like variety and change. The Italians display varieties of home environment.

The Irish neighbourhood maintains a unifying atmosphere and encourages the appearance of the block as one entity. The Irish seem to think of themselves as part of a group. The individual home is considered and decorated as part of a whole neighborhood. Fewer instances of personalization occur in the Irish neighborhood. The Irish, being conservative and consistent with their principles and uniformity, leave the windows and steps unchanged. There is little variation in colors and entry treatments. The houses in this area are of red brick and white trim. The combinations of white cornice, white window sills, and white louvered shutters add to the impression of simplicity and modesty of Irish characteristics. These simple arrangements are matched with a plank-front frame and 1/1 windows, topped by a transom.

The Italians, however, use the facade to express their values and individuality. It may be due to the fact that the Italians are more extroverted and expressive than the Irish. Each house in the Italian neighborhood is unique, distinctive, and expressive. They eliminate steps, windows, even transoms and cornices. They finish off steps and cornice with special treatment of brick. They also add colorful awnings, decorations, and lattice in the front. The facade is used to add touches of individuality to the home and it sometimes functions as a place for socializing with neighbors. The Italians seem to believe that it is important to express themselves in their homes.

Questionnaire: perceptions for the variety and changes in the home

Preference for uniformity/variety of home environments is closely related to population characteristics. Society Hill residents prefer diversity but they are strongly object to the idea of extreme deviation from the neighbourhood and historical characteristics of the site. This does not mean they do not like to put individual touches on the facade. Society Hill residents use the flowers, different colors, and shutters in decorating the front. Fairmount residents do not want to be different, since the majority of working class people dislike the idea of showing off. Most people except the Italians do not want to fix up the house to be different from others, even if sometimes they prefer variety. The Irish prefer a unified environment and do not intend to fix up the house to be different from others. Unlike the people of other three neighbourhoods, the Italians seem to like modifications and being different from others. The Italians feel that since people have different taste and characteristics, their homes should be different as well. The Italians elaborate their homes by modifying several elements of home, whereas the Irish try to keep unity through unifying colors and fronts.

In addition, it is found that personalization reflects a variety of human needs. Four reasons emerge for changing home environment: for need and to update (39.2%), for change (14.0%), for beauty (23.8%), and for suiting their taste (21.7%). Reasons for personalization are significantly different among different groups of people. The working class people make alterations on the basis of need and beauty, whereas a large percentage of professionals change their homes not only to update but also to suit their taste, to show their preferences. Professionals change their homes to reinforce personal identity (Table 1).

1.1 Social Difference Society Hill/Fairmount			1.2 Ethnic Difference Irish/Italian		
	SOC	FAI		IRA	ITA
NEED	19 (46.3)	15 (40.5)	NEED	15 (55.6)	7 (18.4)
CHANGE	1 (2.4)	7 (18.9)	CHANGE	2 (7.4)	10 (26.3)
LOOK BETTER	7 (17.1)	8 (21.6)	LOOK BETTER	5 (18.5)	14 (36.8)
SUIT TASTE	14 (34.1)	6 (16.2)	SUIT TASTE	5 (18.5)	6 (15.8)

Table 12.1 Reason for change

Interviews with the residents further support the results of questionnaire surveys. Many Society Hill residents mentioned that they modified their homes to express themselves. They regard their homes as an extension of self and want to change their homes to suit their tastes and preferences. Society Hill residents mentioned as follows:

> I change my home to make it more suitable for my taste.
>
> Home is an expression of myself. I want to reflect my personal taste and styles.
>
> As an architect, I would like my home to look somewhat different. I want to exercise my ideas.

Most Fairmount residents said that they modified their homes to update and change the appearances. They just want to maintain a good appearance. Fairmount residents said as follows:

> I would like to change the atmosphere. I am tired of sameness. I am tired of red brick.
>
> I want to make my house look better. I like to keep up a better appearance.
>
> It is needed. My house is rather old. It has to be done.

To the Irish, alterations to dwellings arises from practical motives and needs. The Irish residents mentioned that they altered their homes just because it was needed. They changed their living space since they want to have comfortable, uncluttered, and clean atmosphere. The Irish mentioned as follows:

> For clearer looking and feeling comfortable.

I want my house to be better looking. I am very pleased with changing home.

I am tired of the old look. I have lived here ever since I was born. My home needs to be updated.

The Italian residents mentioned that they modified their homes to have nice and different looks. As was seen from the questionnaire survey, they like the idea of looking different and want to have their own styles. The Italians said as follows:

I want my own style. I want to have more contemporary style. I am tired of my home. I want to change.

I have my own preference. I want to have a different colors and fronts from other neighbors.

I want to have a better appearance. I want to my house to look nice.

I want to have a change. I like to keep my house nice. It is the same as keeping myself nice. I want to my house to look clean and neat.

Interview: images of home

Many people concede that home reflects their ideas, tastes, value, personalities, and characters (Table 2). The Majority of professionals mentioned their homes as reflections of themselves.

Everything in here all speaks to me. Everything in here speaks all part of me. The way my house is decorated reflects everything, my personality, education, income. My home is a reflection of my professional values(skills), ethnic background, education, income, personality.... Sure, I would like to express myself through the house like the way you dress. It's inherent. I don't have to express. The home is expressive itself. (Society Hill)

This is me. It reflects my taste. Home is reproduction of my taste. I decorate my home the way I like it. I am really enjoying. (Society Hill)

... reflect what I am, what I am enjoying, what I feel comfortable. (Irish)

My home is decorated the way my mother likes to. And the way Mother decorates reflects herself, her color preferences. (Italian)

SOC	FAI	IRI	ITA
Character	Me	Taste	Me
Me	Taste	Personality	Taste
Personality	Character		Mother's Pref
Professional	Wife's Pref		
Ethnic Value			
Education			
Income			

Table 12.2 Home as reflection of?

People want their home to look good, cosy, clean, lived-in and well-maintained. Many professionals want their houses to look like themselves, while many working class people want their houses to look comfortable and pretty (Table 3).

The residents in Society Hill are interested in displaying their individuality through the home.

> I want my house to look like the combination of high quality. I want my house very eclectic and tasteful. (Society Hill)
>
> I want my home to look like myself. The way I feel about it. (Society Hill)
>
> The house has its own life. We should make that to look like what that is. (Society Hill)

The Fairmount residents want to have a nice and clean environment. Working class think it is very important to keep house clean and attractive.

> I want to make it provincial and elaborate. It will be nice that my home looks attractive, nice, neat, and clean. (Fairmount)

The Irish residents pursue relaxing and clean environments, whereas the Italian residents want to have something different. However both of them agree that home should be comfortable and pretty.

> I want my home comfortable, relaxing, and country-looking.I would like to make it lovely. (Irish)
>
> I just want it to be comfortable. When other people come in my house, I just want them to feel at home. I want my home clean and well-maintained. (Irish)
>
> Home as interesting, artistic, and welcoming. (Italian)

I want to have a different look. I like differences.. Everybody is different. (Italian)

SOC	FAI	IRI	ITA
Myself	Clean	Comfort	Comfort
Tasteful	Elaborate	Pretty	Pretty
Clean	Nice	Clean	Differ
Creative	Attractive	Traditional	Modern
Eclectic	Provincial	Well -Maintained	Good
High Quality		Lovely	Artistic
Simple			Welcoming
Spacious			Country

Table 12.3 Pursuing image of home

Summary and conclusion

The results from this study support the following conclusions. First, home environments are used in self presentational performances and function to symbolize and display the personal as well as sociocultural identities. Home environments are chosen, modified, decorated, and maintained to communicate identity. Data collected from observation constitute first source of such support. It includes variety of exterior modifications; door, window, colour, shutter, step, cornice.... Data collected from the questionnaire and interview further support the central hypothesis of this study. A majority of residents agree that their homes express their identity. It is evident that the home environment is a reflection of ideas, attitudes and needs of its occupants.

Second, it is also proved that the form of houses varies between different sociocultural groups. Different sociocultural groups have different tastes, perceptions, and use of space. The categories to be used to describe self, personality, and social identity vary between the groups.

References

Altman I. & Chemers, M. (1980), *Culture and Environment*, Brooks/Cole, California.

Cooper, C. (1975), *Easter Hill Village*, Free Press, New York.

Csikszentmihalyi, M. & Rochberg-Halton, E. (1981), *The Meaning of Things*, Cambridge Press, New York.

Duncan, J.S. (1973), 'Landscape Taste as a Symbol of Group Identity', *The Geographical Review*, vol. 63, pp. 334-55.

Duncan, J.S. (ed.) (1982), *Housing and Identity: Cross-Cultural Perspective*, Holmes & Meier Publishers, New York.

Goffman, E. (1959), *The Presentation of Self in Everyday Life*, Doubleday, New York.

Low, S. & Chambers, E. (eds.) (1989), *Housing, Culture, and Design*, University of Pennsylvania Press, Pennsylvania.

Rapoport, A. (1982), *The Meaning of the Built Environment*, Sage, California.

13 Changing lifestyles, changing housing form: Japanese housing in transition

S. Kose

Introduction

With the rapid growth of economy in recent years, the Japanese housing has experienced and is still experiencing a great change. The traditional house plan and the relationship of spaces within a house were affected with the modernization of life styles, and modern plans emerged. The move came along with the Japan Housing Corporation, established in 1955, which played a decisive role in popularizing westernized life styles through design and construction of multi-story public collective housing, a completely different style from traditional Japanese houses. These dwellings had, however, been thought as intermediate steps before suburban detached houses could be obtained.

A trend in recent years is the general acceptance of collective housing as a type of long-lasting nest for the nuclear family, partly imposed by the sharp rise in land prices, but partly positively acknowledged as a new attitude toward life.

The plan of detached houses by local carpenters still retains traditional design concepts. They are, however, challenged by industrialized housing manufacturers who aim at getting a nationwide share in the market with houses of superior quality.

The aging of Japanese society will further affect the life style and eventually the design of dwellings. It will first change traditional detailed design, but will further affect the plan of dwellings.

The present paper attempts to discuss these points. However, before going into detailed description, some basic information is given, which will perhaps assist the reader to understand the discussion that follows.

Background

Population

In 1990 the Japanese population was approximately 124 million, with 7.5% between 65 and 74 years old and 4.5% 75 years and older. Those who are between 15 and 64 years were about 69.5%. In 1986 the National Institute of Population Studies projected that by the year 2020 the population would be up to 135 million of which 12.3 % would be 65 to 74 years old, and 11.3% would be 75 years and older. The estimated proportion of those between 15 and 64 will be about 60%. This is to be compared with the figure in 1935, when the proportion of people between 15 and 64 was 58.5%, and 65 and over was mere 4.7%.

There were 37.5 million households in 1988 with the average number of persons per household being 3.1, compared with 5.03 in 1935, 4.97 in 1955, and 4.05 in 1965.

It is important to note that in 1950, 62.7% of total population lived in rural areas, but only 36.7% in 1960, and in 1988 76.7% lived in urban areas. This dramatic shift of the place of life from the countryside to cities along with the diminishing size of the household affected the housing situation.

Housing

Since 1966, the number of housing units being constructed annually has been between one and 1.5 million, which roughly paralleled the economic growth annually in Japan. Recently, the rate of construction of privately owned units has been between 0.6 to 0.7 million per year. The most notable trend is that collective housing became the mainstream of supply in recent years. As late as in 1968, 53% of all existing housing units were single storied according to the government housing condition survey, and only in 1973 the ratio of single storied housing became the minority, with 43%. More detailed description on Japanese housing is to be found in two government publications (1987; 1988).

Traditional housing forms

Historically, there are several precedents of Japanese housing forms. Most houses and dwelling units inherited some part of the concept of these house forms (Yoshida, 1955; Nishi & Hozumi, 1985). However, three archetypes can be pointed out as the mainstream of traditional Japanese houses.

One is the Samurai-warrior house which is a detached house with a garden that surrounds the house. After the Meiji Restoration in 1968, this form became the standard for government officials and white collar workers of major corporations in the city. It was basically comprised of two parts in the house itself: public space and private space. The public space was reserved for accepting formal guests, seldom used by the family members. An example is given in Fig. 1. Please note that the size of the rooms and the house can be estimated from the size of Tatami mat which is 1.8m x 0.9m (6 shaku x 3 shaku: one shaku is a Japanese unit almost equal to one foot).

The second comes from the farmer's house which normally housed an extended family living under one roof. Everything was to be done in the house so that a large meeting room was available by removing the sliding paper screens that separated the room into smaller ones (typically into four). This space was not for daily use, either. It was usual to have an earth floor, part of which was the cooking area with a furnace. Figure 2 gives an example of this. For the grandparents, a kind of granny annex might be prepared away in the garden.

The third comes from the tradition of townhouse, the norm in the cities. They were built eaves to eaves, directly facing to the street, sometimes having the garden at the back. Typical examples still survive in Kyoto machiya house where the houses are built along the narrow street (Fig. 3), leaving no gaps between but having a small garden opposite to the street.

This is to some extent similar to houses in a city surrounded by walls. The complete difference is that the land lot was usually not shared, for the building or for the garden. It was normally for exclusive use, and it was rare to have different households living on different floors of a building. The dwelling units of townhouse were separated by thin walls. They were called 'Nagaya', long housing.

Housing situation

Before the Second World War, it was not difficult to rent a house in the city, even in Tokyo. Rather, it was the norm. Leasehold was also quite popular and people built houses of their own as a leaseholder. There was a clear distinction of classes in Japanese society, which was associated with the way of living and the area in which one lived. The 'white collar' and the 'blue collar' working classes had different standards and values, which were not easily mixed.

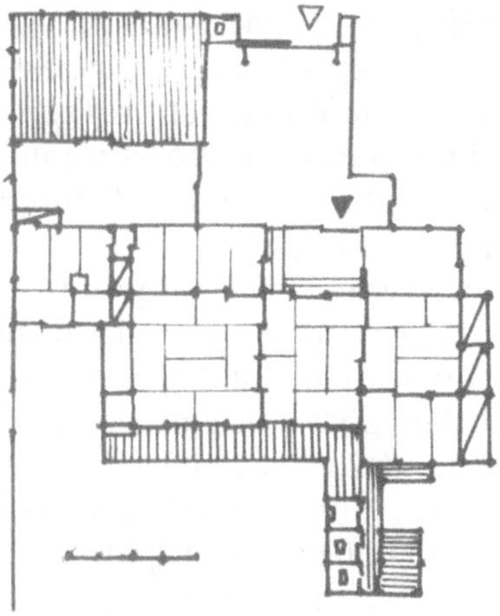

Figure 13.1 A Samurai warrior house

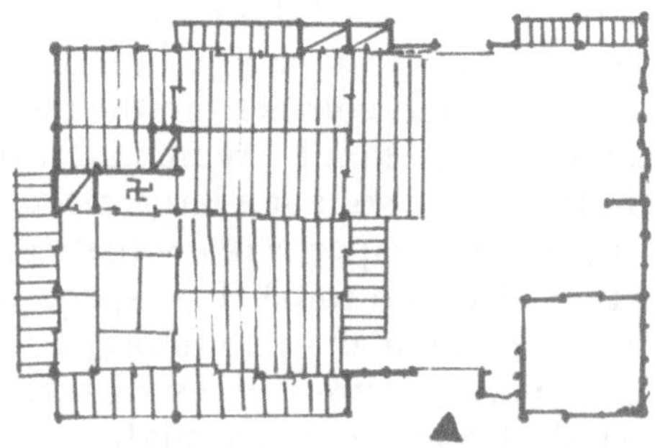

Figure 13.2 A Farmer's house

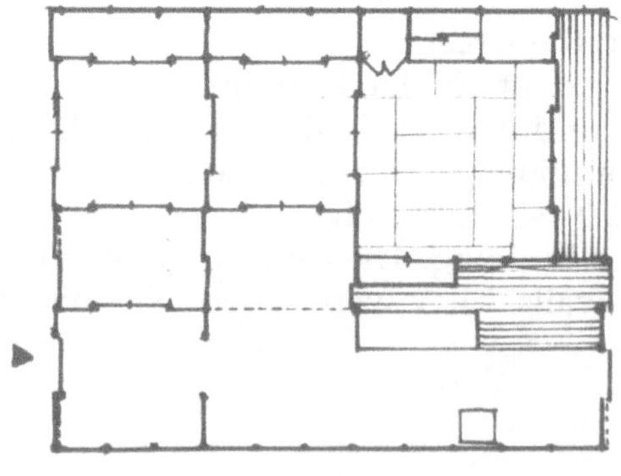

Figure 13.3 Kyoto Machiya house

After the War, Japan had to re-start housing construction from the ashes in the cities. Publicly operated rental housing (PORH) was the first to be built through the initiative of the government by the local governments. It was only in 1950 when the Japan Housing Loan Corporation (HLC) was established, which assisted the prospective dwellers to build/purchase with loans from the government. Japan Housing Corporation (JHC: now HUDC, Housing and Urban Development Corporation) was set up in 1955 to construct public collective housing for rent and for purchase. This partly took over the role of the PORH.

The government policy for housing was that owner-occupied houses be constructed. Land also tended to be self-ownership as opposed to leasehold before the War. This emphasis on self-construction was partly due to lack of public funding (thus relying heavily on private money of the prospective dwellers), partly due to expectation of the contribution of the construction activities toward economic growth. Rapid recovery of the economic capacity after the War owes to the heavy investment on housing construction in the private sector.

The role the Japan Housing Corporation played

Although some collective houses were built with reinforced concrete after the Great Kanto Earthquake in 1911, such as the Dojun-Kai apartment blocks, they were quite small in number, and the War prevented it from becoming the main stream. This meant that the move PORH and afterwards the JHC took was the first major step toward multi-story collective housing.

As the fund was quite limited, PORH and the JHC mainly supplied smaller dwelling units with the floor area of about 40 m^2. Figure 4 is a plan layout at an early stage. This size persisted for quite a long period after which standard size of the dwelling became larger. To make best use of this small floor area, many ideas were introduced in the design and construction of the dwelling units.

First is the adoption of a dining-kitchen (DK), which changed the style of having meals from sitting on the Tatami floor to using table and chairs (Fig. 5). This made it possible to separate the functions of space within a dwelling which were previously somewhat ambiguous.

Second is the introduction of western type toilet stool, thus eliminating the need (and space) of male urinal stool. This was so vital for space saving that it quickly spread all over Japan, for detached houses as well.

The underlying concept of the JHC housing is thus very much different from the traditional one. It basically phased out the possibility of living in it as an extended family, mainly due to its size. Dwelling types supplied were called n-DK, which meant that the unit had a dining-kitchen, a bath, a toilet, and n rooms, which usually was 2, at least at its beginning when average number of people in a nuclear family was about 4 or 5 (father, mother, and two or three children). Those fathers and mothers mostly came from rural areas to work in the metropolitan area because that was virtually the only place to find jobs. They left their parents in their home places.

Most dwellers of the JHC housing in the early years took it for granted that they would move out to the suburban detached houses, partly because the apartment unit was too narrow for a family with bigger children, and partly because the detached house with a small garden was their dream house. They were not prepared to accept such apartment units as their long-lasting dwellings. As they grew up in the rural area, they were never taught of the manner of living in cities: Japan has never had intramural cities in her history.

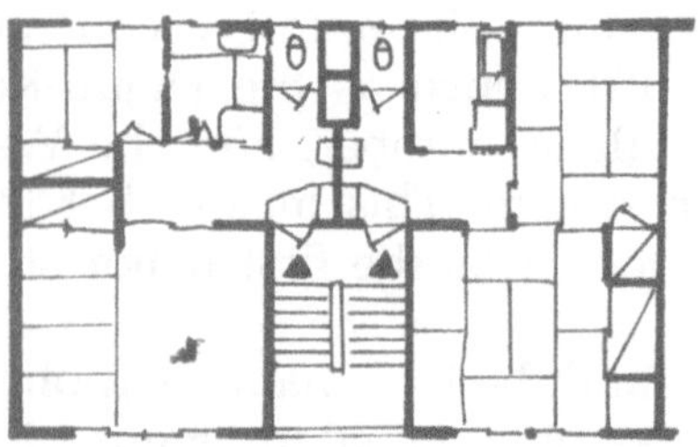

Figure 13.4 An early plan layout of PORH dwelling unit, Takanawa, 1948

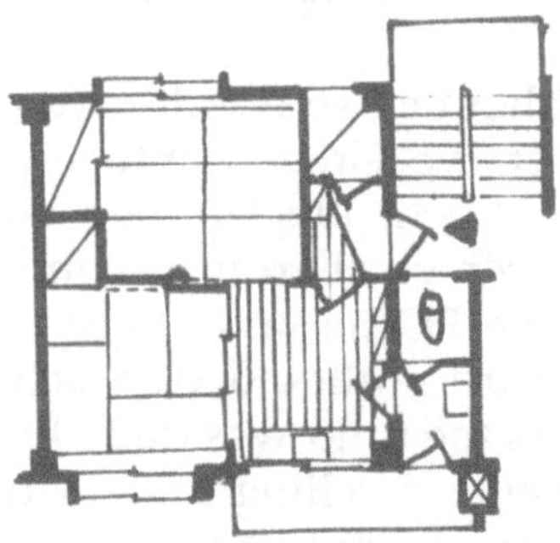

Figure 13.5 Introduction of dining-kitchen (DK) into PORH 1951

The Japanese cities were rather rural cities without city walls and multi-story housing with different families living on different floors has never been a tradition. Japanese people also stick to the self-ownership of land for their houses. The joint ownership of larger lots with multiple dwelling units is not so common. The townhouse form as owner-occupied units has never been popular, either. Due to the fact that Japan never experienced an invasion by enemies, the ownership of land has never lost its legitimacy.

Effects on the design of detached houses

The steady economic growth and the acceptance of the nuclear family as standard family type led to the 'family-first' principle, and the change in plan layout of houses in urban/suburban areas. Most importantly, the space reserved for guests gradually disappeared, and was replaced by a living room. Other major changes are attributable to the mechanization of household work.

The plan of detached houses mainly built by local carpenters still retains traditional characteristics . This is probably because they follow their own know-hows, and their clients are also conforming to the traditional idea of how a house should be designed and organized. Local culture has been quite difficult to change.

It is now being challenged, however. The industrialized house manufacturers are competing to get a nationwide share in the market. Their selling points are that their houses are modern, higher in quality, and quicker to build. Mass media and TV programs in particular have been effective in persuading local people to accept (or yearn for) a 'modern' concept of dwellings.

The industrialized housing manufacturers started their activities as providers of less expensive 'prefabricated' houses, but with the growth of national economy, clients shifted their emphasis to diversity: The readiness to respond to personal preferences became essential. The manufacturers are now capable of doing as requested. They produce the houses with the help of CAD/CAM system, and the slightest difference can be met such as variation in the size of windows, etc. which arises just from preferences of the client. They lost, however, their prime virtue of building low-cost housing.

They succeeded in getting more ground in the market partly because of their publicity as was already pointed out, and partly because the local carpenters were losing their tradition of craftmanship. The long established master-apprentice training system is disappearing. On the other hand, some industrialized house manufacturers are trying to include the craftsmen under their own umbrella. This will surely accelerate the disappearance of local tradition in construction and house design, while a move toward centralization (modernization) of housing culture will become more evident.

Figures 6 through 8 show typical plan layouts of recently designed and built detached houses for sale. A clear difference in concept between traditional carpenters and industrialized manufacturers is visible in the relationship between living room and tatami room. North entrance type almost invariably places living room and tatami room next to each other, while about half (10 out of 19) of south entrance type layouts separate tatami room from the living room. A closer look reveals that local carpenters put the two rooms together (5 out of 6), but industrialized manufacturers made them more independent from each other (9 out of 13).

The difference in these two layouts of course reflects two different ideas in the use of space. Whether the dwellers will accept the new idea of separating two rooms is another matter.

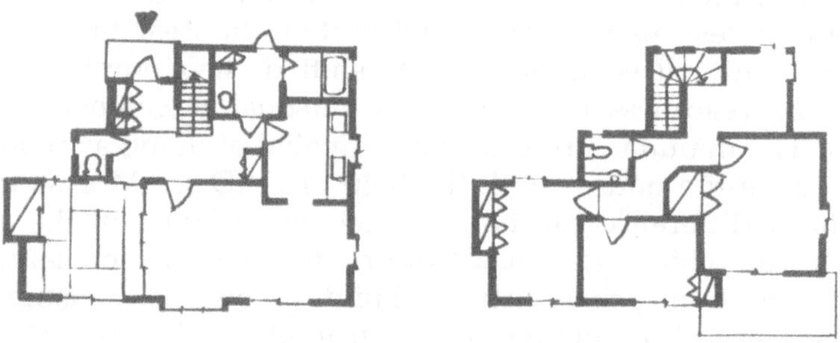

Figure 13.6 A detached house of north entry

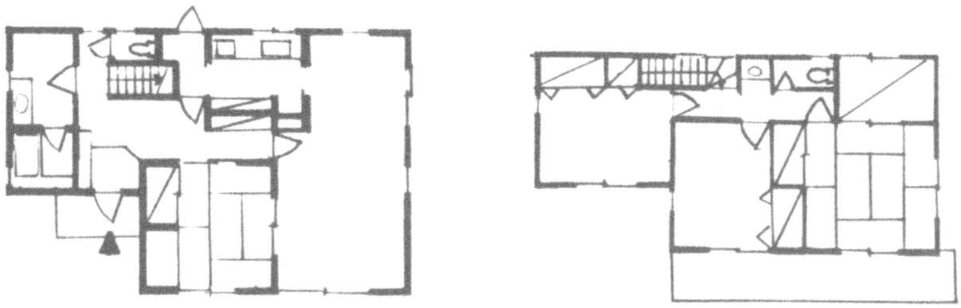

Figure 13.7 A detached house of south entry in which living room is connected with the tatami room

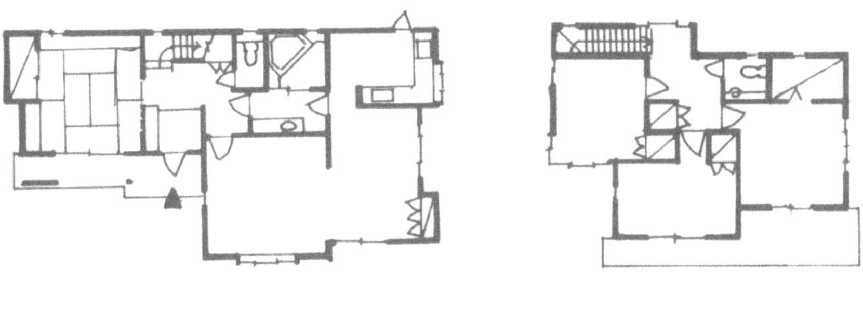

Figure 13.8 A detached house of south entry in which living room is separated from the tatami room

Change in life styles: collective housing as long-lasting nest

The situation is however again gradually changing. Recent movement is toward the general acceptance of collective dwelling units as a lifelong dwelling form among urban dwellers.

One reason is that it is acknowledged as an acceptable way of life for a nuclear family. The number of children is decreasing. Children move out from the house when they enter the university or when they go into a job, so there is less need for a family to get out of the present dwelling unit to obtain a larger house.

Another reason is that the sharp rise in land prices makes it nearly impossible to purchase a land for a detached house within a reasonable distance from the workplace in larger cities. It will cost about 8 times of one's yearly earnings to purchase a house in the suburban metropolitan area, while 3 or 4 times is assumed to be the feasible cost which is still the case in small local cities. Even if one bought such an expensive house, one has to commute two hours one way. This will make people reconsider whether they should buy a house. There are several possible alternatives: One is to obtain a house in a very remote area and the breadwinner lives in a very small unit near the city during weekdays (someone named this 'multi-habitation'); another is to live in a collective housing unit (perhaps a high-rise) which is wide enough to enjoy life as a family.

The positive attitudes toward collective housing as in the latter form led to the requirement of higher quality units from the viewpoint of residents. A single solution would never suffice. Rather, such needs will be met through diverse plans and designs, including the adoption of some specific characteristics of detached houses: personalization in design, allowing dwellers' free choice in various aspects; enhanced sense of privacy around units through provision of second entrance door to kitchen, etc.; and creation of intimate relationship among neighbours, such as giving residents the power of control over the environment (built-in flower pots to be taken care of by the residents).

The impact of the aging society

The next important trend is the aging of the society which was already pointed out. The traditional system to cope with the aging of one's parents -the extended family- is shrinking due to smaller number of children, and the paternal society system is dissolving. As to three generations living together, the most common has been the parents living with their son's family, which frequently leads to conflicts between the son's mother and his wife in the kitchen. Today, more and more wives refuse to live with their husband's mother. The wife's parent(s) living with their son-in-law as an extended family -maternal line- has never been common in Japan. (Some examples of social housing for extended families are given in Kose & Nakaohji, 1990.)

What clearly illustrates this trend is the varied proposals of two-family dwelling design for parents and children's couple. An organization named Institute of Two-Family House Design (Nishotai Juutaku Kenkyusho), affiliated to an industrialized house manufacturer, did extensive studies and design proposals of two-family dwellings. Their findings suggest that two families try to live independently from each other as long as they can. Their relationship is rather similar to that of neighbours or friends. Only when the aged person (usually the grandmother) becomes more frail, she tends to share her living space with that of the children. Thus, it is different from what people traditionally assumed to be.

The key issue that will further affect the design of dwellings is the Japanese 'Age Wave' (Dychtwald, 1988), the aging of the baby-boomers in Japan. They are brought up in the age of westernization, or more precisely, the age of Americanization, and have become accustomed to their way as opposed to traditional Japanese life styles.

The baby-boomer generation prefers the dining-kitchen, and men do not hesitate to cook (their fathers mostly kept themselves away from the kitchen, even from washing dishes). This made the kitchen to be placed nearer toward the center in the layout plan of the dwelling. The kitchen, the dining room and the living room are usually more closely connected than they traditionally were as Figs. 6-8 have shown.

The rooms (bedrooms in particular) on the other hand became separated by hard walls, thus securing more independence. This is in contrast to traditional design of room layouts which allowed provision of larger space by removing paper screens between connected rooms (Takeshita, 1990). In local areas it is still preferred but it will gradually change.

Associated with the move toward introduction of hard walls between rooms is the inclusion of the two household concept in the plan, thereby enabling the unit to be separately used by two independent families. What was first planned for the extended family might become a house with an accessory apartment unit or a granny annex, with assistance to the aged household from the younger, or completely independent two households sharing the space under the same roof without any significant interference. This will make it possible for the aged generation to have some earnings from the rent as well as providing some sense of security in case of need (just like being looked after by a warden). Examples of this kind are emerging.

The baby-boomer generation do not insist on having tatami room. They would rather have carpeted rooms with table, chairs and beds. Many do not have special preferences to sliding paper screens, either. This will further accelerate the trend away from traditional Japanese design. Such design features will be adopted from personal preferences of the residents, and won't be the norm any more.

Detailed building design for the needs of the aged

Traditional design was almost always targeted to young and healthy dwellers. There seems to have been an assumption that people will only live up to the age of 50, while actually the average length of life is now nearing 80. Research into the decreasing capability of people with age demonstrated the importance of design modifications for the aging society from the viewpoints of safety and usability (Kose, 1990).

Two major requirements have been suggested as crucial: elimination of level differences, and installation of handrails. The former is quite essential because traditionally they exist between wooden floor and tatami areas. Other design needs of the aged will include door lever handles, larger switches, easily operable facilities, etc., (Kose & Nakaohji, 1991; Nomura et al., 1990).

As to the first point, the existence of tatami, and traditional detailed design of tatami rooms made it normal to have height differences between wooden floor and tatami area. The difference is quite dangerous to the aged persons because it induces falls by tripping on the floor and results in fractures. As fractures in lower limbs and hips are known to be the most troublesome injury for the aged, the elimination of level differences (including the elimination of door sills) will greatly benefit the aged population. It however requires changes in the cultural tradition. Handrail installation is essential to assist balanced body movement, but handrails often interrupt (as architects say) design consistencies in the space. It will perhaps take some time before architects and designers are prepared to accept the design requirements of the aged persons.

Conclusion

Japanese society has dramatically changed after the War along with the economic recovery. Housing form was affected as well but only moderately. Dwelling design still retains some of its historical characters. It is now the time to change.

The baby-boomers almost always struggled hard to get what they needed for the past years. They will continue to do the same as they grow older, and by doing so, they will reshape the environment according to their wishes. Their requirements will be the requirements of the society, and in the years to come, the baby-boomer, the future aged, will change the housing design to one that is livable for them.

References

Dychtwald, K. (1988), *Age Wave*, Bantam Books, New York.

Hirai, K. (1980), *Zusetsu Nihon Juutaku no Rekishi (Illustrated History of Dwellings in Japan)*, Gakugei Shuppansha, Kyoto.

Housing Bureau of the Ministry of Construction, Housing & Urban Development Corporation, and Building Center of Japan (1987), *A Quick Look at Housing in Japan*, 2nd Ed., The Building Center of Japan, Tokyo.

Housing Policy Division of the Ministry of Construction (1988), *A Historical Review of Japan's Housing Policy*, The Ministry of Construction, Tokyo.

Kose, S. (1990), 'Koureisha no koudou nouryoku to juutaku sekkei' (Activity capability of the aged and detailed dwelling design), *Kenchiku Gijutsu*, no. 474, pp. 226-233.

Kose, S. & Nakaohji, M. (1990), 'Housing the Elderly: Past Present and Future', Policy development by the Ministry of Construction, in Pamir, H., Imamoglu, V. & Teymur, N. (eds.), *Culture, Space, History*, Middle East Technical University, Ankara, vol. 3, pp. 258-266. (A revised version appeared in *The Journal of Architectural and Planning Research*, vol. 8, no. 4, pp. 296-306).

Kose, S. & Nakaohji, M. (1991), 'Design guidelines for dwellings for an ageing society-a Japanese perspective, Japanese housing policy for ageing society', *Building Research and Information*, vol. 19, no. 1, pp. 24-30.

Lawrence, R. (1987), *Housing, Dwellings and Homes*, John Wiley and Sons, Chichester.

Nishi, K. & Hozumi, K. (translated by Horton, H.M.) (1985), *What is Japanese Architecture?* A survey of traditional Japanese architecture, with a list of sites and a map, Kodansha International, Tokyo.

Nishiyama, U. (1975), *Nihon no Sumai* (Japanese Housing), vol. 1, Keiso Shobo, Tokyo.

Nomura, K., Kose, S., Kodama, K., Nishizawa, H., Tanaka, Y., Kido, M. Ishikawa, A. (eds.) (1990), *Koureika Taiou Juutaku Reform Manual* (Dwelling Rehabilitation Manual for the Aged), Nihon Juutaku Reform Center & Juutaku Kin'yu Fukyu Kyoukai (Japan Housing Reform Center & Housing Loan Service Association), Tokyo.

Takeshita, T. (1990), 'Gendai no juutaku no heimen kousei no tokucho to sono shiteki zanshisei (Characteristics of plan layout of contemporary Japanese houses and their historical background)', *Kenchiku no Kenkyu*, no. 81, pp. 1-5.

Yoshida, T. (1955), *The Japanese House and Garden*, The Architectural Press, London.

14 Continuation of vernacular in squatter settlements

G. Saglamer

Introduction

Several field studies have been carried out in squatter settlements and some urban/rural settlements from where the inhabitants of squatter settlements came, in order to find out the relationships between these settlements in cultural terms.

It has been observed that when migration takes place, the newcomers are affected by their social relations, social and cultural backgrounds, basic needs and income levels in the course of choosing the settlement place. As they mainly build their dwellings themselves by the help of craftsmen, they try to build the familiar plan types with the familiar construction systems under present conditions. Consequently the new environment reminds them of the old one and thus they feel at home.

In this paper, similarities and differences between squatter settlements and rural settlements have been analysed on dwelling and neighbourhood scales, thus a formal base has been obtained to discuss the continuation of vernacular in squatter settlements. These discussions have not only been based on the field studies carried out since 1982 but also the evolution of house forms which have existed in Anatolia since the Bronze Age.

Throughout history, endless efforts have been made with the aim of providing shelters to save mankind from the unpleasant effects of the environment in physical, social and psychological terms. The cultural, social, technological, geographical and economic differences, which occurred in different times and different places have had significant effects on dwelling and settlement forms.

Although many of these forms have not survived in physical terms till now, they have affected their successors in many åspects. Many research projects have been carried out on vernacular architecture. Comparative studies have been used to demonstrate the differences and similarities between settlements depending mainly on cultural aspects (Rapoport, 1969).

In vernacular architecture 'basic' and 'conventional' design and construction processes have been used. In the basic process of design, the user gives his or her requirements a physical form, whereas in the conventional design process, the user informs the designer or the constructor directly about his/her requirements and priorities. In squatter settlements almost mostly 'basic' but in some cases 'conventional' design and construction processes have been observed as in vernacular architecture.

In the 1980s several research projects were carried out on the layout patterns of squatter settlements both on the dwelling and the settlement levels to find their origins. The goals of these projects were to define the present layout patterns and their predecessors by carrying out historical studies into the vernacular architecture in Anatolia (Saglamer, et al, 1983, Saglamer & Erdogan, 1989, Saglamer & Dinçel, 1990).

It was interesting to observe close relationships between the dwelling units in the squatter settlements and in the rural settlements from where the inhabitants of the squatter settlements under investigation came. Two different squatter settlements have been chosen for this investigation; the first one is the Kuruçesme/Istanbul settlement and the second is the Eskişehir squatter settlement. The inhabitants of the squatter settlements in Istanbul have come from all parts of Anatolia. The biggest share in this migration process belongs to the Black Sea part. On the other hand, Eskişehir, which is a medium size city in cental Anatolia has migrants from its immediate neighbouring towns and villages; therefore is has completely different characteristics from the squatter settlements in Istanbul.

A morphological approach to layout analysis

Starting from the neolithic period, many dwelling types and settlement forms have emerged in Anatolia. The individual shelter was the first step in this process. As subsequent steps, individual shelters began to constitute groups to set a social environment and they also acquired different characteristics to meet the requirements which mainly emerged as a consequence of social and cultural developments.

Typological analyses can be carried out on dwellings and settlements according to the different attributes of dwellings and settlements. For example, if we try to analyse plan layouts these attributes can be the number of rooms or spaces, types of relationships between these rooms, types of rooms, grouping of rooms, specialisation of rooms according to activities etc. In this study, a morphological approach based on geometrical and topological attributes of dwellings has been developed.

In its simplest form, a dwelling unit contains a single space which is used for all sorts of activities. The number of rooms is obviously a function of the well-being of the inhabitants as well as the cultural constraints. Therefore, dwelling units which have a large number of rooms in a single space organisation in vernacular architecture are excluded in this study, as the inhabitants of squatter settlements have low incomes and they usually use primitive space organisations. The maximum room number has been accepted as 4 rooms which constitute a connected graph (Figure 1).

Since spaces generally have rectangular shapes in most of the vernacular architecture in Anatolia, this property has been used as a constraint in this study.

Dwellings that have more than four rooms in the investigated settlements, have generally been obtained by adding one group of spaces to the other. Thus instead of setting complex space organisations, users preferred to use simple groupings of spaces for their changing requirements. Adding an individual unit or a group of spaces to the existing layout demonstrates the feature of expandibility of the dwellings in rural and squatter settlements.

The plan type 1a is the basic form for dwelling units. This type of dwelling was used in the neolithic settlements in the seventh millennium BC in Catalhoyuk. The type 2a is the meçaron type, the early samples of which were seen in Troy (3000 BC). Types 2b and 3b are the types which have been used since the Bronze Age in Anatolia. The plan type 3a, which is called the hairpin megaron (Kostof, 1987) and the type 4b, which has a more complex structure emerged in 700 BC. The types 3c and 4g which were called prostas types have been used since 500 BC in Anatolia (Usman, 1958). The types 4c and 4f can be observed in traditional Turkish houses.

We may call these space organisations 'grouping patterns' or 'basic units'. Each pattern may constitute a dwelling unit by itself or it may combine with some other patterns, or it may repeat itself to generate larger organisations. They can be combined in a courtyard house around a courtyard like the peristyle houses in the Hellenistic Period or they can generate a compact building shape by one being added to the other. Figure 2 shows a dwelling unit from the neolithic settlements (a) (Kostof, 1985, p. 51); a courtyard house containing several individual units (b) (Kostof, 1985, p. 1414); and types consisting of combinations of different patters (c) (d) (Kostof, 1985, p. 51, Akin, 1985).

Although some of the researchers who are interested in architectural languages claim that there are no clear dependencies between spatial organisation and articulated style (Fleming, 1987). Therefore, analysing an architectural language in terms of spatial organisation could not give sufficient information about the whole.

If we were to carry out a research on the taxonomy of styles that have emerged through centuries, we would have the chance of observing the distribution of plan types among these styles or we would be able to observe the grouping of styles. Unfortunately, such a work has not yet been carried out. Different plan types within the same style or the same plan types within the different styles do not mean that there is no connection between them, because each style can house a certain type of plan layouts which suit its articulated form. For example, traditional Turkish houses have certain layout patterns (Eldem, 1978). Therefore, the morphological analysis of plan types and their associative styles can be used to demonstrate the cultural continuation through architectural languages.

In this study it is not claimed that the plan types observed are unique for these settlements. The main argument is that there is strong dependencies between squatter settlements and the rural settlements from where the inhabitants of the first group migrated.

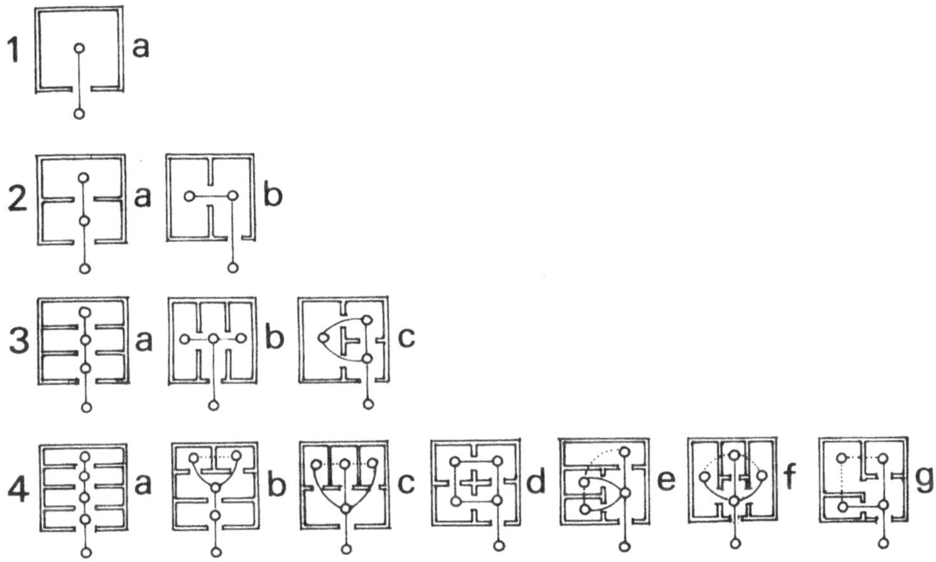

Figure 14.1 Topological diagrams of simple plan layouts

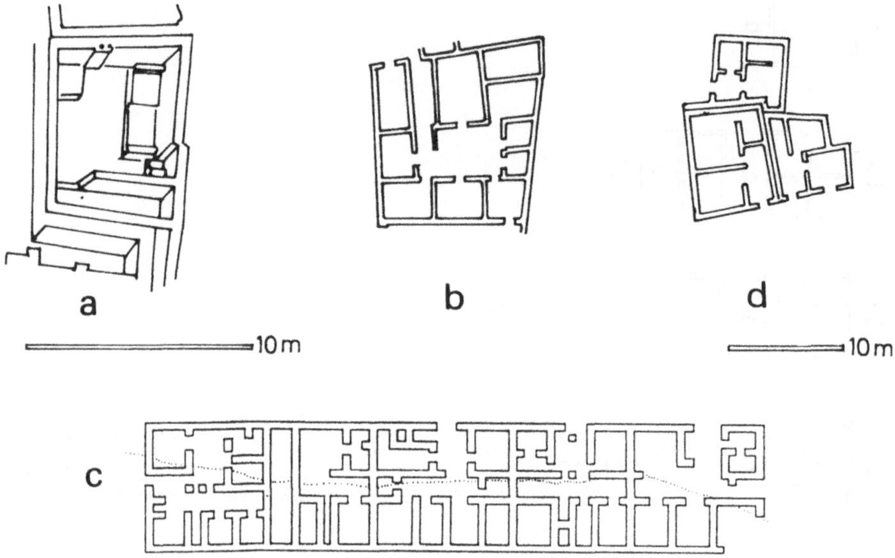

Figure 14.2 Some examples of combinations of different patterns

Layout patterns in squatter settlements and their origins

In this paper, two squatter settlements investigated in the 1980's will be used to demonstrate the similarities between squatter settlements and vernacular architecture. Two different types of dwelling groups have been used to analyse these similarities. The first group of dwellings are taken from the squatter settlements and the second group of dwellings are taken from the towns or villages that the inhabitants of the first group came.

Case Study 1: Kuruçeşme

Kuruçeşme is one of the oldest settlements on the Bosphorus. There used to be a tea-packing workshop and a coal distribution centre on the coast. These two functions as well as a fire that destroyed most of the historical wooden houses have caused the living standard of the settlement to decline and a squatter settlement has developed just behind the main settlement area. Despite its poor living conditions this settlement has retained the visual characteristics of the Bosphorus by building mostly only one or two storey houses, by preserving the trees and greens and by not spoiling the topography and surface characteristics of the earth to a great extent.

The first survey was carried out on this settlement in 1983 in order to assess the construction systems of the dwellings (Saglamer, *et al*: 1983). The second survey which is based mainly on the users' cultural background, social attitudes, family structures has been carried out since 1988. In the first survey, 16 dwellings were investigated. In the second survey the dwellings which were not taken into consideration before, have been considered and the measurement drawings of these dwellings have been prepared, thus a more comprehensive site layout has been obtained. In this part of the study, the social survey has been carried out on 25 families. As 16 of the families out of 25 came from Alucra, the analysis is mainly based on these families (Saglamer & Erdogan, 1989).

The characteristics of the site layout: The land on which the squatter settlement is built belongs to the municipality and a religious foundation. The land has a steep slope of 80% and the ground consists of sandstone. Building on a steep slope needs a great deal of site preparation, such as excavations and loose fill work and retaining walls, which means an expensive substructure. The squatter units are generally one- or two-storey buildings located in a linear form along the contour lines of the terraces obtained as a result of site preparations. They are oriented towards the magnificent scenery of the Bosphorus and do not obstruct each other in terms of scenery. Each dwelling's location demonstrates the good relations between the neighbours. One of the most important factors in this formation of dwelling units in this way is the care taken not to disturb the neighbours (Figure 3).

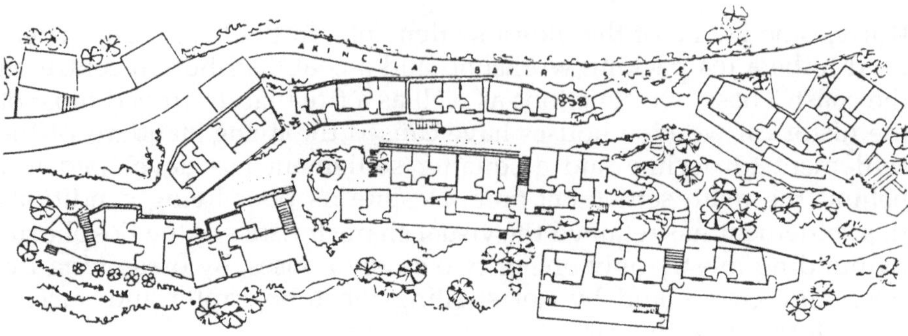

Figure 14.3 The site layout of Kuruçeşme

The Layout Patterns of Dwellings: Three types of plan layouts have been observed in this settlement. In the first group, a dwelling unit consists of two spaces; the hall and the room (Figure 4a). A dwelling unit of the second group consists of three spaces, the hall and two adjoining rooms (Figure 4b). The third group, a dwelling unit has more than three rooms usually obtained by adding an independent group of rooms to the existing spatial organisation (Figure 4c).

The rooms are not specialised for certain activities in these dwellings. As the number of the rooms are very limited, the different activities have to be housed in the same rooms at different times of the day. In all the houses, drainage and waste disposal systems are built individually. The toilets are generally located in a corner of the garden. All the houses have entrance through their balconies which are located in front of the houses.

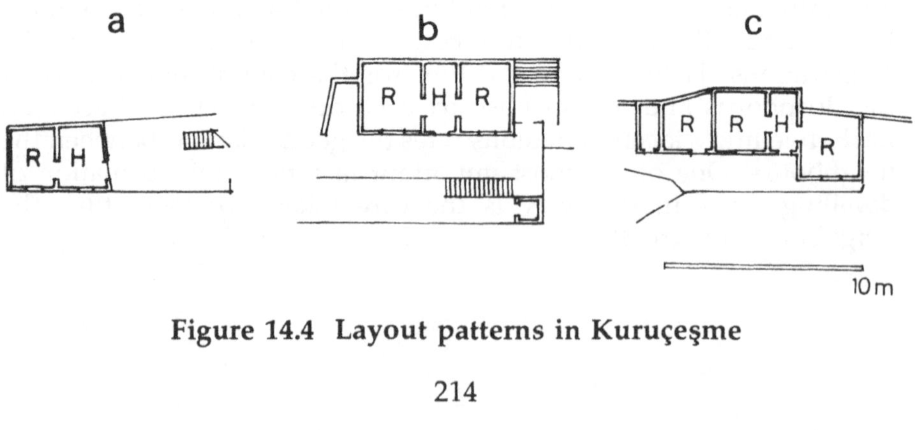

Figure 14.4 Layout patterns in Kuruçeşme

Case Study 2: Alucra

The inhabitants of Kuruçeşme came from the villages of Alucra in Giresun in the Black Sea region. Although Alucra is county located within the territory of the city of Giresun, there is no similarity between Alucra and Giresun in terms of geographical features, climate, social and cultural structures. Alucra is one of the oldest settlements in north east Anatolia, dating back to the Hittite Period (1340 BC). It is located in the Kelkit valley near the old city Sebinkarahisar. The Kelkit valley has different characteristics from the Black Sea region and central Anatolia. The field study has been carried out in the Bayirköyü, Sarpkaya and Gürcali villages of Alucra. The interviews and the questionnaires have been applied to 14 families in these villages as a pilot study.

The characteristics of site layout: The villages consist of a set of small neighbourhoods. The families which are all close relatives, prefer to live in the same neighbourhood. Each neighbourhood usually contains 4 to 10 dwelling units. The land on which the dwellings are located in this area has a steep slope. All the houses are oriented towards the Kelkit river. Because of the topographical conditions, the houses are located on the terraces prepared by their owners. As there is plenty of land available to build houses, the dwellings are separated by large gardens. Only some close relatives have adjacent houses. In front of each house there is a large place for the harvest. Barns and stables are usually located under this place.

The layout patterns of the dwellings: Four types of plan layouts have been observed in the villages of Alucra. In the first group; a dwelling unit consists of a single room, which is called 'Ev' in this area. The 'Ev' houses all sorts of activities except for toilet facilities. There is a fire place made of the local stones in the 'Ev' to be used for all cooking activities (Figure 5a). In the second group the dwelling consists of two spaces, the hall and the room (Figure 5b). The hall houses several activities like the 'Ev'. In the third group a dwelling unit has three spaces; the hall, the 'Ev' and the room (Figure 5c). The dwelling units in the fourth group are a combination of the first three types (Figure 5d).

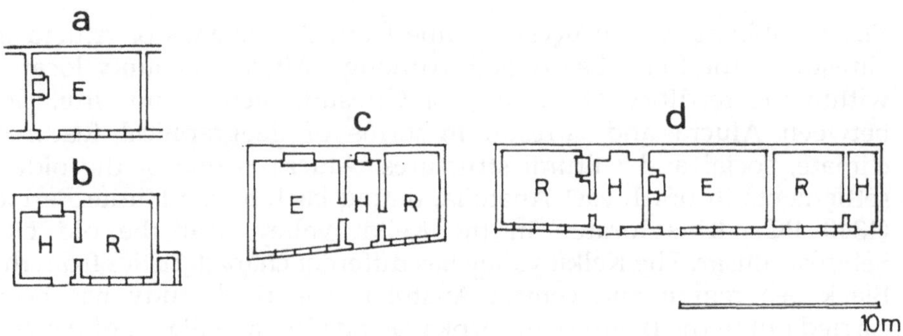

Figure 14.5 Layout pattern in Alucra

Case Study 3: Eskişehir

Eskişehir is a middle-size city in the west part of central Anatolia with a population of approximately 700,000. Eskişehir has a position suitable for industrial development, therefore it can be seen as a potential city which will be faced with severe migration problems in the near future. The squatter settlements in Eskisehir are mainly located on the outskirts of the city, especially near the inter-city transportation network, which has connections to the rural areas where the inhabitants of the squatter settlements usually come from.

The characteristics of the site layout: A part of the squatter settlement investigated in Eskisehir is shown in Figure 6. As the land had been dissected before it was used, the site layout demonstrates the characteristics of the grid system. It has a regular street pattern which has no similarity with the Turkish city structure but it is similar to the antique city patterns in the region.

Figure 14.6 The site layout of the Eskişehir squatter settlement

The layout patterns of the dwellings: The layout patterns of the dwellings are based on the grouping patterns analysed above. In these layouts, garden (the open space) and the rooms constitute the dwelling unit altogether. At the first step, the user constructs a wall around his/her land to define his/her territory. Afterwards, the rooms are located along this wall to obtain a courtyard. In this case, the clustering of spaces within the defined outlines is used as a way of providing space differentiation in the dwellings. This location process sometimes begins from the side of the garden opposite the street or vice versa. In any case the users prefer to have access from the street into the garden and through the garden into the dwelling unit or directly into the individual rooms (Figure 7a, 7b). The desired privacy is obtained by the enclosed wall of the garden in which the user accommodates some activities based on his/her rural life style. As squatterisation phases proceed, the number of located rooms increase, and consequently the area of the garden decreases and thus the garden becomes enclosed by the rooms instead of the walls (Figure 7c).

As seen in Figure 7, the garden can be accepted as the main circulation area besides the other activities accommodated in it. At each step of the development process of these dwellings, all the spaces can change their functions and consequently their connections. Therefore unusual connections can emerge. Courtyard houses have been used for thousands of years in Anatolia. In Figure 8 some courtyard houses built in different periods are shown (Usman, 1958, pp. 197, 199).

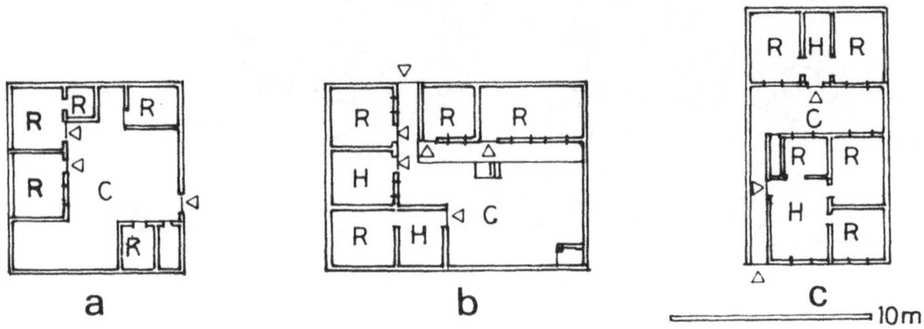

Figure 14.7 Layout patterns in the Eskişehir squatter settlements

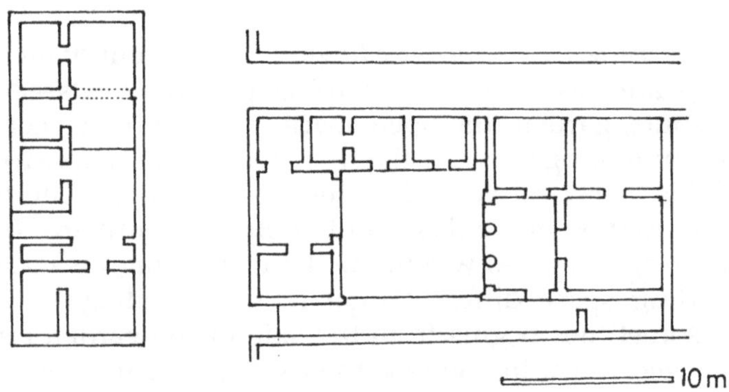

Figure 14.8 Some examples of courtyard houses in Anatolia

Conclusions

In this paper several field studies which have been carried out to investigate the similarities and differences between rural settlements and squatter settlements have been discussed in a historical context. A theoretical framework has been proposed to define the solution domain for particular dwelling types, and some best known house forms have been examplified within this framework. It has been observed that simple space organisations having no more than four rooms have been used since the Bronze Age in Anatolia and these are still in use in rural and squatter settlements. Space organisations seem to have many similarities in vernacular architecture and squatter settlements.

When migration takes place the newcomers are affected by their social relations, social and cultural backgrounds and basic needs in the course of choosing settlement place. As they mainly build their dwellings themselves with the help of craftsmen, they try to build the familiar plan types with the familiar construction systems under the present conditions consequently the new environment reminds them of the old one and they feel at home. At the first step of the migration, social and cultural backgrounds play very important roles. As they stay in urban areas longer the importance of these factors decrease gradually, their dwellings are expanded horizontally or vertically and new space organisations are created step by step according to changing requirements. Migrants from different parts of Türkiye have been building different squatters according to their cultural backgrounds. As cultural, social, physical and economic constraints have great effects on architecture, one can easily observe the continuity of architectural languages through centuries in Anatolia. Cultural continuation may be disturbed by some political, social or economic events throughout history but it has always had the tendency of returning to its roots even with some distortions.

References

Akin, G. (1985), *Güneydogu Anadolu'daki Tarihsel Ev Tiplerinin Anlami*, PhD. Thesis, iTÜ, Mimarlik Fakültesi.

Eldem, S.H. (1984), *Türk Evi*, TAÇ Vakfi.

Fleming, U. (1987), 'More than the Sum of Parts: The Grammar of Queen Anne Houses', *Environment and Planning B.*, vol. 8, pp. 269-293.

Kostof, S. (1985), *A History of Architecture: Setting and Rituals*, Oxford University Press.

Rapoport, A. (1969), *House Form and Culture*, Prentice Hall.

Saglamar, G. Yürekli, H. & Çagdas, G., (1983), *Assessing the Present Construction Systems in Slum Areas*, IAHS World Congress on Housing, Miami, USA.

Saglamer, G. & Erdogan, N. (1989), 'Effects of Users' Cultural Background on Squatter Settlements', Sixth Inter-Schools Conference on Development, Emerging Trends in the Third World Housing Policies, 1990's and beyond, Sheffield.

Saglamer, G. & Dinçel, H. (1990), 'The Analysis of Layout Patterns in Squatter Settlements', *International Journal for Housing Science and its Applications*, vol. 14, no. 2, pp. 107-114.

Usman, M. (1958), *Antik Devir Küçük Asya Evleri*, İTÜ, Mimarlik Fakültesi, Güven Basimevi.

15 Life in between residential walls in Islamic cities

R. Samizay and B. Kazimee

Introduction

The quest for cultural identity versus the drive for modernization through emulation of Western ways of life is a conflict that is challenging ideas and practices of contemporary architects and planners in Muslim cities. This conflict has resulted in a crisis which is rapidly changing the socio-historical characteristics of these societies and their built environments.

The need for a deeper knowledge and understanding of the Islamic society is crucial for comprehending its indigenous architectural forms and urban layouts with their intended meanings and uses. If cities of the Islamic world are to survive the negative pressures of modernization that threaten their fabrics, then an understanding of the traditional orders of the city and their appropriate application is essential.

Traditionally, the residential quarters in these cities have been intimately-bonded communities accommodating extended families and clans who are brought together by a cohesive culture and its belief systems. One aspect of the traditional cultural norms is the unique relationship between the male and female sectors of the society. The discouragement of the two sectors from intermixing and interacting in the public spaces, and the consequential separation of their domains, bring about two divergent spatial orders one may call *introverted* and *extroverted*. These ordering systems are very important for the richness of life that happens in between buildings.

The examples used in this investigation are from traditional residential sections of three cities in the Muslim world: Kabul in

Afghanistan (Fig. 1), Lahore in Pakistan (Fig. 2), Al-Qala in the Qatif region of Saudi Arabia (Fig. 3). These three cities, although different in terms of local culture and climate, have similarities shaped by the general tenets of the Islamic faith. In this respect, they are appropriate urban specimens for the study of Islamic socio-spatial concepts.(1)

Figure 15.1 Traditional residential settlement in the old town of Kabul, Afghanistan. (Source: Kazimee)

Figure 15.2 Traditional residential segment in the old town of Lahore, Pakistan. (Source: Qureshi)

Figure 15.3 Traditional residential segment in Al-Qala, Saudi Arabia. (Source: Talib)

The family and its role in the larger social order

Before one can understand the socio-spatial relationships in the built environments of traditional Muslim societies, it is essential to understand the role of the family in the larger social order under the Islamic jurisprudence. The family, as an influential social unit with its unique influence on the individual and the community, has been the central factor behind the development of the spatial order of the Islamic city.

In Islamic society, the survival of the extended family structure has only partially been caused by the need for economic dependency; the socio-cultural and religious requirements often played a more important role. Despite the opportunity for economic autonomy in the newly oil-rich societies, social needs remain as the strong bonding agent in the structure of the extended family. In fact, the new wealth and power have continuously been concentrated in the extended family through intermarriages and other bonds. Religious and social taboos which discourage women from participation in public affairs have reinforced the need for the male-dominated extended family which limits duties and activities of women to the domestic domain. Thus, the family precinct remained an important social unit for the female sector of society. Within this social order, the individual and even the nuclear family is subservient to the larger social order which starts at the extended family (*khanawada*) and expands to the clan (*taefa*), the tribe (*qabila*) and the society of believers (*umma*). While the individual is privileged with the economic support and moral virtues of khanawada, he/she in turn is burdened for their safeguard.

It is this influential role of the extended family and the particular gender relationship which have been a powerful image maker in the morphology of residential environments. This social pattern is clearly translated into a physical order that differentiates between the inner and private and the outer and public dimensions of life. While the outer dimension is seen as uncertain, unreliable, insecure and a constant source of struggle, the inner dimension centered around family life, provides security, serenity and trustworthiness. Understanding this stable *introverted order* against the unpredictable *extroverted order* and the physical forms they engender is crucial for understanding the life which is interwoven in Islamic cities. As this paper concentrates on residential quarters, its main focus is naturally the introverted order. However, this introverted order cannot be separated from the extroverted order, which is explained briefly as well.

Life in the family: the introverted order

The introverted order is intertwined with life within the family. This inward-looking microcosm is formed by a series of spaces that start at the alley or dead-end alley leading to the family compound and extends to the intimate corners of the house (Fig. 4). These functional and ritualistic places form a procession of spatial experiences necessary for understanding the introverted order.

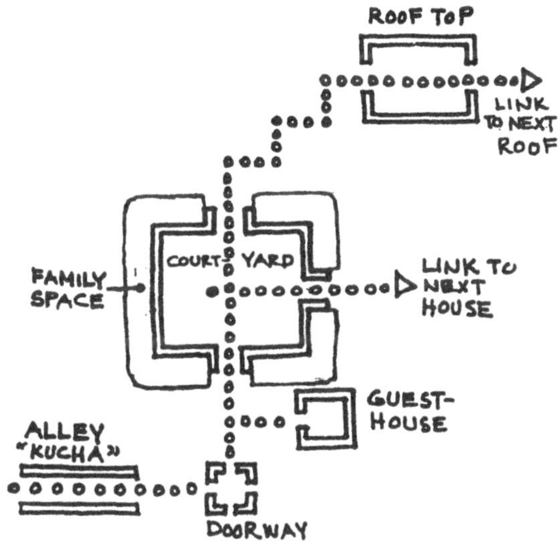

Figure 15.4 Diagram of introverted spatial progression

Alley (Kucha)

Alley (*kucha*) is a mediating space in Islamic cities which falls between the extroverted and the introverted orders of life and functions as an overlapping semi-private/semi-public space. It is a transitional space which on one side one may slide to the exposed realm of the public, and on the other may penetrate through the guarded domain of the family. Walking through the old sections of Kabul, Lahore or Al-Qala, one is struck by the intimate scale, richness of form, spatial quality and the mysterious effects of light and shadow in these alleys. The Kucha provides for casual encounters and the discrete comings and goings between neighbours. The high walls, the small punched windows, the thick entry doors and the narrow sectional proportion, reinforce this role (Fig. 5). Due to their semi-private nature, alleys are cleaned and maintained by the residents whose houses border on them. On the private side, entryways (*dar* or *dargh*), and guest houses (*mehman khana*) are located. Above, one finds the upper story projections and punched windows which allow women to peep on the public without being seen. In this respect, the alley is passive, and symbolically falls between the inside (identified with the soul *batin*) and the outside (identified with the appearance *zahir*). To children, for whom the issues of gender separation has not yet become relevant, the kucha is a socially active space animated by neighbourly encounters and games. For male adults, it is a passage to public spaces where they may pause to knock at a door while being careful not to infringe on the privacy of secluded women. The massive walls of the kucha provide the visual, the auditory and thermal insulation necessary between the outside macrocosm and the inside microcosm.

Figure 15.5 Alley in Lahore

Family compound (Manzil, Serei)

On the private side of the *kucha* lies the family compound (variously referred to as *manzil* or *serei*). The configuration of manzil is the result of the progressive evolution of the complex of residences and smaller dwelling sub-units. The compound may start as a large piece of land bordered on the alley and owned by the patriarch of the family. In this case, it may originally have one unit built on a side or divided into several units to accommodate different families of the clan, depending on the stage of family growth. For those who have inherited the compound over decades or a century, the origin is often buried in the past and the growth pattern is complex. For others, it is the result of instant development to accommodate different members of their family who have moved in from elsewhere. Population growth has played an important role in this process. Since these cities were built as walled cities and therefore expansion outward was limited, new growth was accommodated vertically in the form of third and fourth floors and through the subdivision of existing units.

As the examples from Kabul, Lahore and Al-Qala indicate, the end result is a series of courtyards and living quarters, linked together horizontally or, in the most populated areas, vertically. There are other housing types such as apartments and row houses in these cities which have grown out of the heterogeneity of population and differences of local cultures. The social quality of interaction between families is lively and rich; especially since women may move from their house throughout the entire residential block without being exposed to the eyes of the public or strangers thus allowing them to socialize with neighboring women. Architecture sensitively reflect this subtle social order.

Doorway (Dar, Dargah)

The architectural expression of the introverted order begins with the doorway as an element of transition between the outside public spaces and the ambient environment of the inside. The symbolic meaning of doorway (*dar* and *dargah*) is associated with the transition from the ephemeral world of the outside (*zahir*) to the enduring spiritual order of the inside (*batin*). People are brought up to understand that this sacred passageway should not be violated or trespassed by the outsiders. This symbolic passageway is more pronounced in the iwans of shrines of holy men in which reaching the *dargah* is a means of achieving spiritual communion.

The entry door has a pocket space on the inside, often both on the outside and the inside. The outside pocket allows a visitor to identify himself with a particular house and yet be partially protected not to disturb the privacy of the alley. The inside pocket creates a turn before entering the private courtyard to allow the women to hide away or provide seclusion from the alley in the event the door is left open (Fig. 6). This is also the space where a family member, often a man or a child, stands to open the door and determine the nature of the visit. The respect for this cultural function of the doorway in maintaining the peace and privacy of every family is the required duty of every individual in the society. Due to its symbolic function, doorways are carefully designed and intricately decorated. However, in most cases, due to the secular nature of residential doorways, they are humble by standards of the portals of the shrines which are monumental and richly decorated to commemorate the divine.

Figure 15.6 Doorway off the alley in Al-Qala

Guest house (Mehmankhana)

Whether in Kabul, Lahore or Al-Qala, the guest house is located immediately adjacent or above the entry, a location that again relates to the issue of privacy and protection of women. In certain instances, they may span over the street, a feature called *sabat* in Arabic (Fig. 7). Guesthouses are set aside for use by guests (including relatives) who sometimes come from another town or village to stay for a few days; or they may be used to entertain short time local visitors. The guest house is the domain of the male. Female visitors are entertained in a room inside the house. Guest houses become particularly active in festive holidays when inter-familial and extra-familial visits increase. The size of *mehmankhana* varies with the size and status of the family. In some instances, it is a simple room; at other times, it is a complete unit with its own patio. The rooms are well decorated and embellished, often better than the rest of the house, to bring comfort to guests as part of a long tradition of hospitality and care for others.

Figure 15.7 Underpass Sabat with guest room above in Al-Qala

In a series of adjoining houses inhabited by an extended family, a common guest house serves all.

In the hierarchical order of spaces, the guest house functions as a link between the extroverted order of the public spaces and the introverted order of the private spaces. Socialization in this space is formal. Historically, the guest house has played a mediating and peacemaking role bringing together different clans and families at times of conflict and disputes, thus functioning as a counseling podium for the community.

The courtyard (Hawyeli)

The courtyard as a spatial concept, although used in other cultures, has deep-rooted historical importance in Islamic residential architecture providing the essential need for privacy. Furthermore, the concept has been used as an ordering mechanism in other building types such as mosques, madrassas and leisure gardens. In residential prototypes, it takes a smaller and more intimate scale expressing the essence of the introverted spatial order which in turn encourages active social participation. In contrast to the uncertain and inert character of the *kucha*, the courtyard brings a sense of delight and security. It is a reflection of authentic social values rising above the limits of ordinary consciousness. The term *hawyeli* (courtyard) in this sense means more than the space and often refers to the entire house. It is therefore the hub of the family that epitomizes the entire dwelling and its life.

The courtyards may be square or rectangular in shape and are wrapped around by rooms or units of variable architectonic character and configuration. In Kabul, a single unit may be formed around a courtyard; or a multiple of row houses may be clustered around a larger common yard (Fig. 8). Similar configurations exist in Lahore. In Al-Qala, the single unit prototypes are more the norm. Since the periphery of the house is sealed with thick walls from adjacent houses and the street, the courtyard becomes the essential source of light, air and view. It is designed with colonnades, verandas, terraces and adorned by fenestrations, protrusions and spatial pockets. The courtyard may have one or two trees, a reflecting pool, or as is common in Al-Qala, a *sakooncha* which is a raised resting platform. Courtyard space essentially becomes the extension of the interior space accommodating domestic activities in good weather or taking the overflow during ceremonial functions (Fig. 9).

Figure 15.8 Courtyard cluster housing from Kabul

The social quality of the courtyard is further signified by various types of inter-family and neighbourly interaction. The patterns of activity throughout the day vary in quality and intensity alternating in use between different members. In the daytime, when men leave early for work, women, children and the elderly from the entire cluster may gather in the space to have breakfast and plan for the daily chores. In later hours of the day, the going and coming of neighbouring women from one house to the next take over. The courtyard thus becomes a means of social exchange where news and gossip are passed on; or it turns into a learning workshop for crafts and literacy programs.

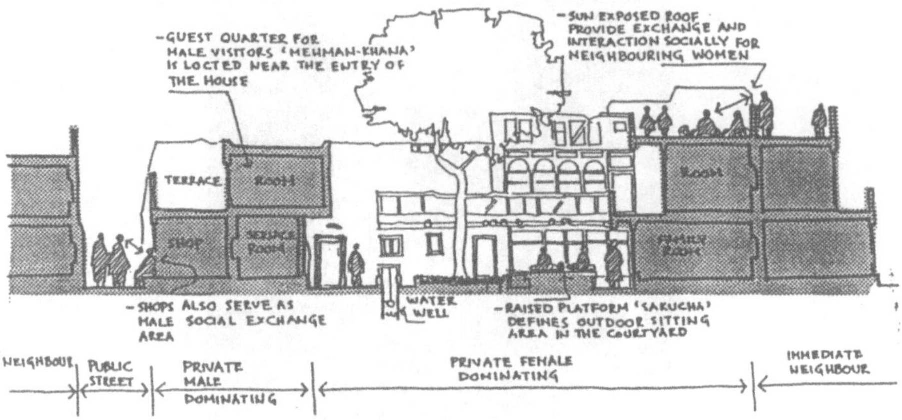

Figure 15.9 Section of a traditional courtyard house in Kabul showing the introverted spatial order

The interior family spaces (Utaq)

Rooms around the courtyard are arranged anywhere from one to four wings. In multiple wings, various functions such as cooking, storage and servant living are separately accommodated. In some houses, the main living spaces may have north-facing summer rooms and south-facing winter rooms.[(2)] In larger houses, a wing may be a sub-unit where a family member such as a newly-wed son and wife may live. Despite the existence of a hierarchy of use and level of privacy between the habitable rooms which may distinguish them as sitting/living or sleeping, rooms in the average house accommodate multiple functions. A room during the day may be used for sitting and entertaining, but may turn into a sleeping chamber at night. Flexible floor furnishings suit well to this variation in function.

Rooftop spaces (Bam)

In Islamic cities, such as Kabul and Lahore, due to circumstances of climate and indigenous culture, rooftops become spaces of architectural significance. It complements the spaces of alley and courtyard in use and social function. In the summer, they could be used for sleeping to escape the heat of interior spaces; in the winter when the alleys are muddy or courtyards are shady, it can function as a sun deck where similar social activities, which happen in the courtyard for women or in the alley for children, take place. Roofs may link to other roofs into a complex network accommodating another level of neighbourly interaction. These spaces are well defined and richly adorned by privacy parapet walls and decorative grills (Fig. 10).

Figure 15.10 Rooftop spaces in Lahore

Life beyond the family: the extroverted order

If *kucha* is the mediation space which borders the introverted order of the family on one side, it also forms the beginning of the extroverted order of the public life that extends into the city and beyond. This network starts from the kucha, extends into the street (*jada*), leads to the bazaar, and goes to the city square. The network further connects to the local mosque, the Friday Mosque, and the public bath; ultimately, it leaps beyond to the suburban gardens, shrines, fields and orchards (Fig. 11).

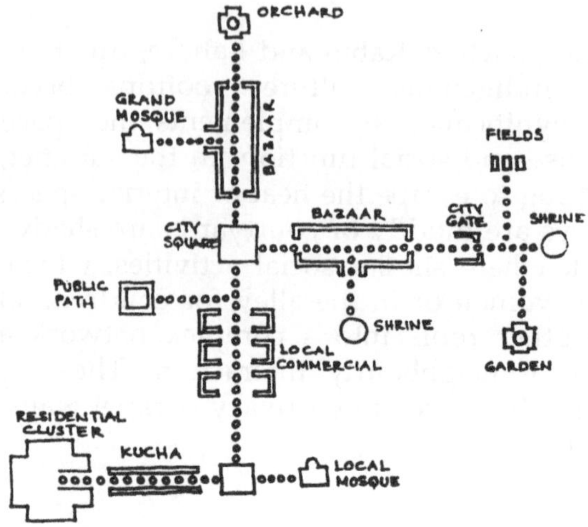

Figure 15.11 Diagram of extroverted spatial progression

Street intersections are nodes where a local shop or a local mosque may occur. A widened street or a pocket in the corner may add to this communal and public function where male adults gather to socialize. The bazaar (*suq*) is perhaps the more active stretch of these public spaces accommodating commercial and artisan activities. Engagement in commerce and artisanship is predominantly a male activity, with the exception of weaving and sewing that are done by women in the houses. Workshops (*karkhana*) and commercial stores/shops (*dukan*) are run by men who dominate the life of the bazaar. It is in the bazaar that the larger social interaction and commercial exchange between different social groups occur. The tea house (*chaikhana*), where men sit around to discuss business, in this respect, plays an additional important role. The intersection of the bazaars, often centrally located, forms the town square (*chouk*). Here major business transactions and social deals are made in the more prestigious shops which cluster around it.

The local mosques and the Friday mosques form a contrasting nucleus for religious and community interchange. In their outreach, they go beyond the family and the clan; they cut across the issues of race and creed by bringing together the larger society (*umma*) fostering its solidarity and brotherhood. They may reinforce the basis of the central government which, in connection with the clergy, regulates larger life. In Kabul, the Pul-e Khishti Mosque and in Lahore the Padshahi Mosque plays this larger role.

Since the houses in the city are tightly built and the courtyards are intimate family spaces, public gardens (*bagh*) foster enjoyment of nature and allow opportunities for picnicking. As such, they play another important role in bringing people together within the network of an extroverted social order. They may be used alternately by male and female populations on different days of the week, or may be separated by different sections to be used by the different population groups. The Babur Gardens in Kabul and the Shalimar Gardens in Lahore are good role models.

Within this larger order, the shrines (*ziarat*) play a similar role. Although pilgrimage to shrines have a religious function for people wanting forgiveness for their sins or mercy for their miseries, at the same time, the spatial settings of shrines give ample opportunity for men and women to mingle in the larger public realm.

Contemporary applications

Understanding the intricacies of these introverted and extroverted socio-morphological orders is a prerequisite for life-giving design and development. Its negligence will cause disruption of the culture that forms the lifeblood of the people and their culture--a culture which has been handed down to them through the centuries nourishing cohesion of their environments. While progress is a necessary element for contemporary life, its implementation should not be enforced at any cost to replace the traditional order. Ideas prevalent in these traditional environments can be reformulated for contemporary application with equal strength. The model briefly discussed here is an attempt to make this transition from the old to the new healthy and peaceful. It makes an effort to reinterpret these ideas for contemporary application in Saudi Arabia.(3)

The model is proposed for the eastern province of Saudi Arabia. It promotes an introverted residential pattern which incorporates the traditional values and virtues of the past with their proven principles of design. It attempts to liberate the designers and users from the current dilemma of conflicts between contemporary and traditional cultural norms. In pragmatic terms, it responds to the contrasting needs of both sexes in the context of a larger life system. The design includes a series of courtyards and private spaces which offer a range of opportunities for social interaction for female members of the community, as well as a variety of controlled spaces for children to play. Modern amenities, such as parking, are carefully located. While the model encourages valuable contact between the families in a modern setting, at the same time it conforms to the continuity of a time-honoured tradition of the introverted spatial order which animates the community and fosters new identities (Figs. 12 and 13).

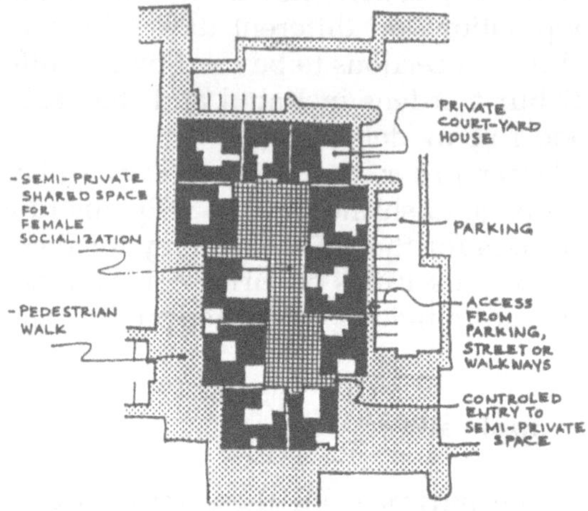

Figure 15.12 Proposed residential model for contemporary application in Saudi Arabia. Cluster plan. (Course: Hilton and Kazimee)

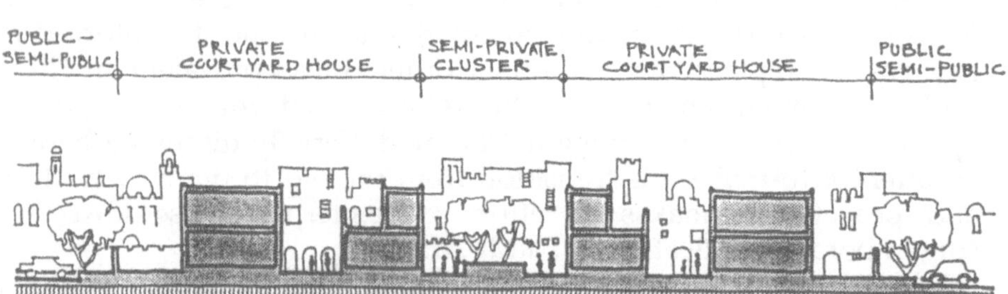

Figure 15.13 Cross-section of the proposed residential model for contemporary application in Saudi Arabia

If change is not to disrupt the fabric of the Islamic city, understanding the introverted and extroverted orders of life and their balanced incorporation in new communities are essential. Change is both unavoidable and necessary. But we have learned that change without continuity brings social disruption and environmental fragmentation. Continuity without change, on the other hand, brings stagnation, which is equally undesirable for developing societies with masses in desparate need for getting out of the cycle of poverty and yearnings for social mobility. The challenge to architects and planners today is how to incorporate change within continuity and continuity within change.

Notes

1. For a discussion of climate and residential patterns for the three cities, see: Stanley Hallet and Rafi Samizay, *Traditional Architecture of Afghanistan*, New York, 1980, pp. 175-194; Parvez Qureshi, *Dwelling Environments, A Comparative Analysis*,Thesis, MIT, 1974, pp. 20-27. Kaizer Talib, *Shelter in Saudi Arabia*, New York, 1984, pp. 83-92.
2. The extremes of summer and winter climate in Kabul have often called for this feature.
3. The model was developed as part of studio work in King Faisal University in Saudi Arabia.

References

The material in this study is based on the author's field research: 1975-80 in Kabul, 1980-1981 in Lahore, 1984-89 in Eastern Saudi Arabia. However, the following have provided the background references.

Hallet, Stanley & Samizay, Rafi (1981), *Traditional Architecture of Afghanistan*, Garland STPM Press, New York.

Hilton & Kazimee (1987), 'Change & Tradition: Towards a Housing Model for the Eastern Province of Saudi Arabia,' *Open House International*, vol. 12, no. 4.

Kazimee, B. A. (1986), 'Traditional Housing Pattern: The Old City of Kabul', *Open House International*, vol. 11, no. 1.

Qureshi, Parvez L. (1979), *Dwelling Environments: A Comparative Analysis*, MIT Thesis, Lahore, Pakistan.
Samizay, Rafi, (1981), *Islamic Architecture in Herat: A Study Towards Conservation*, Government Press, Kabul.
Samizay, Rafi (1990), 'Order and Randomness in Patterns of Islamic Architecture and Urbanism', in Pamir, H., Imamoglu, V. & Teymur, N. (eds.), *Culture, Space, History*, METU, Ankara.
Talib, Kaizer (1984), *Shelter in Saudi Arabia*, Martin's Press, New York.

16 What makes a house a home: The garden?

J. Sime

This paper argues that while the boundaries of a house are its walls, and a home is often viewed in the same way, for many people the area of ground outside a house and yet inside the psychological and social boundary of a property, as defined by a garden fence, hedge, wall or symbolic borderline, is a significant part of their 'home'. The paper suggests that two apparently disparate areas of recent environment and behaviour research and literature, need to be integrated, namely: (a) attachment to house and home and (b) the meaning of gardens. Attention to the dialectic and symbiotic relationship of individuals to the house and garden as a locus of place attachment, is likely to increase understanding of the temporal experience of 'dwelling' (the link between self and physical world). The paper illustrates the psychological and phenomenological significance of home gardens by quotes from an exploratory set of interviews with three generations of women (a grandmother, mother and daughter). Implications for housing research, design education and practice are briefly considered.(1)

Introduction

> 'If a home has not a garden and an old tree, I see not whence the everyday joys of life are to come' (Ch'en Hao-tsu, 1783, translated).

The title of this paper is intended to highlight the lack of attention to the garden in recent environment and behaviour research and literature on the concept of 'home'. The question 'What makes a house a home?' is one which has been posed by Lawrence (Lawrence, 1987a, b) in relation to the design, meaning and use of home interiors. The growing attention to the meaning of the 'home' in other publications has generally concentrated on home as an interior space, associated household activities and the meaning of a 'place' circumscribed by the walls of the house (e.g. Altman and Werner, 1985, Giuliani, 1991). In contrast, it will be argued that a home often extends to the territorial boundary of land characteristically surrounding a house. If anything, the house as home in recent academic literature, is contrasted with the wider neighbourhood beyond the house, almost as if the garden does not exist. In some cases, of course, a garden does not exist or is not significant to the inhabitants. The antithesis of home is arguably 'housing' without gardens or a surrounding personal territory (e.g. high-rise housing). The 'home garden' as a significant part of the home and a physical locale for homemaking and 'dwelling', has been neglected in housing literature.

This lack of attention to the garden contrasts with the recent research and writing about the meaning of gardens (see Francis and Hester, 1990). The literature on people's psychological relationship to the garden provides an increasingly rich source of understanding of the significant role of gardens in people's lives (e.g. Kaplan 1973, 1983). This literature by definition is concerned with the meaning of the garden, rather than the house, and is circumscribed by the perimeter of the house and the boundary of the land considered to belong to the house. The garden is viewed as a psychologically significant locale for a householder's activities and experience. This paper is concerned with the significance of the relationship between the house and garden as the psychological locus or centre of a person's world: the home. In this respect, the boundaries of the garden constitute the territorial and psychological dividing line between the home and the outer world beyond the home. A greater integration and extension of the evolving literature on home and the meaning of gardens, is not only likely to lead to significant insights into the relationship between people and the physical world, but to provide an appropriate basis for social, psychological and cultural principles adopted in the interface between housing design and planning.

Home gardens

While this paper adopts the premise therefore that the garden is a significant part of home as an emotional bond to a place, it is also considered that the landscape of a garden is an intermediary link between the house (used as a generic term for a form of housing most likely to have a garden) and the the outer world. The garden is in many respects a living entity, in contrast to a house which is essentially inanimate. We may assume that while a house has been regarded as a metaphoric extension of a person's self-identity (e.g. the house as body metaphor: see Dovey, 1985), the home garden may be attributed with comparable properties. At the same time it is an inner and outer world.

One of the striking features of the recent research academic literature on 'home' and 'dwelling' is the degree to which many of the evolving concepts could be applied equally to the 'home garden'. The house and home literature provides concepts and approaches which could extend our understanding of the significance of gardens as part of the home and the process of dwelling. Thus, a starting point for considering in what way the provision of a garden and involvement in gardening could 'make a house a home', is to consider how concepts and research approaches being applied to the house as a physical manifestation of home, could be extended to the garden. In seeking to gain a greater understanding of the relationship between people and home gardens, this paper adopts the strategy of drawing on the theoretical and methodological research framework underpinning the study of people's relationship to the house as home.

Lawrence's article: 'What makes a house a home?' emphasises the need to elucidate the cultural, sociodemographic, and psychological dimensions underlying the relationship between people and housing. It is clear that a comprehensive appraisal of home gardens would need to consider the home garden from a similar range of perspectives. For example the garden, as a semi-public or semi-private space around housing, represents an area where social interaction with neighbours potentially takes place. Access to, or through a garden, provides a transition space between the interior of housing and exterior world on a privacy gradient from the most public (street) to the most private rooms. Lawrence discusses this privacy gradient primarily in relation to house interiors (Lawrence, 1987b). In one paper he also includes the garden in an illustrative diagram. In contrasting different housing types, the 'garden' is labelled as a 'collective' space in two examples and as a 'private' space in another example (see Lawrence 1982, figure 3, p.44).

Cultural similarities exist in the widespread provision of gardens next to housing and differences in the specific form of the garden and privacy attained within cultures. For example, there are marked differences in the characteristic demarcation of boundaries between suburban 'home gardens' and street in North America (boundary at the front of a house least demarcated), Britain (low fence) and Japan (high fence). Indeed, there are cultural differences in the degree to which the space in front of a house is perceived as a private space and the degree to which there is a distinction between house and garden (e.g. less distinct in a Japanese than American home). The issue of the degree of privacy desired and afforded by home gardens in different cultures and cultural variations in garden styles (e.g. American and British in contrast to Japanese and Chinese) is discussed in detail elsewhere (see Sime and Kimura 1988, Sime 1990).

Access to home gardens is also related to climatic, ecological, socio-economic and historical factors. This paper is primarily concerned with the psychological significance of a garden as part of the home. Lawrence (1987b) advocates a dual historical perspective or approach to the study of the design, meaning and use of home interiors, namely, the study of the reciprocal relations between a 'macro'-social history of house designs and 'micro'-social history in the form of the residential biographies of individuals. This is an approach which would also seem to be apposite in relation to the study of the design, meaning and use of home gardens. In adopting a biographic approach (considering changes and continuity over a person's life span), this paper is also concerned with the psychological and temporal significance of the home (garden).

Lawrence (1987a) defines 'dwelling' as the link between house and home, 'a process of defining the relationship of individuals to the physical, social and psychological spaces around them'. For another characterisation of 'dwelling' and potential source of understanding the relationship between people and home gardens, it is worth examining recent phenomenological literature concerned with the home. A number of humanistic researchers (e.g. Dovey 1985) have emphasised the notion of 'dwelling'- the process by which people make their place of existence a home. An important assumption, which they and others (e.g. Bachelard 1969) make, is that the 'home' is the place of greatest significance in people's lives. Indeed, it is through personal attachment to the home, as a geographic setting, that people acquire a sense of belonging and purpose which gives meaning to their existence.

Since an important focus of phenomenology is the nature of human experience, the 'lifeworld' and 'being-in-the-world' (Seamon 1982), it is perhaps surprising that greater attention has not been directed to the garden as part of the home and world. The dialectic relationship between inside-outside, order-chaos, home-journey, which is considered to characterise a phenomenology of place experience, attachment, and a home coming into being (Seamon, 1982, Dovey, 1985) is relevant to the home garden. The dialectic movement between house and garden is illustrated by the following verse and a biography of the poet (Brown, 1987):

> 'This little space which scented box encloses
> Is blue with lupins and is sweet with thyme
> My garden all overblown with roses,
> My spirit all is overblown with rhyme,
> As like a drunken honeybee I waver,
> From house to garden and again to house,
> And, undetermined which delight to favour,
> On verse and rose alternatively carouse.'
> (V. Sackville-West, 1921)

It is possible that movement between the house and garden represents movement within an ordered world of the home, as well as a journey to a symbolically distant landscape beyond the protected shelter of a house. It is also possible that movement into the garden and back, is a means of release from the confines of a house, a means of enhancing feelings for a house or finding a different place in oneself (a spiritually uplifting place to go to without moving very far). In this respect, another dialectic, used to characterise a distinction between a house and elsewhere, sacred-profane (Dovey, 1985) can be applied to feelings about a home garden. Eliade (1959) refers to the house as sacred space, at the centre of the cosmos. In keeping with cosmic symbolism, 'settling in a territory is equivalent to founding a world' (Eliade, 1959, p. 47). The garden too has often been regarded in different cultures and religious writings as a sacred place. Indeed, Cooper-Marcus (1987) views what she regards as a current resurgence in gardening as a shift in consciousness, a reaction against modern technology: 'A yearning for the symbolic place of innocent beginnings and blissful homecoming - the Garden of Eden'.

Figure 1 graphically represents the relationship between an individual and home garden in terms of the argument that a garden is part of the home and an 'inner' landscape. As a graphic representation figure 1 could be compared with diagrams of the person-home relationship which seem to concentrate on the house as the locale for activities, personal meanings and place attachment (see Werner, Altman and Oxley, 1985, Dovey, 1985). The inner circle in figure 1 represents an inner personal world in which the garden is considered to be a symbol of the self as much as the house (Cooper-Marcus, 1974). The garden, like the house, provides a fixed point of reference for structuring the world. The garden can be characterised as 'nearby nature' in an urban context (Kaplan, 1983, Kaplan and Kaplan, 1989). It is an inner and outer world. For different individuals a house and/or garden is the centre of our world and a symbiotic locus of place attachment, a reflection of self and world and temporal experience. If the outer world of nature and the daily and seasonal rhythms of time are displaced by settlement (i.e., there is not ready access to the 'natural world'), then the home garden takes on a phenomenological significance as a locus for 'sparing and preserving' and 'heightened environmental encounter' with the natural environment (Seamon 1984). The development of an emotional bond to a home garden can be likened to a 'field of care' (Tuan 1974), a connection to a place that grows over time through everyday dwelling and care.

The forces of nature and the human world are not always benign. A garden in the sense of place attachment (i.e., garden as part of a person's home) might be characterised as:

(a) a personal and private territory;
(b) a protected (cared for) world;
(c) a protective world;
(d) a natural world under control;
(e) a natural world rendered comprehensible.

Francis (1988) lists a number of meanings of the garden on the basis of in-depth ethnographic interviews with people in California and Norway:

The garden as: a setting for creativity, a retreat from the outside world, a private activity, a social place, a connection to one's personal history, a reflection of one's personality, a productive landscape, a symbol of caring and a declining landscape. Underlying many of these meanings are references to the past and present, and aspirations for the future.

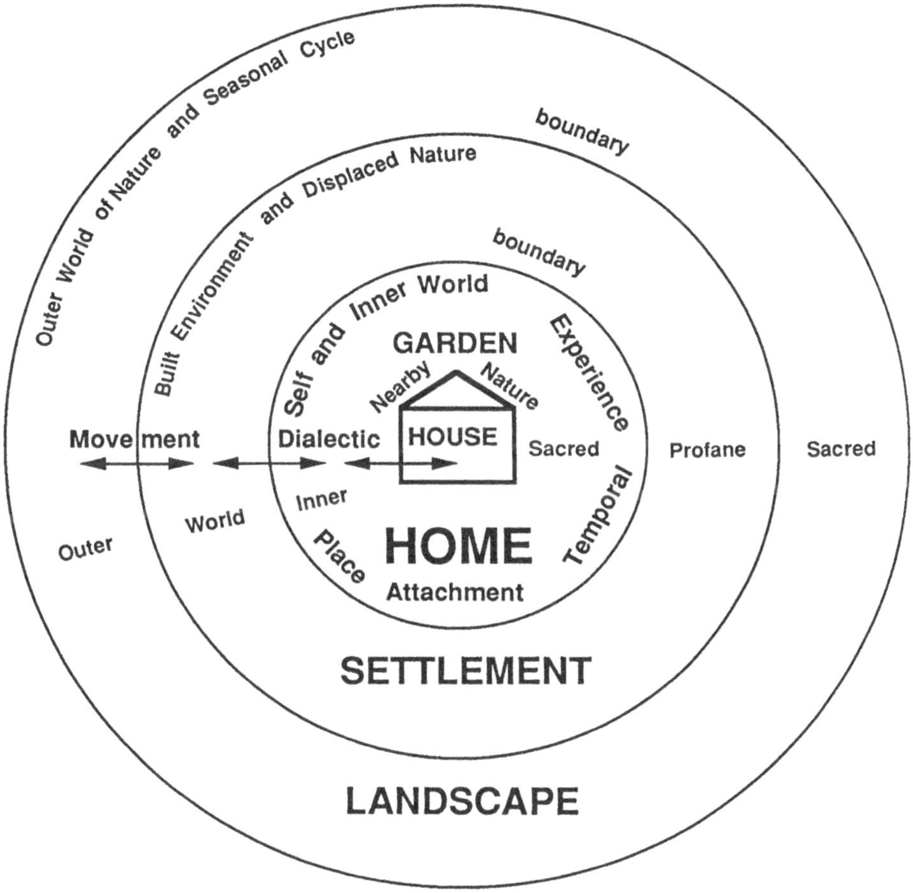

Figure 16.1 **Home as house and garden: the centre of a person's world and a symbiotic locus of**

Place attachment:	emotional bond of person to setting;
Self and world:	maintained by a dialectic within the Home as an inner and outer World (House↔Garden), between Home and outer world (Home ↔ Settlement ↔ Landscape);
Temporal experience:	cyclical time (daily and seasonal birth-death-rebirth), linear time (childhood, adulthood, old age), ecyclical-linear time (past memories, present experience, future aspirations).

A temporal dimension of garden meaning

The remainder of this paper is concerned primarily with exploring the temporal dimension underlying the meaning of home gardens. It is considered that the temporal dimension is likely to be the most important aspect of people's relationship to the physical world of the home garden. While not referring directly to home gardens, Werner, Altman and Oxley (1985) advocate a transactional holistic approach to the study of home, involving three major aspects as a focus of attention: people/psychological processes, environmental properties and temporal qualities. Three factors are considered particularly important in the way people 'invest places with meaning and significance and act in ways that reflect their bondage and linkage with places': appropriation, attachment and identity. They suggest that the linear (past, present, and future) and cyclical, or spiraling, recurrent features of temporal events represent an essential aspect of a comprehensive study of home.

It is not the aim of this paper to debate the similarities and differences between phenomenological and transactional approaches, beyond citing Seamon (1990) who considers a transactional perspective, while putting an emphasis on a unity between people and the environment, 'continues to maintain a subject-object and person-world split' in a way in which the notion of a 'lifeworld' and 'immersion, beginning with bodily self', does not. What is of interest in this paper is the inclusion in the transactional framework of a temporal dimension in studying the relationship between people and the physical environment.

Mugerauer (1985) has hinted at the phenomenological significance of the American 'yard' (equivalent to the English home 'garden') and different zones of the yard, in terms of self, body, and social interaction with neighbours. A phenomenology of home gardens, in terms of the self-world experiential relationship, is yet to be articulated or explored in any detail. One question is in what way it is the protective walls of the house or the boundary of the garden itself which symbolically represents the self and/or body. The habit, body, time-space routines involved in the act of gardening, may actually be a means of getting 'in touch' with the temporal life forces of the physical world and nature. Seamon (1990) suggests that sometimes habitual patterns of gardening may be pursued to the point that 'the garden is so much part of the person, he or she must be in it working '(see also Seamon 1979 p.54).

If the house is a 'symbol' or mirror of the self (Cooper-Marcus 1974), it is possible that the garden is a place where the distinction between self and world dissolves. Adopting the temporal classification suggested by Werner et al (1985) our feelings about a home garden, and the degree to which we feel it is part of the home, can be distinguished in terms of cyclical time (daily and seasonal birth-death-rebirth), linear time (our evolving biographies from childhood to adulthood to old age), cyclical-linear time (past memories, present experience, future aspirations) (see figure 1).

In a series of environmental autobiographical exercises conducted with landscape architecture students, Cooper-Marcus found that two major themes stood out: 'the significance of outdoor environments' and 'the need for hiding places'. While landscape students would be expected to be sensitive to past garden experiences, there is other evidence that a home garden (or yard) represents a particularly significant place in childhood (see Hart 1979) and for this reason is likely to be easier to recall than the interior of houses. For an infant who has little experience of a wider landscape beyond the home, the home garden in many ways is the world.

Similarly, the world of a very elderly person, in terms of ability to move (or journey) may be reduced to the perimeter of a home garden. The geographic world of direct experience in this way expands and contracts at different ends of our life span. As Riley (1988 p. 137) suggests: 'The garden is where we deal with the basic dialectic of our existence, the tension between life and death. Gardens, we all know are about life and ever-promised renewal'. There is the idea that the garden is a source of life and final resting place for the body - burial under the earth: It (the garden) 'cannot be false, for it is both womb and grave and as such a part of the original mother' (Krall 1990). Bachelard (1958) suggests that there is a powerful relationship between the house we were born in and the dream of a house towards which we may strive. Dovey (1985) likens 'home' to a 'mnemonic anchor' which 'enables us to participate between present and past, between experience and memory' (Dovey 1985). Again, these notions make sense not only in relation to our feelings about particular houses, but also home gardens.

There is not space in this paper to consider the temporal aspects of experience, which distinguish a child's relationship to the physical world (present oriented) from an adult (future and progressively past oriented as one gets older), and the temporal symbolism of oriental gardens (e.g. attempts to recreate the mountainous terrain of the immortals in Chinese gardens). In the home gardens of some cultures there is a clearer symbolic represention of distant landscapes beyond human settlement (for example, rocks and sand representing mountains and water in Japanese gardens: see Sime and Kimura (1988). Cultural meanings of home gardens and associated temporal experiences are considered in more detail in Sime (1990).

Biographic continuity over a lifetime: the home garden as reality in a changing world

To illustrate a number of the points made in this paper, and provide an example of a method of interviewing people about the home which could be extended in future studies, some quotes are briefly presented from a series of interviews conducted by the author of this paper in the Spring (April) of 1990. Since it is unrealistic to conduct a series of interviews with one person over their life span, it was decided to interview three women, 3 generations of the same family who live separately: Interviewee A (aged 96), who has one daughter, interviewee B (aged 65), who in turn has one daughter, Interviewee C (aged 32). In a sense, this might be considered as the closest one can get, at one point in time, to interviewing a person at an interval of approximately 30 years (a biographic chain of relationships). The semi-structured interviews were tape recorded (in two cases in their home gardens, in one case in the house next to the garden). Clearly, this is not intended to be a representive sample, and if anything is 'biased' towards one culture (British) and individuals who are particularly sensitive to the garden being part of the home.

Nevertheless, further research may well reveal that the garden is a significant part of the home for many other people.

Each of the interviewees was adamant in open-ended questionning about what a home is, that a garden is a more significant feature of 'home' than a house . Similarities in the interviewees responses were clearer than differences which might be attributable to age and experience.

A: 'I would be very unhappy if I hadn't got a garden, if I had just got houses to look at. I really love the garden. It's peaceful. It's beautiful and of course with the seasons it changes ... I should be lost without a garden ... I wish I could give all day to the garden. I wish that very much ... It's a duty to do the house but its a pleasure to do the garden.'

B: 'I could not live in a house without a garden ... I find lots of jobs in the house an absolute chore, but there's nothing I can think of in the garden which I find a chore.'

C: 'I couldn't live without a garden ... the caravan is just somewhere to live. The garden is created around the caravan. The caravan is not created for the garden. When it comes to a house, the garden is more important than the property.'

Another theme of the interviews, partly prompted by the interviewer's line of questionning later in the interviews, was in terms of a self-other-world relationship . A thinks of her present home garden as her friend and hopes she is a friend to the garden: 'It's company.' When A, B and C were asked what they would like to say to their garden, and if they were the garden it might say to them, the garden seemed to have less of a self-referential personality than the house. C referred to her garden as her own private oasis:

C: 'nobody else can really enter into it, unless you give them the right to . .. You just listen to the wind and the trees, everything going on around you. I mean talking to it spoils it. That's why I like it. I don't have to communicate with it. It's not at all like a person. That's the beauty of it. It has no mental demand over me.'

Another feature of the interviews was the way in which their feelings for a home garden have a temporal dimension . Particularly striking is the future and cyclical oriented nature of the following response from A (the 96 year old): For her the return of Spring is always an occasion for renewed optimism:

A: 'Spring- the first snowdrops .. bring a lot of joy. Life goes on. It's beautiful. I look forward ... with spring there's hope again.'

In many ways a biography of A constitutes a biography of her relationship to a series of eight home gardens as significant mnemonic anchors in her life, starting from her childhood, through her married years, to the 27 years following her husband's death.

The linear and circular biographic thread between early and later gardens, the affinity with and recall of a garden of her childhood, is clear in statements by B:

B: 'I think there is a theme running through my life in which the garden has been absolutely vital.'

B: 'The garden was much more important than the house. I wasn't awfully interested in the house. It was nice , but it wasn't mine and I was their niece and not really their family. I had a lovely room, but it was the garden which was important...'

B: '...The basic important thing for me over the gardens I've really liked is a sense of not only present, but a future and a past. The garden at Lamas Hall had a past, present and obvious future, because even if the family got out, that garden would go on and on and on. It would always be there as a garden. It is no longer in the family and I did go back to see it a couple of years ago and I was sad because it was dilapidated and nobody had really cared for it, but the basic garden was still there. The age long place was still there . The trees were still there. The roses had grown and gone wild, but it didn't seem to matter very much. The vegetable garden was in full swing as usual, still walls around it ...'

B has the same feelings about the garden she now has. She feels she has come home and does not wish to move again. When asked why she regularly goes into her garden to do gardening, B replied: 'It's my idea of reality'.

Conclusion

The degree to which the reader feels that a garden is part of the home is likely to be influenced by personal history. Many of one's deep feelings about a house or garden are at a subconscious level and not always easy to articulate. The view that the interviews conducted are unrepresentative of a wider population might be compounded by revealing that interviewees A, B and C are my grandmother, mother and sister, respectively. Further research should help to reveal how widespread, personal and culturally bound the feelings expressed are. Now that my grandmother has died at the age of 97 (in May 1991), it is interesting in visiting her house and garden to experience that, whilst her house and its contents resonate with a feeling of the past, the garden still lives. The reason I started writing about 'home gardens' in the past few years is that I have instinctively begun to be drawn towards 'my' home garden as a source of solace, as a restorative experience (see Kaplan 1973) in a search for meaning beyond my house. It seems worth asking whether the close affinity a child may have with the physical world of a garden, may be lost in adult years and increasingly sought later in life.

A rich source of phenomenological information on home gardens are biographies and autobiographies of people who have felt closely attached to their gardens (Sime 1990). Further research using in-depth biographic interviewing (particularly of a cross-cultural kind) is likely to extend our understanding of people's relation to home gardens. The provision of a home garden seems particularly important for children and elderly people. Surveys of residents suggest that immediate private or semi-private outdoor spaces are a particularly important corollary of housing satisfaction (see Cooper-Marcus and Sarkissan 1986). Mass urban high-rise housing schemes with impersonal public spaces have often been a response to the principle that everyone should have a roof over their heads. It is worth asking whether every home unit should be required to have an adjacent territorial space which people can modify, change and make part of their home. Private gardens should as far as possible have primacy over public spaces. Architectural and Planning students need to be alerted to their own environmental histories and associated preferences, as well as the sensitivities of users. The temporal significance of home gardens suggests a more humble role for the landscape design professional than a master planner, one of a facilitator and supporter of people's involvement in their gardens.

Deprivation of a home garden is at best experienced as a mild or temporary inconvenience; at worst it fosters a pervasive form of environmental anomie and personal 'dislocation': a life-world without a centre and devoid of feeling. For an increasing number of people, concerned about ecological damage to the world, the home garden has significance as an intimate landscape. Through gardening an attitude of caring for a patch of land is fostered. The argument in this paper has been that, for those who are custodians of a home garden, it is the garden which makes a house a home.

Notes

1. I would like to thank Irwin Altman, Mark Francis and David Seamon for comments on a more lengthy unpublished manuscript on Home Gardens (Sime 1990) from which some of the material in this paper is drawn.

References

Altman, I. & Werner, C. (eds.) (1985), *Home Environments*, Plenum, New York.

Bachelard, G. (1969), *The Poetics of Space*, Beacon Press, Boston.

Brown, J. (1987), *Vita's Other World: A Gardening Biography of V. Sackville-West*, Penguin Books, Harmondsworth.

Cooper, C. (1974), *The house as symbol of the self, in Designing for Human Behaviour*, J. Lang, C. Burnett, W. Moleski and D. Vachon (eds.), Dowden, Hutchinson and Ross, Stroudsberg, Penn.

Cooper Marcus, C. (1978), 'Remembrance of landscapes past', *Landscape*, vol. 22, no. 3, pp. 35-43.

Cooper Marcus, C. (1987), 'The garden as metaphor', in Francis, M. and Hester, R.T. (eds.), *op. cit.*

Cooper Marcus, C. & Sarkissan, W. (1986), *Housing as if People Mattered: Site Design Guidelines for Medium-density Family Housing*, University of California Press, Berkeley.

Dovey, K. (1985), 'Home and homelessness', in Altman, I. and Werner, C.M. (eds.), *op. cit.*

Eliade, M. (1959), *The Sacred and the Profane: The nature of religion*, Harcourt Brace and World, Chicago.

Francis, M. (1988), 'Gardens in the mind and in the heart' in van Hoogdalem, H., Prak, N.L., van der Voordt, T.J.M. and van Wegen, H.B.R. (eds.), *Looking Back to the Future,* IAPS 10/1988 Proceedings, Vol. 2, Delft University Press, Delft.

Francis, M. & Hester, R.T. (1987), (eds.), *The Meaning of Gardens,* MIT Press, Cambridge, Mass. and London.

Giuliani, M.V. (1991), 'Towards an analysis of mental representations of attachment to the home', *Journal of Architectural and Planning Research,* vol. 8, no. 2, pp. 133-146.

Hart, R. (1978), *Children's Experience of Place,* Irvington, New York.

Kaplan, R. (1973), 'Some psychological benefits of gardening', Environment and Behavior, vol. 5, no. 2, pp. 145-162.

Kaplan, R. (1983), 'The role of nature in the urban context', in *Behaviour and the Natural Environment,* Altman, I. and Wohlwill, J.F. (eds.), Plenum, New York.

Kaplan, R. & Kaplan, S. (1989), *The Experience of Nature: A psychological perspective,* Cambridge University Press, Cambridge.

Krall, F.R. (1990), 'Spring, Summer, Fall and Winter', In Francis, M. and Hester, R.T. (eds.), *op. cit*

Lawrence, R.J. (1982), 'A psychological-spatial approach to architectural design and research', *Journal of Environmental Psychology,* vol. 2, no. 1, pp. 37-51.

Lawrence, R.J. (1987a), *Housing, Dwellings and Homes: Design Theory,Research and Practice,* Wiley, Chichester.

Lawrence, R.J. (1987b), 'What makes a house a home?', *Environment and Behaviour,* vol. 19, no. 2, pp. 154-168.

Mugerauer, R. (1985), 'Midwestern yards', *Places,* vol. 2, no. 2, pp. 31-37.

Riley, R.B. (1988), 'From sacred grove to disney world: the search for garden meaning', *Landscape Journal,* vol. 7, no. 2, pp. 136-147.

Sackville-West, V. (1921), 'Sonnet', Long Barn, 1917, in Sackville-West, *Orchard and Vineyard,* John Lane, London.

Seamon, D. (1979), *A Geography of the Lifeworld: Movement, Rest and Encounter,* Croom Helm, London.

Seamon, D. (1982), 'The phenomenological contribution to environmental psychology', *Journal of Environmental Psychology,* vol. 2, no. 2, pp. 119-140.

Seamon, D. (1984), 'Emotional experience of the environment', *American Behavioural Scientist,* vol. 27, no. 6, pp. 757-770.

Seamon, D. (1990), Personal Communication.

Sime, J.D. (1986), 'Creating places or designing spaces?', *Journal of Environmental Psychology* , vol. 6, no. 2, pp. 49-63.

Sime, J.D. (1990), *Home gardens, place attachment and the experience of time*, unpublished manuscript (being revised).

Sime, J.D. & Kimura, M. (1988), 'Home gardens: attachment to the natural environment and the experience of time from a Western and Japanese perspective', in Lawrence, D., Habe, R., Hacker, A. and Sherrod, D. (eds.), *People's Needs/Planet Management Paths to Co-existence* , Proceedings of 19th Annual EDRA Conference, Pomona, California, 11-15 May, EDRA, Washington D.C.

Tuan, Y.F. (1974), *Topophilia: A study of environmental perceptions, attitudes and values*, Prentice Hall, Englewood Cliffs, N. J.

Werner, C.M., Altman, I. & Oxley, D. (1985), 'Temporal aspects of homes: a transactional perspective' in Altman, I. and Werner, C.M.

17 Architectural education and architectural careers: The views of students in three countries

M. Symes

Introduction

The way architects approach design problems is partly conditioned by the education they have received. Since the systems of architectural education in different countries vary quite considerably, one can anticipate that students' views on their future careers will vary as well. As architectural practice becomes increasingly international in its scope and organisation, this variation will take on a practical as well as an academic meaning. To study this question considerable methodological problems arise: not only must questionnaires be translated and researchers trained but contextual factors which may affect the interpretation of results must somehow be addressed.

A brief chapter such as this one can do no more than act as an illustrated introduction to this topic and to some of the issues it raises. The chapter is based on information gathered when the principal author, who had previously edited a collection of papers on architectural education which included papers on the views of students in Britain and Israel, visited Japan. A questionnaire was devised, using questions drawn from studies reported in the earlier collection, translated, and given by Japanese collaborators to students in two of the leading Japanese University schools. The questions covered students' interests, their ideas about the work they were asked to undertake in their studies, and their career expectations. Some emphasis was laid on the different nationalities' attitudes towards the technical aspects of architectural design. The responses obtained to this questionnaire are then compared with responses obtained in the earlier studies. Although the conditions under which this work was undertaken hardly allow for the drawing of statistically significant conclusions, it seems clear that this work could usefully be followed up in future in more extended studies.

Some issues in architectural education

In a recent discussion of research on architectural education, the princpal author suggested that the human context of a school influenced the transmission of knowledge within it.(Symes, 1989). The treatment of theoretical issues and the preparation of the school's students for the world of practice were structured by the human relationships set up within the school. The educational system could be looked at as a network of communications. Its functions would include those of making students' interests relevant to staff, and staff interests relevant to students. Again, different emphases in the communication systems of particular schools (for example the promotion or discouragement of scientific approaches to design problem-solving) could lead the staff to rather different ways of attempting to transform student interests into professional capabilities. International comparisons between the attitudes of students in the schools of different countries would be likely to suggest interesting differences between the processes concerned.

One of the issues for cross-cultural comparison is indeed whether other countries' systems of architectural education bring scientific and technical knowledge closer to the centre of their students' area of concern and this is one of the features of students' attitudes to their education which is investigated in this chapter. Given the popularly held view that Japanese companies dominate the markets in technology in Western European countries, one might be forgiven for expecting to find a strong technological orientation amongst those Japanese students preparing to enter their architectural profession.

Student attitudes in Britain and Israel

One of the studies mentioned was carried out in Britain. In it Mikellides (1989) used a standard psychological test (the interest-profile) with a number of cohorts of architectural students entering the Oxford Polytechnic. He found their strongest interest to lie with aesthetics. This may be unsurprising (unless one were to consider architecture to be no more than building well) but it does contrast with the second strongest interest which was outdoor activity. Only weakly represented were literary, musical, practical and (sadly, perhaps - or perhaps not!) persuasive interests. Mechanical, computational and scientific interests seem not to have figured in the first preferences of the Oxford sample. If British architectural profession were looking for technologists, it would find only reluctant heroes here.

In another study, Tzamir and Churchman (1989) developed their own questionnaire to investigate the sources of knowledge used by Israeli students in the middle of their course at Haifa Technion, and relate them to, inter alia, the design facets they felt they were addressing in their project-work. The authors reported that these students used their own feelings and personal experiences to guide their work. They ignored objective or abstract knowledge but did pay attention to the opinions of their teachers. This knowledge was applied to the achievement of user experiences, functionality and environmental quality in the students' designs. Less attention was paid to symbolic and moral values. The technological factors were hardly considered at all, a lack of interest similar perhaps to those of the British beginners.

Tzamir and Churchman also asked their students whose position they would adopt if there were a conflict between their own and that of a client when they were in practice. They were inclined to respect client views regarding functional aspects af a design but to wish to stay with their own views on aesthetics. The Israeli authors regretted their students' unwillingness to pay attention to objective sources of information. In doing so they may also have been regretting the fact that clients' views of their needs may be just as personal as architects' views of aesthetics. It would seem to the present author that Israeli educational system they studied may have as much difficulty in coping with the transmission of social-scientific insights as it, and the British one, may have with the transmission of technical information.

The Japanese system of architectural education

Japanese schools of architecture are normally located in the Engineering Faculty of their University. They are thus implicitly technological in their orientation. Students must gain entry to higher education in direct competition with their peers who wish to pursue a career in applied science and technology. In the first year and a half of their university course they will normally take the same subjects and be judged by the same criteria. Once the architectural students have been separated out, they are still likely to be taught by staff with a specialisation in technological aspects of the subject. Japanese professors are expected to establish research 'laboratories' not unlike those of other teachers in their faculty and of course the emphasis is almost always on applied science. Students proceeding beyond the first degree stage, to a taught Masters' are encouraged, but not always willing, to specialise in the same way as their elders.

If conditions in the educational sector seem more conducive to a scientifically oriented set of interests among architectural students than they are in the West, conditions in practice might be thought to provide a strong rationale for these arrangements. Dodd (1970), a British architect who worked for some years in Japan, explained how:

> Practical work in offices allows for all kinds of degrees of specialisation....it is only by the decision of the individual that he or she concentrates, on graduation, on architecture, advanced engineering, or construction site supervision.

The 'Architects' Law' provides for a common qualifying examination for membership of a profession which in Britain and elsewhere in the West is more commonly subdivided. Structural engineering, environmental engineering and town planning are normally considered as specialisations within architecture in Japan, rather than as separate fields. As a result, a country which has roughly twice the population of the United Kingdom has almost eight times as many registered architects![(1)] If the prospect of a career provided all the motivation required for students to develop an interest in the application of technical knowledge to architectural production, then the vast majority of Japanese architectural students would be strongly oriented towards just that.[(2)]

Responses to a questionnaire

A short questionnaire was constructed by collating some of the questions reported in the studies mentioned above and translated into Japanese. In addition a question was included concerning students' preferred career destinations. All the students in the third year of their degree course in two Japanese university departments of architecture were asked to complete it and in each place about half the students agreed to do so. 60 responses were obtained, 24 from Tokyo and 36 from Kyoto. As numbers were small, and there seemed little difference between the responses obtained from the two schools, they have been aggregated. As the original questions came from different studies, the comparisons which could be made were sometimes with British responses and sometimes with those from Israel.

Interests

The question asked for a ranking of twelve possible areas of interest. Six categories had accounted for 89.5% of first choice interests in the Oxford study and the same six categories accounted for 87.3% of Japanese first choices. The order of popularity is roughly the same, although the Japanese consider themselves less literary and more practical, but the spread of responses is very different. The Japanese are less strongly focussed on aesthetic interests, a good proportion choosing other interests first. The suggestion that this might be a result of their engineering faculty background is reinforced when it is observed that the next most popular choice (i.e. the seventh, made by a further 5%) is Computational. In Mikkelides' tables for Oxford architecture students this interest is the least liked.

	Japanese	**Oxford**
Aesthetic	30.0	69.0
Outdoor	20.0	11.0
Literary	6.7	2.5
Musical	11.7	3.5
Practical	15.0	3.5
Persuasive	5.0	0.0

Table 17.1 First choices of interest, (%)

Sources of knowledge

The question specified 8 possible sources of knowledge students might use in their designs and offered the possibility of answering 'a great deal','partially' or 'not at all' for each one. The Japanese students admit to using more of these sources of knowledge to a greater extent but their greatest reliance (on personal feelings) is a little stronger than the Israeli students reliance on personal rational formulations. The Japanese are more willing to use empirical research and to refer to projects seen. These tendencies seem quite consistent with the engineering design context of architectural education in Japan.

	Japanese	Haifa
Architectural style	13.3	4.0
Theoretical approaches	25.0	6.0
Empirical research	33.3	8.0
Opinions of non-professionals	11.7	2.0
Specific projects seen	33.3	9.0
Teachers instructions	31.7	26.0
Personal feelings and experience	81.7	69.0
Personal rational formulations	46.7	80.0

Table 17.2 Sources of knowledge used a great deal, (%)

Design facets

Here students were given a list of nine facets they might address in their designs and asked to answer in the same way as they had for the question on sources of knowledge. On two facets which were addressed by some of the Israelis (economic cost and energy and maintenance) the Japanese gave no response at this level.On two other facets (symbolic messages and environmental quality), the Japanese response was more enthusiastic than that received in Israel. For the other four facets it was less enthusiastic. It seems that the Japanese students focus more narrowly on some parts of the design task than do their Western peers: a tendency at odds both with the breadth of interest expressed in their response to the earlier question concerning the sources of knowledge they use and, somewhat surprisingly, with much of their technological background.

	Japanese	Haifa
Economic cost	0.0	8.0
Energy and maintenance	0.0	21.0
Technology	5.0	27.0
Moral values	25.0	39.0
Symbolic messages	48.3	37.0
Aesthetics	51.7	73.0
Environmental quality	81.7	78.0
Functionality	56.7	84.0
User experience	66.7	96.0

Table 17.3 Design facets addressed a great deal, (%)

Relationship between sources of knowledge and design facets

The relationship between the somewhat surprisingly different answers given to these two questions by Japanese students was explored by means of a number of cross-tabulations. These suggested that two particular sources of knowledge (Teachers' instructions and Personal feelings) and four of the design facets which could be addressed (Symbolic messages, Aesthetics, Environmental quality and Functionality) were related to each other. A particularly strong relationship was indicated between the second of these sources of knowledge and the students' propensity to address environmental quality in their designs. A large number of the Japanese respondents say they address the quality facet : they are also approximately twice as likely to say they do so if they use their personal feelings to guide them as they are if they look to their teachers for help. They might be thought of as taking up these issues if they are rejecting the institution's values.

Symbols	no yes	9 10	22 19	25 24	6 5
Aesthetics	no yes	8 11	21 20	23 26	6 5
Environment	no yes	10 19	1 30	10 39	1 10
Function	no yes	6 13	20 21	22 27	4 7
	yes	no Teacher	yes	no Personal	

Table 17.4 Facets addressed a great deal against sources

Conflict situations

The ambiguous feelings Japanese students may have towards their personal feelings about design issues appeared again when they were asked which of two positions they would adopt if faced with a conflict with their client. Japanese respondents are much more likely to take the client's side on the questions of cost and functionality than are Israelis. They are much less likely to side with the client on moral issues or aesthetics. It might be thought that they have greater self-confidence (or less humility) on the aspects of design for which their academic background prepares them least.

	Japanese		Haifa	
	Client's	Own	Client's	Own
Functionality	23.3	23.3	8.0	66.0
Cost	45.0	1.7	10.0	47.0
User experience	28.3	36.6	18.0	31.0
Moral values	1.7	48.3	38.0	6.0
Aesthetics	73.3	34.0	32.0	

Table 17.5 Preferred position in conflict situations, (%)

Careers

The Japanese students were also asked a question which had not been put to the groups surveyed elsewhere. This sought their ranking of potential types of employer. For the majority, their choice falls on the independent design firm. Given the structure of their industry, this is unlikely to be the normal outcome.

Independent design firm	51.7
Construction company	21.7
Another type of company	8.3
Government department	3.3
School of architecture	13.3

Table 17.6 First choices of career, (%)

Conclusion

The authors of the earlier studies on which the questions asked here were based argued, firstly, that architects' interests are broad enough to fit them for a wide range of careers outside architecture, and, secondly, that architectural education should develop more effective methods of training in the use of 'external, objective information'. The Japanese system seems designed to meet both these needs: it expects students of architecture to come to their studies with a broad background in the applied sciences and it provides a wide range of career outlets for them in construction and building management. This study of the students' own ideas about their work suggests however that they hold a rather different view of their future careers and that they rely surprisingly strongly on their personal feelings in undertaking the work required of them on their course. The educational experiences they have had may have affected their reported interests and the scope of knowledge they say they use in addressing design projects but it does not appear to affect their perception of the issues they attempt to address, or their image of their own future role. Contrary to some ideas held in the West (and perhaps even in the East: see Dore, 1986) teachers instructions do not count for a great deal. If it can be suggested that Japanese students form their own views on what they should be trying to do, it may be concluded they may move further intellectually from the structures of thought encouraged by their seniors than their Western counterparts, who often learn in a less technologically oriented environment. Again, the conditions of their later employment , usually in conglomerate organisations, may come as something of a shock, but at least while they study they seem to try to determine some of their own priorities. It may be that some future research will investigate the way in which this happens.

It appears from this study that Japanese students may have broader scientific interests than their Western counterparts but nonetheless use their personal feelings more often in approaching design projects. Surprisingly, perhaps, their teachers' influence does not seem to determine these attitudes. A question not asked in the earlier studies shows that Japanese students'career preferences lie with independent design practice but background studies of the profession in that country suggest that this is unrealistic for most of them. Further comparisons between the attitudes of architectural students in Japan and those in the West might usefully focus on the way in which attitudes towards the technological determinants of design change during the students' time in school and again when they leave. In this way we may learn more of the influence of their educational system on the growth of career expectations.

Notes

1. In March 1990 there were 223,983 first-class architects registered in Japan. There were also 504,666 second-class architects, who have received a less sophisticated training and are restricted in the functions they can perform. Wooden-building architects, who seem more like tradesmen than professionals in Western terms, numbered 11,609, but they should not be confused with carpenters, who are counted quite separately and inherit the great tradition of Japanese vernacular building. These figures were kindly provided for me by Ryoichi Shimada, whose speciality is the study of the Japanese architectural profession.
2. 12,293 graduated from 114 courses in 1984. Since a number of these courses are in home economics, it is also useful to know that 995 graduated from 83 graduate courses in architecture in the same year. Post-graduate study is however not a requirement for registration so direct parallels with Western

educational structures are difficult to establish. This information was kindly provided by Takashi Takahashi.

References

Dodd, J. (1970), 'The Architect in Japan', *Journal of the Royal Institue of British Architects*, vol. 77, no. 11, pp. 499-504.

Dore, R. (1986), 'Where will the Japanese Nobel prize winners come from?', *Science and Public Policy*, vol. 11, no. 6, pp. 347-361.

Mikellides, B. (1989), 'Some Questions Concerning the Interest-Profiles of Prospective Architects', *Journal of Architectural and Planning Research*, vol. 6, no. 3, pp. 240-250.

Symes, M. (1989), 'Research on the Human Problems of Architectural Education: an Introduction', *Journal of Architectural and Planning Research*, vol. 6, no. 3, pp. 181-185.

Tzamir, Y. & Churchman, A. (1989), 'An Ethical Perspective on Architectural Education', *Journal of Architectural and Planning Research*, vol. 6, no. 3, pp. 227-239.

18 Housing projects designed by students of architecture

H.L. Hentila

Motto: Who's afraid of the Big Bad Wolf?

Background and introduction

The values that guide problem solving in design may be understood by studying housing projects designed by architecture students. The discussion is in three parts: the individual starting point of each student, decisions made during the design process, and interpretation of the projects.

Interaction between people and their physical surroundings is most intensive in their place of residence. This is where people spend a lot of their time: for some it is here 'living' really takes place. That is why it is interesting to consider the value basis upon which designers make their decisions when designing housing.

Compared to professionally realized projects, students tend to design more personally. They are not affected so much by the codes, clients, contractors and other such factors relating to practice. Therefore it might be more possible to discover ideals and other sources of inspiration in the design of students than in the solutions of hard boiled practitioners.

I refer in this paper to my experiences during the four years as an assistant teacher at the university of Oulu, Department of Architecture (Contemporary Architecture), in housing and design. The concept of housing is restricted in this study to small scale housing (single person flats, leisure time cottages, and groups of dwellings arranged around a central courtyard).

Starting point

The exercises within contemporary housing are intended as an introduction to composition and the planning of functions associated with daily or leisure time living. When each single student begins to sketch the project, some factors already exist that will affect the final result.

- deep-rooted personal experiences of housing and its meaning for people;[(1)]
- practical experience of housing design (e.g. age, working experience, knowledge of construction);
- reasons to take up careers as architects;[(2)]
- attitudes on the role of the architect.[(3)]

Design process

When design process is considered as an heuristic search within a problem space the decisions made are value-based. An inexperienced designer (student) uses the same kind of human problem solving methods as an older designer (trial and error, induction, deduction). Only his/her design tactics do not yet allow as long decision chains - one has to learn by experience.

There are many decisions (both unconscious and conscious) to make while designing - for example finding a problem to be solved from design context is not always readily done. Values do control the hierarchy between different decisions. Some of the problems students struggle to solve are:

- image of design;[(4)]
- form or function - which should come first, or can some kind of balance exist;
- use of a prototype (vernacular housing, Laplander's hut, classical atrium) or an abstract form (circle, triangle).

The very first idea is often an analogy (nature: shell; object: boat) or the student is predetermined on some architectural element (light above, veranda, big country kitchen).

When sketching further solutions are tested against the opinions of other students and teachers, existing requirements (design program, codes), published examples - and the most important fact - against the student's own growing knowledge and skills.

In the project studio the student becomes acquainted with the silent knowledge of the profession by listening to the teachers' points of view. In Finland almost everyone acting as an assistant in housing earns his/her living also as a practising architect.

The relationship of housing research and the projects done is weak. There are two main reasons for this:

- not too much research, which can be applied by architects, is done within the housing branch;
- the professional attitude of architects is that his or her own knowledge achieved in practice is good enough.

Results

When interpreting the student projects one has to remember that the skill of presentation varies and the ideas are not necessarily clearly presented. To receive a complete picture of the students' projects one really needs to follow them throughout the design process.

However, some architectural elements are often represented in the housing projects. The importance of playing with space reflects a modernistic attitude (Corbusier). The artist's atelier or a study room, added to a house is a characteristic image of the architect's own way of life. A traditional ethnic feature in Finland is the sauna (many of the students want to have a sauna even in a single person's tiny flat of 32-45 m^2). Primitive elements, such as fire (fireplace, positive image of gathering together) or water (leisure time cottage) seem to be constant sources of inspiration.

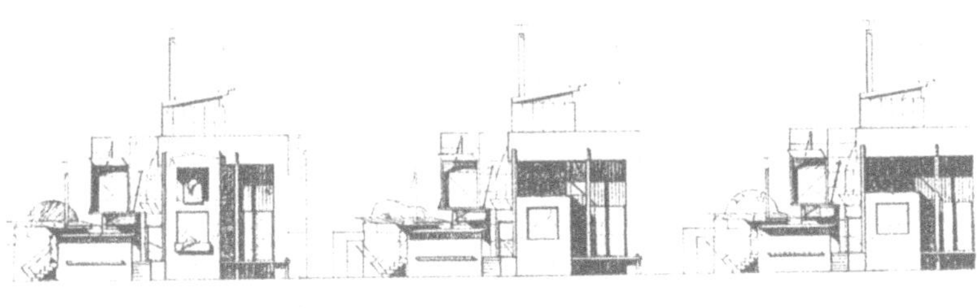

Figure 18.1 Kyösti Meinilä: a detached house. 2nd year exercise in dwelling house design. The task was to design a group of terraced, semidetached or detached houses for a freely adaptable environment

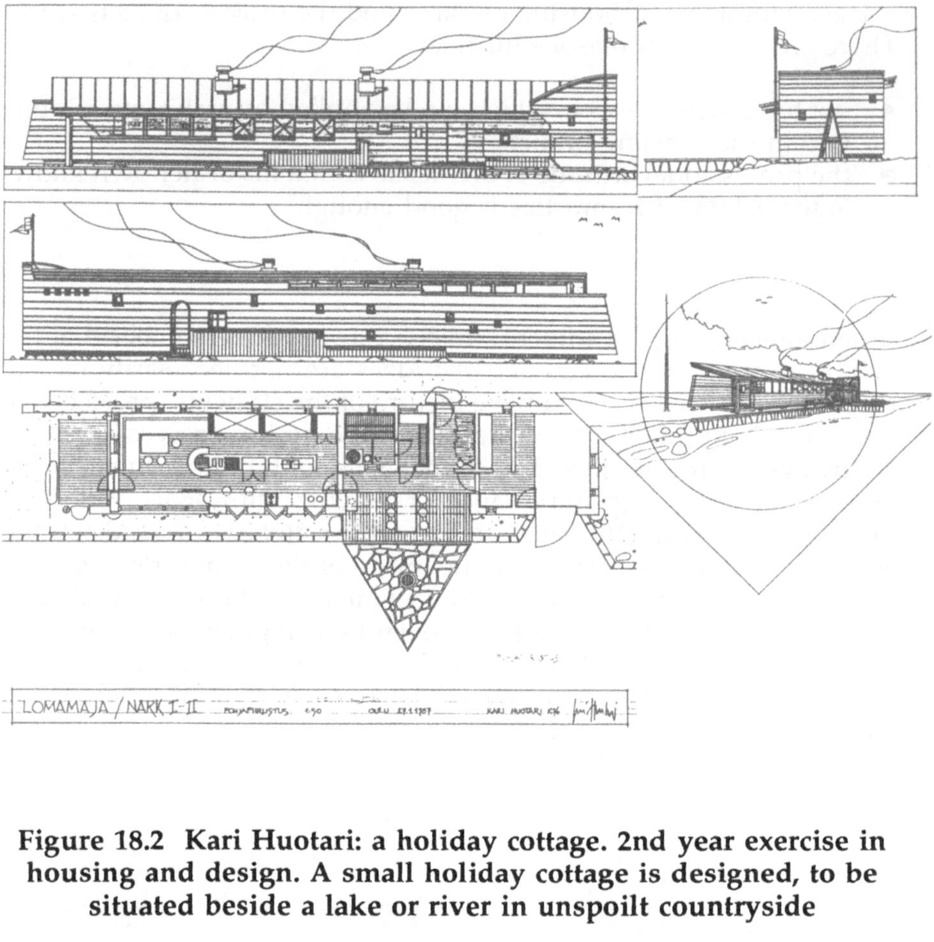

Figure 18.2 Kari Huotari: a holiday cottage. 2nd year exercise in housing and design. A small holiday cottage is designed, to be situated beside a lake or river in unspoilt countryside

Figure 18.3 Kari Kehus: a holiday cottage. 2nd year exercise in housing and design

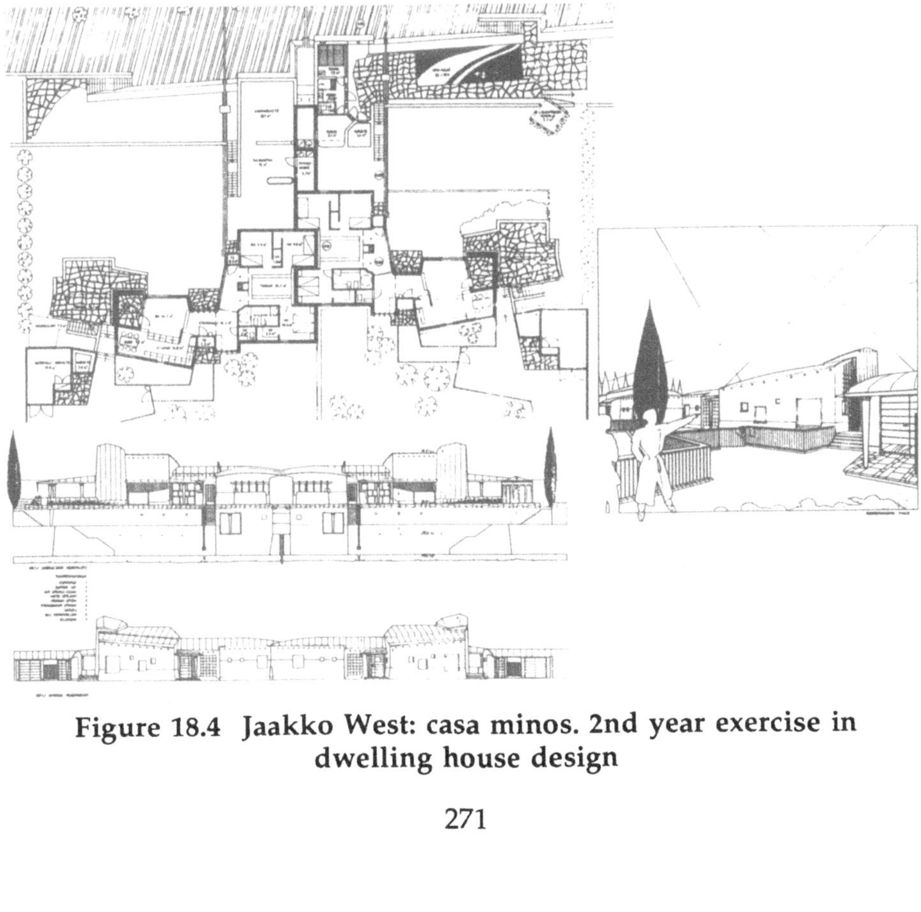

Figure 18.4 Jaakko West: casa minos. 2nd year exercise in dwelling house design

Figure 18.5 Juha Kylliö: a holiday cottage. 2nd year exercise in housing and design

Besides these physical facts there are to be found different design philosophies reflecting the intellectual values. For example students can find Steiner's philosophical principles (forms, colours, community) so important when designing housing that functional necessities are ignored.

Classification of different design philosophies and intellectual values guiding decisions could be:

- theoretic (ecology, classicism);
- realistic (practical, economical);
- artistic (object, sculpture, heroistic, self expressive);
- technologic (laws, structure, systems);
- fashionable (up-to-date);
- anarchistic (neglecting everything);
- imaginary (searching models from romantized history, Disneyland).

Epilogue

What has this to do with the three little pigs and the Big Bad Wolf?

Within certain limits and circumstances (threat from the Wolf) there might be only few ways to design a house. Nowadays the operative field is so wide that one has to both figure out the problems and make solutions in an informaton chaos. Education of an architect should give subjective capability to handle design action but also an open mind for information (research, users opinions, other consults) outside ones own experiences. Once capable of connecting both requirements with the context of design, there is no longer any need to be afraid of any kind of Big Bad Wolves.

Notes

1. Andersson & Olsson (1986) have been using the psychoanalytical method to find a connection between the choice made by adults over their residence and environment wherein to grow up. One could think that a designer also uses the positive elements of his or her childhood environment in housing designs.
2. In her research on the world view of Finnish architects, Komulainen (1985) reported that some had wanted to be architects, because they wanted to build better environment. Some had wanted to use their creativity in their profession, and some had just wanted to get a good salary and a respectable profession.
3. Ödmann (1986) has researched the Swedish students of architecture. She discussed the point that attitudes on the role of the architect varied from the traditional practitioner to the idealistic reformer.
4. Image of design goals can be very vague at the beginning of the studies. Students do not have schemes how to design and what to do. Usual comment 'I did not invent anything new' reveals that students think innovation and creativity is expected.
5. Illustrations used in this book are taken from publications of the Department of Architecture and are therefore of high quality - both in presentation and architecture.
6. The phrase 'Architecture is not only a profession - it is a way of life' is presented during the first lectures.

References

Andersson, T. & Olsson, E. (1986), *Hitta hem. Sambandet mellan vuxnas bostadsval och deras upvö xtmiljvö.* (Find your wayhome.The relationship between choice of dwelling as an adult and the previous childhood environment.) Rapport 4093, Formlrä, KTH, Stockholm.

Komulainen, T. (1985), *Arkkitehdin ammatti ja maailmankuva.* (The Architec.t's Profession and World View.) Suomen Teknillinen Seura, Helsinki.
Odmann, E. (1986), *Bakom fasaden - om arkitektelevers kunskaper och vrderingar.* (Behind the Facade. The Knowledge and Values of Architecture Students.) Liber, Stockholm.

Illustrations

Exercises in Flight (1987) Exercises produced at the Department of Architecture in Oulu 1983-1987. Architectural Exhibition 1987, University of Oulu, AO C 26.

University of Oulu. Department of Architecture. (1989) Autumn 1987-Spring 1988. AO C 28, Oulu.

Contributors

Iris Aravot
Faculty of Architecture and Town Planning Technion ITT
HAIFA 32000, ISRAEL

Iris Aravot is Lecturer at the Faculty of Architecture and Town Planning, Technion I.I.T., Haifa, Israel. She received her B.Arch, MSc in Architecture and DSc in Theory of Architectural Knowledge from the Faculty of Architecture and Town Planning, Technion. Additional Studies: Department of Philosophy, Haifa University, Israel and the Architectural Association Graduate School, London. Her current research deals mostly with approaches to urban design.

David N Benjamin
Norwegian Institute of Technology, Division for Architecture
7034 Trondheim, NORWAY

David N Benjamin is a member of The Norwegian Institute of Architects; a PhD candidate at The Norwegian Institute of Technology; M.Arch. 1982, Washington University, St. Louis, USA.

Yvonne Bernard
CNRS, Paris, FRANCE

Yvonne Bernard is research scientist in the Institute of Psychology of University PARIS V and National Council of Scientific research. Her research includes environmental psychology and more specifically housing research.

Edwin S. Brierley
School of the Built Environment, Department of Architecture, De Montfort University
PO Box 143, LEICESTER, LE1 9BH, GREAT BRITAIN.

Edwin S. Brierley is a Senior Lecturer at the Department of Architecture, De Muntfort University. He has held both a SSRC Research Fellowship and a Leverhulme Faculty Fellowship. Research work has been supported by both the RIBA and the Michael Ventris Memorial Fund.

Marjorie Bulos and Waheed Chaker
School of Land Management and Urban Policy, South Bank University
Wandsworth Road, LONDON, SW8 2JZ, GREAT BRITAIN.

Marjorie Bulos teaches research methods and sociology at South Bank University. Research interests and activities in the past two years have been focused on exploring a variety of aspects of homeworking.

Waheed Chaker is a Lecturer in Urban Studies at South Bank University currently doing research into the urban development process.

M Vittoria Giuliani
Istituto di Psicologia del C.N.R.,
Viale Marx 15, 1-00137
ROMA, ITALY.

Gilles Barbey
Ecole Polytechnique Federale,
11 bd. de Grancy, CH-1006
Lausanne, SWITZERLAND.

M Vittoria Giuliani is senior researcher at the Institute of Psychology of the Italian National Research Council (C.N.R.) in Rome. She is currently involved in several research projects, including the study of the residential experience in urban environment, and the relationship between attachment to home and life cycle. She is presently member of the board of IAPS.

Gilles Barbey has practised as an architect in Switzerland and abroad. He currently teaches at the Polytechnic of Lausanne. His research work is focused on housing, adopting a perspective both historical and sociopsychological, including the social history of housing and the phenomenological analysis of home.

Helka-Liisa Hentila

M.Arch., Licentiate of Technology (Univ. of Oulu). Guest researcher at Royal Institute of Technology (The Department of Form and Environment of the School of Architecture). Stockholm, Sweden. Assistant teacher in housing and design at University of Oulu 1986 - 1990. Own architecture office in Helsinki. Helka-Liisa Hentila.

Bob Jarvis
School of Land Management and Urban Policy, South Bank University
Wandsworth Road, LONDON, SW8 2JZ, GREAT BRITAIN.

Jyung Hwa Jin
119A Long Lane, Upper Darby, PA 19082, USA

Senior Planner, Datamap, PA, 1989-present. PhD City and Regional Planning, University of Pennylvania, 1989. M.Arch & MCP, University of Pennsylvania 1985. BE Architectural Engineering, Yonsei University, Korea, 1982.

Satoshi Kose
Head of Building Design and Use Division, Building Research Institute
Tatehara, Tsukuba Science City 305, JAPAN.

He graduated from the Department of Architecture of the University of Tokyo, joined the Building Research Institute of the Ministry of Construction in 1972 and received his Doctor of Engineering in Architecture from the University of Tokyo in 1986. He is specialized in safety and human factors in buildings. His current research interests include dwelling design for the aging population.

Roderick J. Lawrence
Centre for Human Ecology and Environmental Sciences, University of Geneva
Box 226, 1227 Carouge, GENEVA, SWITZERLAND.

Jeanne Moore and David Canter
Psychology Department, University of Surrey
Guildford, GREAT BRITAIN.

Jennie Randall

Jennie Randall is a part-time doctorate student with the Open University for whom she teaches foundation and Psychology courses, and 'Women into Management'; also other management and work-related courses in the past. She did research in school of architecture for a year.

Gülsün Sağlamer

Istanbul Technical University, Faculty of Architecture

Taskisla/Taksim, 80191 ISTANBUL, TURKEY.

Gülsün Sağlamer graduated from ITU, Faculty of Architecture in 1967, got her PhD Degree in 1973 from the same University and was appointed a full Professor in 1988. She is presently Deputy Vice-Chancellor there. She has been teaching architectural design and lecturing on architectural design theories, models of design, architectural morphology and CAAD. Her main research areas are: morphological studies of house forms, 'gecekondus', CADD of dwelling units, simulation of parametric design procedures, circulation in buildings. She designed several buildings, and organised a symposium on 'Housing for the Urban Poor' in September 1991 in Istanbul. She is the author of two books on architectural design theories and over 50 papers as well as the co-editor of the proceedings of 'Housing for the Urban Poor'.

Rafi Samizay and Bashir Kazimee

School of Architecture, Washington State University,

Washington, USA.

Rafi Samizay is the Chairman of the School of Architecture at Washington State University.

Jonathan D. Sime

Jonathan Sime Associates (JSA), Environmental and Social Research Consultants,

26 Croft Road, Godalming, SURREY GU7 2BY, GREAT BRITAIN.

and

School of Architecture, Kingston University,

GREAT BRITAIN.

Jonathan Sime is an environmental psychologist with 20 years experience in research, design education and consultancy. He has 50 publications. He is director of JSA, a research consultancy which specialises in crowd safety and psycho-social aspects of architecture, design and planning. Dr. Sime is a visiting lecturer at the School of Architecture, Kingston University and IAPS Secretary (International Association for People-Environment Studies).

Martin Symes
in collaboration with Takashi Takahashi, Massami Kobayashi and Yurika Imai.
School of Architecture, University of Manchester,
MANCHESTER, M13 9PL, GREAT BRITAIN.

Martin Symes is an architect and planner who has published extensively on urban design and regeneration as well as on architectural education. He is currently Head of School of Architecture at Manchester University where he holds the British Gas Chair of Urban Renewal. In 1990 he was Monbusho, Visiting Professor at the University of Tokyo, where his host was Takashi Takahashi, and Yurika Imai was research assistant. Massami Kobayaski teaches in the Department of Global Environment Engineering at the University of Kyoto.

Necdet Teymur
Centre for International Architectural Studies,School of Architecture, University of Manchester
MANCHESTER, M13 9PL, GREAT BRITAIN.

Necdet Teymur is Director of the *Centre for International Architectural Studies* at University of Manchester. He has practised as an architect, taught design and theory and done research on design, theory and education. He is on the Executive Committee of IAPS and the Council of Design Research Society. He is the author of *Environmental Discourse* (1982) and *Architectural Education* (1992), co-editor of *Rehumanizing Housing* (1988) and *Culture Space History* (1990) and an Associate Editor of *Journal of Architectural and Planning Research.*